T0194539

Sven Pastoors · Lars Meyer

Das Konzept „Starke Sprache"

Wie Sie mit klaren, wirksamen Formulierungen Ihre Ziele erreichen

Sven Pastoors
Düsseldorf, Deutschland

Lars Meyer
Düsseldorf, Deutschland

ISSN 2197-6708 ISSN 2197-6716 (electronic)
essentials
ISBN 978-3-658-30691-5 ISBN 978-3-658-30692-2 (eBook)
https://doi.org/10.1007/978-3-658-30692-2

Die Deutsche Nationalbibliothek verzeichnet diese Publikation in der Deutschen Nationalbibliografie; detaillierte bibliografische Daten sind im Internet über http://dnb.d-nb.de abrufbar.

Planung/Lektorat: Marion Kraemer
Springer ist ein Imprint der eingetragenen Gesellschaft Springer Fachmedien Wiesbaden GmbH und ist ein Teil von Springer Nature.
Die Anschrift der Gesellschaft ist: Abraham-Lincoln-Str. 46, 65189 Wiesbaden, Germany

Was Sie in diesem *essential* finden

In diesem Buch finden Sie Tipps und Anregungen...

- Wie Sie erfolgreich mit anderen kommunizieren, verhandeln oder diskutieren und Ihnen jeder gerne zuhört.
- Wie Sie Missverständnisse vermeiden.
- Wie Sie komplexe Zusammenhänge im Beruf, der Lehre oder in wissenschaftlichen Arbeiten gut verständlich formulieren.

Zudem erfahren Sie...

- Wie Sie Sie Ihre Gedanken ordnen können.
- Wie Sie sprachlich Vertrauen schaffen
- Wie Sie Ihre Sprache von Ballast befreien.

Danksagung

Bei diesem Buch haben uns viele Menschen mit Ihren Anregungen unterstützt. Unser Dank gilt den Klienten, Coachees und Seminarteilnehmern der CLM Business School Düsseldorf, wie auch Dozenten und Studenten der Fontys International Business School in Venlo, die uns bei diesem Buch aktiv mit Beispielen unterstützt haben. Das Buch ist ein Spiegelbild jahrelanger Begleitung von Projekten mit Klienten und Studenten.

Des Weiteren bedanken wir uns bei Anke Meyer-Cours und Kristina Laubeck, die uns beim Konzipieren und Schreiben dieses Buches geholfen haben, sowie allen Menschen, die dieses Buch lektoriert haben.

Viel Spaß beim Lesen und Umsetzen!

Düsseldorf
Mai 2020

Sven Pastoors
Lars Meyer

Inhaltsverzeichnis

Was kennzeichnet eine ausdrucksstarke und überzeugende Sprache?

Egal, ob im Studium oder im Beruf: Erfolgreiches Schreiben, Verhandeln oder Diskutieren setzt eine klare und deutliche Sprache voraus. Wie kompetent und glaubwürdig Ihre Gesprächspartner Sie einschätzen, hängt maßgeblich vom Gebrauch Ihrer Sprache ab. Dabei kommt es nicht nur darauf an, was Sie sagen, sondern auch, wie Sie es sagen. Wenn Sie klare Aussagen treffen und andere zu Wort kommen lassen, dann hören diese Ihnen gerne zu. Zudem helfen Ihnen kurze und klare Aussagen, Missverständnisse zu vermeiden. Die Art und Weise wie Sie kommunizieren ist somit entscheidend für Ihren privaten und beruflichen Erfolg. Wer die Grundregeln einer ausdrucksstarken und überzeugenden Sprache berücksichtigt, verleiht seinem Standpunkt Nachdruck und Bedeutung. Der Fokus dieses Buches liegt deshalb auf den verbalen Aspekten der Kommunikation.

Grundsätze für erfolgreiche Gesprächsführung

Der Kommunikationswissenschaftler Paul Grice hat sich mit den Erfolgsfaktoren für eine gelungene Kommunikation auseinandergesetzt. Sein ursprüngliches Ziel war es, das menschliche Gesprächsverhalten besser zu verstehen und mögliche Unterschiede zwischen Gesagtem und Gemeintem zu erklären. Grice kam dabei zu dem Ergebnis, dass der Erfolg einer Kommunikation maßgeblich davon abhängt, ob eine Person ihr Gegenüber verstehen (bzw. mit ihm kooperieren) möchte oder nicht (vgl. Grice 1967). Auf der Basis dieser Erkenntnisse bestimmte Grice neun Grundsätze (Konversationsmaximen), die für den Erfolg menschlicher Kommunikation erfüllt sein müssen. Bei diesen Grundsätzen handelt es sich um Regeln, die die meisten Menschen in der Kommunikation unbewusst anwenden.

© Springer Fachmedien Wiesbaden GmbH, ein Teil von Springer Nature 2020
S. Pastoors und L. Meyer, *Das Konzept „Starke Sprache"*, essentials,
https://doi.org/10.1007/978-3-658-30692-2_1

Hintergrundwissen: Konversationsmaximen nach Grice (1967)
Maximen der Quantität:

- Mache deinen Beitrag so informativ, wie (für den gegebenen Zweck) nötig.
- Mache deinen Beitrag nicht informativer als nötig.

Maximen der Qualität:

- Sage nichts, was du für falsch hältst.
- Sage nichts, wofür dir angemessene Gründe fehlen.

Maxime der Relevanz:

- Sei relevant.

Maximen der Modalität:

- Vermeide Unklarheit.
- Vermeide Mehrdeutigkeit.
- Fass Dich kurz.
- Achte auf eine klare Struktur und kommuniziere der Reihe nach.

Diese Grundsätze erklären, wie die in einem Gespräch ausgetauschten Informationen für die Kooperationspartner einen Sinn ergeben. Dabei gehen alle Beteiligten wechselseitig davon aus, dass ihre Gesprächspartner diese Grundsätze berücksichtigen. Zudem leitete Grice aus diesen Grundsätzen das Kooperationsprinzip ab: „Gestalte deine Äußerung so, dass sie dem anerkannten Zweck dient, den du gerade zusammen mit deinem Kommunikationspartner verfolgst" (Grice 1967). Er entdeckte, dass Menschen selbst dann noch kooperieren müssen, wenn sie miteinander streiten. Zur Kooperation gehört beispielsweise der Grundsatz, nur Relevantes zu sagen. Im Streit nehmen die Konfliktparteien immer noch Bezug auf das, von dem sie glauben, dass es für die andere Partei wichtig ist.

Anwendung im Alltag
Im alltäglichen und beruflichen Miteinander begegnen Ihnen immer wieder Menschen, die sich und ihre Interessen nur schwach vertreten können. Sie verwenden Füllwörter, Verniedlichungen, lassen eine klare Struktur vermissen und senden keine eindeutigen Botschaften. Dadurch wirken sie schwach, unsicher, fast schon unbeholfen. Das führt dazu, dass ihre Mitmenschen ihnen wenig zutrauen, und sie teilweise nicht ernstnehmen.

Dies lässt sich mithilfe der oben genannten Konversationsmaxime vermeiden. Aus diesen Maximen lassen sich sechs einfache Regeln für die tägliche

Kommunikation ableiten. Diese helfen Ihnen, souverän aufzutreten und Sie Ihre Ziele leichter zu erreichen:

- Ordnen Sie Ihre Gedanken (Maxime der Modalität)
- Formulieren Sie so einfach wie möglich (Maxime der Quantität)
- Schaffen Sie Vertrauen (Maxime der Qualität)
- Stiften Sie Sinn (Maxime der Relevanz)
- Sprechen Sie Klartext (Maxime der Relevanz)
- Befreien Sie Ihre Sprache von Ballast (Maxime der Modalität)

Diese sechs Regeln sind zugleich die zentralen Merkmale einer (ausdrucks-) starken Sprache. In diesem Buch geben wir Ihnen einen Überblick, wie starke Sprache funktioniert und wie Sie diese nutzen können, um selbstbewusst und geradlinig aufzutreten. Hierzu werden diese sechs Regeln in den folgenden Kapiteln erklärt und anhand konkreter Beispiele erläutert. Dabei erlernen Sie Methoden, um auf Augenhöhe mit Ihrem Gesprächspartner zu kommunizieren und sowohl beruflich als auch privat als verlässlicher Partner zu agieren.

Das Buch richtet sich dabei vor allem an Menschen, die sich beruflich verändern möchten, Coaches und Berater, die diese Menschen dabei begleiten, sowie Studenten und Dozenten von praxisorientierten Studiengängen:

- Besonders in Veränderungsprozessen ist es wichtig, dass Sie klar kommunizieren und eine starke Sprache benutzen. Zum einen senden Sie eine Botschaft an sich selbst, dass Sie gut reflektieren und „mit sich im Reinen" sind. Nach außen signalisieren Sie, dass Sie genau wissen, was Sie möchten und auch bereit sind, für Ihre Ziele einzutreten.
- Beratern und Coaches hilft starke Sprache, eine vertrauensvolle Gesprächsbasis mit ihren Klienten aufzubauen und gemeinsam eine wirksame Vorgehensweise zu erarbeiten. Dank der klaren Kommunikation fühlt sich der Klient gut und sicher bei Ihnen aufgehoben.
- Studenten und Dozenten erhalten in diesem Buch Tipps, wie Sie komplexe Zusammenhänge im Beruf, der Lehre oder in wissenschaftlichen Arbeiten gut verständlich formulieren können.

Starke Sprache vermitteltet Vertrauen und Verlässlichkeit. Zum einen Vertrauen in Ihre eigenen Fähigkeiten, zum anderen auch gegenüber Ihren Mitmenschen. Sie nehmen sich selbst ernst und Ihr Gegenüber nimmt Sie als vertrauenswürdigen, kompetenten Gesprächspartner wahr.

Ordnen Sie Ihre Gedanken

2

"Wer zwei Hasen jagt, lässt einen zurück und verliert den anderen."
Indianisches Sprichwort

Niemand kann Ihnen in den Kopf gucken. Und das ist auch gut so. Bevor Sie mit anderen kommunizieren, müssen Sie sich deshalb erst einmal selbst bewusstwerden, was Sie überhaupt erreichen wollen. Denn wie sollen andere Ihre Gedanken nachvollziehen können, wenn Sie selbst nicht dazu in der Lage sind. Machen Sie sich deshalb Ihre Ziele bewusst: Was wollen Sie mit Ihrem Beitrag überhaupt erreichen. Doch achten Sie darauf, nicht zu viele Ziele gleichzeitig zu verfolgen. Sonst ergeht es Ihnen wie in dem indianischen Sprichwort: Sie erreichen keins davon.

Neben klaren Zielen setzt dies auch eine klare Struktur voraus. Hierzu müssen Sie nicht nur wissen, was Sie sagen wollen, sondern auch, welche Informationen der andere benötigt, um Ihre Botschaft zu verstehen. Überlegen Sie deshalb vorab, auf welche Hintergrundinformationen Ihr Gegenüber angewiesen ist, um Ihre Botschaft richtig zu deuten.

Zudem ist es wichtig, sich Gedanken über einen spannenden Einstieg ins Thema zu machen, und sich ein geeignetes Ende zu überlegen, mit dem Sie Ihre Botschaft noch einmal unterstreichen. Dies kann zum Beispiel ein Appell sein, mit dem Sie Ihr Gegenüber zum Handeln auffordern. Eine andere Möglichkeit wäre eine Frage, um den anderen zum Nachdenken zu bewegen.

© Springer Fachmedien Wiesbaden GmbH, ein Teil von Springer Nature 2020
S. Pastoors und L. Meyer, *Das Konzept "Starke Sprache"*, essentials,
https://doi.org/10.1007/978-3-658-30692-2_2

2.1   Machen Sie sich Ihre Ziele bewusst

Ein gut strukturierter Beitrag oder ein erfolgreiches Gespräch setzen klare Ziele voraus. Wenn Sie wissen, was Sie mit einem bestimmten Beitrag erreichen möchten, können Sie diesen besser strukturieren. Falls Sie jedoch neben dem eigentlichen Thema zusätzliche Botschaften einbringen oder die Themen mehrfach wechseln, ist irgendwann keinem der Beteiligten mehr klar, worüber Sie eigentlich sprechen (vgl. Flammer 1996, S. 62).

Überlegen Sie zudem, welche Wünsche und Ängste Sie antreiben, wenn Sie ein bestimmtes Ziel erreichen möchten: Was sind Ihre wahren Motive und Beweggründe? Werden Sie sich Ihrer Emotionen bewusst. Bedürfnisse, die Menschen antreiben, sind zum Beispiel das Streben nach Anerkennung, Freiheit, Harmonie, Rache oder Sicherheit. Werden Sie sich Ihrer Ziele und der Grenzen Ihrer Kompromissbereitschaft bewusst. Wenn Sie keine klaren Ziele vor Augen haben, werden Sie Schwierigkeiten haben, Ihre eigenen Bedürfnisse zu befriedigen (vgl. Ebert und Pastoors 2017, S. 290 f.).

Beachten Sie deshalb folgende Grundsätze, um Ihre Interessen in Gesprächen erfolgreich vertreten zu können:

- Machen Sie sich das Ziel des Beitrags bewusst.
- Kommunizieren Sie dieses offen und ehrlich.
- Werden Sie sich der Erwartungen Ihres Gegenübers bewusst.
- Schaffen Sie einen gemeinsamen Grundkonsens.

2.2   Konzentrieren Sie sich auf das Wesentliche

Eine gute Struktur und ein klarer Fokus auf wenige zentrale Punkte helfen Ihrem Gegenüber, das Gesagte besser zu verstehen. Die sogenannte Fünf-Satz-Technik ist eine einfache und gleichzeitig erfolgsversprechende Methode, dies zu erreichen. Mit ihrer Hilfe können Sie Ihre Texte so gliedern, dass weder Sie, noch Ihr Publikum den roten Faden verlieren.

Diese Technik wurde bereits in der Antike entwickelt. Trotzdem lässt sie sich problemlos auf moderne Reden und Präsentationen anwenden. Sie eignet sich für alle Situationen, in denen Sie Ihr Gegenüber von etwas überzeugen bzw. zu etwas bewegen möchten. Zudem hilft Ihnen die Technik, sich Ihrer Ziele bewusst zu werden, diese zu begründen und in kurzer Zeit eine dementsprechende Rede oder Präsentation zu verfassen. Hierzu gliedern Sie Ihren Beitrag mithilfe der Fünf-Satz-Technik in drei Teile und überzeugen so Sie Ihr Gegenüber von Ihrem Standpunkt:

- Im Einleitungssatz beschreiben Sie kurz die Ausgangssituation.
- Im anschließenden Hauptteil begründen, erläutern und veranschaulichen Sie Ihre drei wichtigsten Argumente.
- Im letzten Schritt ziehen Sie die Schlussfolgerung aus dem bisher Gesagten und fordern Sie Ihr Gegenüber zum Handeln auf.

> **Tipp**
> Gründe für die Überzeugungskraft der Fünf-Satz-Technik (vgl. Scheel 2018):
>
> - Sie sind gezwungen, sich Klarheit über Ihr Ziel und Ihre drei schlagkräftigsten Argumente zu machen.
> - Sie erleichtern Ihrem Verhandlungspartner das Verstehen und Behalten Ihrer Argumente.
> - Außerdem steigt Ihre Chance, ausreden zu können.

Der Begriff „Satz" ist bei der Fünf-Satz-Technik nicht wörtlich zu verstehen. Sie können Sie sowohl für eine Rede, ein Mitarbeiterschreiben oder zum Beispiel ein ganzes Buch verwenden. Der Begriff „Fünf-Satz-Technik" bezieht sich auf die Struktur Ihres Beitrages, die unabhängig von dessen Umfang auf fünf Sätzen aufbaut. Hierzu fassen Sie Ihre zentrale Botschaft in fünf Sätze, bevor Sie mit der Ausarbeitung Ihres Beitrages beginnen. Sobald Sie die Technik beherrschen, können sie mit ihrer Hilfe Briefe, E-Mails, Reden oder Präsentationen übersichtlich strukturieren (vgl. Hölscher 2012):

- Argumentation (Einleitung – 1. Argument – 2. Argument – 3. Argument – Schlussfolgerung): Die einfachste Form der Fünf-Satz-Technik ist die Argumentation. Ziel einer Argumentation ist es, andere von Ihrer Meinung zu überzeugen. Nachdem Sie in der Einleitung kurz das zentrale Problem vorgestellt haben, folgen drei Argumente und am Ende ein kurzes Fazit. Dabei ist es wichtig, sich auf die drei besten Argumente zu beschränken. Mehr können sich Ihre Zuhörer nicht merken und Sie würden sich in Details verzetteln (vgl. ebd.).

- Widerspruch (Einleitung – Argument der Gegenseite – 1. Gegenargument – 2. Gegenargument – Schlussfolgerung): Der Widerspruch ist nötig, um ein bereits vorgebrachtes Argument zu entkräften. Daher ist es sinnvoll, diesem mit zwei Gegenargumenten zu wiedersprechen (vgl. ebd.).
- Kompromiss (Streitpunkt – Pro – Contra – Schlussfolgerung – Appell): Bei einem Kompromiss geht es darum, Pro- und Contra-Argumente abzuwägen und daraus eine für alle Seiten akzeptable Lösung abzuleiten. Stellen Sie hierzu nach der Problemstellung möglichst fair beide Sichtweisen dar und ziehen Sie daraus Ihre Schlüsse. Zum Schluss stellen Sie Ihren Kompromiss-vorschlag vor – mit dem Appell, diesen anzunehmen (vgl. ebd.).
- Lösungsvorschlag (Ausgangslage – Ursachen – Ziele bestimmen – Lösungs-vorschlag – Appell): Bei Besprechungen oder Konferenzen müssen Sie häufig Lösungsansätze für ein Problem skizzieren. Auch in diesem Fall hilft Ihnen die Fünf-Satz-Technik, diese übersichtlich aufzubauen (vgl. ebd.).
- Festtagsrede (Anlass – 1. Anekdote – 2. Anekdote – 3. Anekdote – Schluss-folgerung und guter Wunsch): Sowohl bei guten Anlässen, wie Hochzeiten oder Jubiläen, als auch eher traurigen, wie zum Beispiel Beerdigungen, werden Reden gehalten. Überlegen Sie sich kurz, was Sie erzählen möchten und welche Anekdoten sich am besten eignen, um Ihren Standpunkt zu unterstreichen.

> **Tipp** Bringen Sie Ihr stärkstes Argument bzw. Ihre persönlichste Anekdote immer zum Schluss, damit es Ihren Lesern oder Zuhörern möglichst lange in Erinnerung bleibt (vgl. Scheel 2018).

2.3 Achten Sie auf Ihre Eröffnung und Ihren Abschluss

Um die Aufmerksamkeit und das Interesse Ihrer Zuhörer zu gewinnen, müssen Sie deren Neugier wecken. Ihr Gegenüber merkt sich in der Regel nur den Anfang und das Ende Ihres Beitrages (z. B. Ihrer E-Mail oder Ihrer Rede). Des-halb sollten beide Ihr Gegenüber überzeugen. Der Einstieg entscheidet darüber, ob Ihr Gegenüber dem Vortrag gespannt zuhört bzw. die E-Mail gebannt liest, oder bereits nach wenigen Sekunden abschaltet (Pastoors 2017, S. 62). In der Praxis haben sich unter anderem folgende Einstiegsformen bewährt:

> **Tipp: Einstiegsformen (Mai 2008)**
> **Interaktiv** – Lassen Sie Ihr Publikum selbst über Ihr Thema nachdenken, indem Sie eine rhetorische Frage, am besten aus der Metaebene, stellen: „Was denken Sie: Wie kann ein Redner dafür sorgen, dass ihm sein Publikum zuhört?"
> **Nachrichtlich** – Beginnen Sie mit den Ergebnissen einer aktuellen Studie oder (Branchen-) News: „Sie haben es heute gelesen: Die Konjunktur flaut ab…"
> **Überraschend** – Sie können die Nachricht aber auch bewusst verfälschen und eine Falschaussage treffen, um eine Art Was-wäre-wenn-Szenario aufzubauen: „Die Statistik zeigt: In zehn Jahren ist Deutschland ein Greisenheim."
> **Provokativ** – Überhöhen Sie Ihre Kernthese oder -aussage zum Extrem. Das schafft Reibungsfläche, aber eben auch Aufmerksamkeit: „Wer nicht netzwerkt, findet keinen Job."
> **Vergleichend** – Analogien, Parabeln, Gleichnisse – Geschichten hört jeder gerne: „Vorträge sind wie Stau: Man würde gerne abkürzen, kommt aber nicht raus."
> **Persönlich** – Apropos Geschichten: Erzählen Sie eine Anekdote aus Ihrem Leben: „Sie werden nicht glauben, was mir gerade im Hotel passiert ist…"
> **Humorvoll** – Lockern Sie den Anfang mit einem Witz auf, idealerweise mit einem, der zum Thema passt.

Da sich Ihre Zuhörer am ehesten an den Schluss Ihres Beitrags erinnern, braucht dieser ebenfalls etwas Inspirierendes: Einen Appell, einen Ausblick oder eine provokante Frage (Pastoors 2017, S. 62)(Tab. 2.1).

Tab. 2.1 Praxisbeispiel für starkes Ende

Schwache Sprache	Starke Sprache
„[…] Außerdem führt der Klimawandel zu immer größeren Gewinnausfällen für die Landwirte So, das war es. Vielen Dank für Ihre Aufmerksamkeit."	„[…] Außerdem führt der Klimawandel zu immer größeren Gewinnausfällen für die Landwirte Der Klimawandel bedroht uns somit alle. Helfen Sie deshalb mit, den CO_2-Ausstoß zu senken. Vielen Dank."

Quelle: eigene Zusammenstellung

2.4   Checkliste

Die folgende Checkliste gibt Ihnen einen Überblick, wie Sie Ihre Aussagen klar und gut verständlich strukturieren können (Tab. 2.2).

Tab. 2.2 Checkliste zu Kap. 2: Ordnen Sie Ihre Gedanken

Checkliste	
Machen Sie sich Ihre Ziele bewusst	√
Bevor Sie mit anderen kommunizieren, müssen Sie sich erst selbst bewusst werden, was Sie überhaupt erreichen wollen. Denn wie sollen andere Ihre Gedanken nachvollziehen können, wenn Sie selbst nicht dazu in der Lage sind	
Ein gut strukturierter Beitrag oder ein erfolgreiches Gespräch setzen klare Ziele voraus. Wenn Sie wissen, was Sie mit einem bestimmten Beitrag erreichen möchten, können Sie diesen besser strukturieren	
Überlegen Sie vorab, welche Wünsche und Ängste Sie antreiben, wenn Sie ein bestimmtes Ziel erreichen möchten: Was sind Ihre wahren Beweggründe?	
Konzentrieren Sie sich auf das Wesentliche	√
Eine gute Struktur und ein klarer Fokus auf wenige zentrale Punkte helfen Ihrem Gegenüber, das Gesagte besser zu verstehen	
Die sogenannte Fünf-Satz-Technik ist eine einfache und gleichzeitig erfolgsversprechende Methode, um Ihre Gedanken zu ordnen	
Diese Technik hilft Ihnen, sich Ihrer Ziele bewusst zu werden, diese zu begründen und in kurzer Zeit eine dementsprechende Rede oder Präsentation zu verfassen	
Gliedern Sie Ihren Beitrag mithilfe der Fünf-Satz-Technik in drei Teile und überzeugen so Sie Ihr Gegenüber von Ihrem Standpunkt	
Der Begriff „Satz" ist bei der Fünf-Satz-Technik nicht wörtlich zu verstehen. Sie können Sie sowohl für eine Rede, ein Mitarbeiterschreiben oder zum Beispiel für ein ganzes Buch verwenden	
Achten Sie auf Ihre Eröffnung und Ihren Abschluss	√
Ihr Gegenüber merkt sich in der Regel nur den Anfang und das Ende Ihres Beitrages (z. B. Ihrer E-Mail oder Ihrer Rede). Deshalb sollten beide Ihr Gegenüber überzeugen. Der Einstieg entscheidet darüber, ob Ihr Gegenüber dem Vortrag gespannt zuhört bzw. die E-Mail gebannt liest, oder bereits nach wenigen Sekunden abschaltet	
Um die Aufmerksamkeit und das Interesse Ihrer Zuhörer zu gewinnen, müssen Sie deren Neugier wecken	
Da sich Ihre Zuhörer am ehesten an den Schluss Ihres Beitrags erinnern, braucht dieser ebenfalls etwas Inspirierendes: Einen Appell, einen Ausblick oder eine provokante Frage	

Formulieren Sie so einfach wie möglich

3

> Ein guter Beitrag hat einen guten Anfang und ein gutes Ende – und beide sollten möglichst dicht beieinanderliegen. (Twain, zitiert nach Wöss 2004, S. 157)

Egal, wie lange Sie Ihre Kollegen oder Kunden schon kennen, auch in eingespielten Teams kommt es immer wieder zu Missverständnissen. Folgen Sie deshalb Mark Twains Rat und kommunizieren Sie kurz und klar, um Ihre Ziele zu erreichen und Missverständnisse zu vermeiden. Machen Sie Ihren Beitrag außerdem nicht informativer als erforderlich, sondern passen Sie ihn dem Zweck der Kommunikation an (vgl. Lorenzoni und Bernhard 2001, S. 123).

▷ **Praxistipp: Verwenden Sie eine klare Sprache**

- Verwenden Sie einfache, kurze Sätze
- Verwenden Sie bekannte Worte und verzichten Sie auf Fremdwörter
- Formulieren Sie anschaulich und geben Sie konkrete Beispiele
- Vermeiden Sie Wiederholungen und weitschweifige Erläuterungen
- Seien Sie konkret und vermeiden Sie vage Formulierungen
- Sprechen Sie strukturiert und ordnen Sie Ihre Informationen
- Nehmen Sie jede Frage ernst
  (vgl. Schulz von Thun 2007, S. 33 ff.).

Falls es trotz kurzer Sätze und klarer Botschaften doch einmal zu Missverständnissen kommt, lassen sich diese lösen, indem Sie über den Kommunikationsprozess sprechen. Auf diese Weise können Sie herausfinden, wie die Missverständnisse entstanden sind. Es lohnt sich, im Gespräch kurz inne zu halten, wenn es unbefriedigend verläuft. Reflektieren Sie gemeinsam mit Ihrem Gesprächspartner das Gespräch, um die Störung zu beheben (vgl. Lay 1999, S. 196).

© Springer Fachmedien Wiesbaden GmbH, ein Teil von Springer Nature 2020
S. Pastoors und L. Meyer, *Das Konzept „Starke Sprache"*, essentials,
https://doi.org/10.1007/978-3-658-30692-2_311

3.1   Verwenden Sie einfache, kurze Sätze

Jeder zweite Erwachsene kann gesprochenen Sätzen mit mehr als 14 Wörtern nicht mehr folgen. Jeder Dritte hat sogar schon Probleme, Sätze mit mehr als elf Wörtern zu verstehen. Laut der Deutschen Presse-Agentur dpa liegt die optimale Länge für gesprochene Beiträge bei neun Wörtern, die Obergrenze bei 14 Wörtern pro Satz (vgl. Schneider 2001, S. 89 f.). Das gleiche gilt für geschriebene Sätze. Hier liegt die Grenze je nach Sprachniveau bei 9–18 Wörtern. Entsprechend beträgt die durchschnittliche Satzlänge in der BILD-Zeitung zum Beispiel zwölf Wörter pro Satz. Bei eher anspruchsvoller Literatur wie „Die Buddenbrooks" von Thomas Mann sind es 17 Wörter (vgl. Hesse 2019, S. 55). Die Konzentrationsfähigkeit dürfte aufgrund der Neuen Medien noch weiter gesunken sein. Verwenden Sie deshalb kurze Sätze und verzichten Sie auf komplizierte Satzgefüge: Je kürzer, desto besser.

Lange Sätze sind kein Merkmal für Kompetenz. Ganz im Gegenteil: Sie erwecken bei Ihrem Gegenüber eher den Eindruck, dass Sie von der Materie keine Ahnung haben und dies mithilfe langer Sätze verbergen möchten. Fassen Sie sich deshalb kurz. Egal, ob im Gespräch oder in Texten, lange Sätze und Textblöcke verwirren nur Ihr Gegenüber. Der amerikanische Sprachwissenschaftler und Autor William Strunk brachte dies wie folgt auf den Punkt:

> „Ausdrucksstarke Texte sind präzise. Ein Satz sollte keine unnötigen Wörter enthalten, ein Absatz keine unnötigen Sätze, aus demselben Grund, aus dem ein Bild keine unnötigen Striche und eine Maschine keine unnötigen Teile enthalten sollte. Das bedeutet nicht, dass ein Autor alle Sätze kürzen, Details vermeiden oder Themen nur oberflächlich behandeln sollte, sondern dass jedes Wort von Bedeutung ist" (Strunk und White 2000, S. 32).

Versuchen Sie deshalb, möglichst kurze Sätze zu verwenden (Tab. 3.1). Vermeiden Sie außerdem unnötige Floskeln wie „Abschließend bleibt festzuhalten …", „Dementsprechend stellt sich die Frage …" oder „Grundsätzlich gilt …".

3.2   Verzichten Sie auf Fremdwörter, Abkürzungen und Anglizismen

Verzichten Sie außerdem auf unnötige Fremdwörter und Abkürzungen, wenn Sie möchten, dass Ihr Gegenüber Sie als kompetent und gebildet wahrnimmt. Sie riskieren sonst, dass Ihr Gegenüber Sie nicht versteht oder für abgehoben hält.

Tab. 3.1   Praxisbeispiele für kurze Sätze

Schwache Sprache	Starke Sprache
„Ich hoffe Ihnen meinen Standpunkt ausreichend erläutert zu haben und gebe Ihnen hiermit nochmals die Gelegenheit, den Betrag von 100,00 Euro innerhalb einer Woche nach Erhalt dieses Schreibens unter Angabe des o.a. Aktenzeichens auf eines der u.a. Konten der Stadtkasse zu überweisen." (vgl. Ebert und Fisiak 2018, S. 60)	„Bitte überweisen Sie den Betrag von 100,00 EUR innerhalb einer Woche nach Erhalt dieses Schreibens. // Verwenden Sie dabei das oben angegebene Aktenzeichen als Verwendungszweck. // Die Kontodaten der Stadtkasse finden Sie am Ende des Schreibens. // Wenn Sie hierzu noch Fragen haben sollten, bin ich Ihnen gerne behilflich."
„Demgegenüber steht eine Verringerung des sonstigen betrieblichen Aufwandes im Vergleich zu 2010 um acht Prozent auf 26,7 Millionen Euro (2010: 28,9 Mio. EUR), die insbesondere aus der geringeren Konzessionsabgabe resultiert."	„Demgegenüber verringerte sich der sonstige betriebliche Aufwand um acht Prozent. // Betrug der Aufwand im Jahr 2010 noch 28,9 Mio., Euro, so waren es 2011 nur 26,7 Mio. Euro. // Grund hierfür war die geringere Konzessionsabgabe." (vgl. Ebert und Fisiak 2018, S. 53)
„Ziel der Verbesserung des Instagram-Profils soll eine bessere Nutzung dieses visuellen, digitalen Mediums sein, damit Menschen, die potenzielles Interesse an der Teilnahme an den Veranstaltungen des Unternehmens hätten, auf dem Profil durch emotionale Eventbilder angesprochen werden und sich somit über das Unternehmen, das derzeit neben Facebook bereits Instagram nutzt, aber in Instagram viel weniger Zeit investiert, und dessen Veranstaltungen informieren." (Quelle: studentische Hausarbeit)	„Das Unternehmen nutzt derzeit neben Facebook noch Instagram, investiert aber in Instagram viel weniger Zeit. // Ziel des Projekts ist es, das visuelle, digitale Medium Instagram besser zu nutzen. // Emotionale Bilder von Events sollen potentielle Kunden des Unternehmens ansprechen. // Das Unternehmen hofft, dass diese sich anschließend über das Unternehmen und dessen Veranstaltungen informieren."

Quelle: eigene Zusammenstellung

Setzen Sie deshalb Fachbegriffe, Fremdwörter und Abkürzungen sparsam ein. Erklären Sie die verwendeten Fachbegriffe im Zweifelsfall direkt, oder greifen Sie auf einfachere und allgemein verständliche Formulierungen zurück.

Das Gleiche gilt für englische Begriffe. In der internationalen Unternehmenskommunikation führt kein Weg an der englischen Sprache vorbei. Im Laufe der Jahre haben Unternehmen viele Begriffe aus dem Englischen ins Deutsche übernommen. Nicht immer existieren auch passende Übersetzungen: E-Mail (elektronische Post), Link (Verbindung), Job (Arbeitsplatz), Outsourcen (Verlagern von Aufgaben), Statement (Stellungnahme), Babysitter, Hotline, Wellness, etc.

Denglisch

In der deutschen Sprache gibt es Begriffe, die aus einer Mischung deutscher und englischer Wörter entstanden sind. Diese werden als „Denglisch" bezeichnet: „Die Nachfrage boomt", „das Angebot liegt voll im Trend", „das Unternehmen hat das Ergebnis des Vorjahres getoppt" und aus Kunden werden „Customer", denen Unternehmen maßgeschneiderte „Solutions" anbieten.

Der Duden unterscheidet dabei zwischen Anglizismen (Entlehnungen) und Pseudo-anglizismen (Scheinentlehnungen):

- Zu den Anglizismen gehören zum Beispiel Wörter wie Jeans und Skateboard. Für diese Wörter gab es zuvor keine deutschen Begriffe. Andere Entlehnungen „treten in Konkurrenz zu heimischen Wörtern, verdrängen diese oder aber bereichern das jeweilige Wortfeld": Job und Arbeit/Arbeitsplatz, Jogging und Dauerlauf (Duden 2016, S. 57).
- Pseudoanglizismen werden zwar aus englischen Wörtern gebildet, existieren aber nicht in der englischen Sprache. Ein bekanntes Beispiel ist das Wort „Handy". Weder Briten noch US-Amerikaner verstehen Sie, wenn Sie von den Funktionen Ihres Handys schwärmen. Briten und US-Amerikaner telefonieren mit dem „Mobile Phone". Dieser Begriff findet sich im Deutschen Wort „Mobiltelefon" wieder. Andere Scheinent-lehnungen sind Beamer[1], Body Bag[2], Public Viewing[3], Street Worker[4] oder Show-master[5] (vgl. Duden 2016, S. 57 f.).

Verwenden Sie Fremdwörter, Fachausdrücke und Begriffe aus anderen Sprachen nur, wenn Sie sicher sind, dass Ihr Gegenüber diese auch versteht. Berück-sichtigen Sie dabei, dass nicht jeder Englisch spricht.

3.3   Nutzen Sie aktive Formulierungen

Achten Sie darauf, dass Sie möglichst aktive Sätze verwenden. Dies sind Sätze, in denen die Akteure aktiv handeln. Das Gegenteil sind passive Formulierungen, bei denen den Akteuren etwas widerfährt. Entscheidend ist dabei die Beziehung zwischen dem Substantiv (dem Akteur) und dem Verb.

Aktive Formulierungen und Verben erklären dem Zuhörer oder Leser, wer etwas macht. Auf diese Weise sorgen Sie für Dynamik und kommunizieren Sie klar, was konkret geschieht. Ihre Angaben sind deshalb besser zu verstehen und leichter nachzuvollziehen (Tab. 3.2):

---

[1]Amerikanisch-englischer Begriff für ein Auto der Marke BMW.

[2]Amerikanisch-englischer Begriff für Leichensack.

[3]Amerikanisch-englischer Begriff für Leichenschau.

[4]Amerikanisch-englischer Begriff für Prostituierte.

[5]Sowohl im amerikanischen-, als auch im britischen Englisch unbekannter Begriff.

Tab. 3.2   Praxisbeispiele für passive und aktive Formulierungen

Schwache Sprache	Starke Sprache
„Bei Veränderungsprozessen wird Ihnen geholfen."	„Wir helfen Ihnen bei Veränderungsprozessen."
„Sie werden von uns benachrichtigt."	„Melden Sie sich. Wir rufen Sie zurück."
„Über Ihre Einladung zu einem Vorstellungsgespräch freue ich mich sehr."	„Ich freue mich über die Einladung zu einem Vorstellungsgespräch."
„In diesem Kapitel wird die Tabellenerstellung mit „Word" behandelt."	„In diesem Kapitel lernen Sie, wie Sie mit „Word" eine Tabelle erstellen." (vgl. Ebert und Fisiak 2018, S. 8)

Quelle: eigene Zusammenstellung

Passive Formulierungen wirken vage und leiten die Aufmerksamkeit auf den Adressaten (Opfer) einer Handlung. Sie eignen sich deshalb gut, um hervorzuheben, dass Akteure keinen Einfluss auf das Geschehen haben (vgl. Clark 2015, S. 36–46).

Versuchen Sie sowohl im Gespräch, als auch in geschriebenen Texten, passive Formulierungen nur dann zu verwenden, wenn Sie Ihre Aussage dadurch unterstreichen möchten. Dies ist zum Beispiel sinnvoll, wenn nicht die Handlung, sondern das Erleiden im Vordergrund steht oder wenn der Handelnde keine Rolle spielt. Ersetzen Sie ansonsten alle passiven Formulierungen durch aktive (Englert 2014, S. 106).

Vermeiden Sie Substantivierungen

„Die Schönheit der Landschaft hat uns geradezu geblendet." Dieser Satz ist in der Poesie und der Musik gut angebracht. Vermeiden Sie ihn jedoch im alltäglichen Leben. Was sich lautmalerisch anhört, ist auf Dauer für den Zuhörer oder Leser anstrengend. Die Formulierung „Die Landschaft war sehr schön." ist nicht nur kürzer, sondern auch leichter zu verstehen.

Die Umwandlung von Adjektiven und Verben zu Hauptwörtern wird Substantivierung oder auch Nominalisierung genannt. Dabei bilden Sie aus einem Verb (z. B. gleichen) oder einem Adjektiv (z. B. schön) und bestimmten Endungen ein Hauptwort, das eine Handlung (z. B. Gleichung) oder einen Zustand (z. B. Gleichheit, Schönheit) umschreibt. Sie erkennen Substantivierungen daran, dass sie auf Silben wie „-ung", „-heit", oder „-keit" enden.

Dies klingt nicht nur kompliziert, sondern führt in der Praxis auch dazu, dass Ihr Gegenüber Sie kaum noch versteht. Denn wenn Sie Verben in ein Hauptwort umwandeln (substantivieren), ersetzt dieses Substantiv häufig einen ganzen Satz („Das Ziel wird erreicht" wird zu „Das Erreichen des Ziels"). Weil dadurch die Dichte an Informationen steigt, erschweren Substantivierungen Ihrem Gegenüber das Lesen bzw. das Verstehen. Sie sind somit eine der Hauptursachen für Missverständnisse.

Verwirrende Aussagen

Anhand einiger provokanter Fragen verdeutlichen wir Ihnen, was Substantivierungen bei Ihrem Gegenüber bewirken:

- Ist es Ihnen ein Anliegen, die Frustration Ihrer Zuhörer zu vermeiden?
  → Oder wollen Sie diese schlicht nicht anöden?
- Möchten Sie zur Erörterung der Neugestaltung Ihrer Wohnung einen Freund hinzuziehen?
  → Oder möchten Sie mit ihm besprechen, wie Sie die Wohnung neu einrichten können?
- Wollen Sie Ihre Fahrkünste unter Beweis stellen?
  → Oder wollen Sie beweisen, wie gut Sie Autofahren? ◄

Wenn Sie beim Sprechen oder Schreiben regelmäßig Substantivierungen verwenden, zeugt dies nicht von Kompetenz und Professionalität, sondern von Unsicherheit. Außerdem wirken zu viele Substantive auf Dauer ermüdend. Der Strategie-Coach und Autor Mathias Priebe bringt dies mit folgendem Zitat auf den Punkt: „Die Substantivierung ist der Lebendigkeit ihr Tod" (Priebe 2020). Vermeiden Sie deshalb soweit wie möglich Substantivierungen bzw. Wörter, die auf -ung, -heit oder -keit enden. Verben hauchen jedem Text Leben ein und sorgen dafür, dass Ihr Gegenüber Sie gut versteht.

Mithilfe einiger konkreter Beispiele aus der praktischen Arbeit zeigt Priebe, wie einfach es ist, Sätze interessanter und verständlicher zu formulieren(Tab. 3.3):

Tab. 3.3 Praxisbeispiele, wie Sie Ihre Sätze ent-substantivieren können

Schwache Sprache	Starke Sprache
„Das Produkt besticht durch hohe Belastbarkeit und perfekte Verarbeitung."	„Das Produkt ist sehr belastbar und perfekt verarbeitet."
„Bei circa 75 Prozent aller Menschen werden mittlerweile Kaufentscheidungen von Empfehlungen anderer Kunden beeinflusst."	„75 Prozent aller Menschen werden beim Kauf davon beeinflusst, was andere Kunden empfehlen."
„Wir stehen vor der Herausforderung der Globalisierung."	„Die Globalisierung fordert uns heraus."
„Die Förderung von Kreativität ist unsere Zielsetzung."	„Wir fördern kreative Ideen."

Priebe (2020)

3.4 Checkliste

Die folgende Checkliste gibt Ihnen einen Überblick, wie Sie Ihre Aussagen so einfach wie möglich formulieren (Tab. 3.4).

Tab. 3.4 Checkliste zu Kapitel 3: Formulieren Sie so einfach wie möglich

Checkliste	
Verwenden Sie kurze, einfache Sätze	✓
Kommunizieren Sie kurz und klar, um Ihre Ziele zu erreichen und Missverständnisse zu vermeiden	
Verwenden Sie kurze Sätze und verzichten Sie auf komplizierte Satzgefüge: Je kürzer, desto besser	
Machen Sie Ihren Beitrag nicht informativer als erforderlich	
Vermeiden Sie unnötige Floskeln wie „Abschließend bleibt festzuhalten …", „Dementsprechend stellt sich die Frage …" oder „Grundsätzlich gilt …"	
Sprechen Sie mit Ihrem Gegenüber über den Kommunikationsprozess, falls es trotz kurzer Sätze und klarer Botschaften zu Missverständnissen kommen sollte	
Verzichten Sie auf Fremdwörter und Anglizismen	✓
Verzichten Sie auf unnötige Fremdwörter, wenn Sie möchten, dass Ihr Gegenüber Sie als kompetent und gebildet wahrnimmt	
Erklären Sie die verwendeten Fachbegriffe im Zweifelsfall direkt, oder greifen Sie auf einfachere und allgemein verständliche Formulierungen zurück	
Verwenden Sie Fremdwörter, Fachausdrücke und Begriffe aus anderen Sprachen nur, wenn Sie sicher sind, dass Ihr Gegenüber diese auch versteht	
Nutzen Sie aktive Formulierungen	✓
Achten Sie darauf, dass Sie möglichst aktive Sätze verwenden	
Versuchen Sie sowohl im Gespräch, als auch in geschriebenen Texten, passive Formulierungen nur zu verwenden, wenn Sie Ihre Aussage dadurch unterstreichen möchten. Ersetzen Sie diese ansonsten so weit wie möglich durch aktive	
Vermeiden Sie Substantivierungen	✓
Vermeiden Sie Substantivierungen. Denn wenn Sie Verben in ein Hauptwort umwandeln (substantivieren), kann dieses Substantiv einen ganzen Satz ersetzen („Das Ziel wird erreicht" wird zu „Das Erreichen des Ziels"). Weil dadurch die Dichte an Informationen steigt, erschweren Substantivierungen es Ihrem Gegenüber, Sie zu verstehen	

Schaffen Sie Vertrauen

„Wer es in kleinen Dingen mit der Wahrheit nicht ernst nimmt, dem kann man auch in großen Dingen nicht vertrauen." (Einstein 1957, S. 5)

Kommunikation hilft Ihnen nicht nur, die Handlungen des anderen zu beeinflussen. Sie ermöglicht es Ihnen auch, Rückschlüsse auf die Emotionen des anderen zu ziehen. Dabei ist es wichtig, dass Worte und Taten übereinstimmen. In komplexen Situationen reichen bereits kleine Zeichen, um anderen Vertrauen zu gewähren oder zu entziehen. Ohne Vertrauen ist jedoch keine Kommunikation möglich, ohne Kommunikation kein Vertrauen. Vertrauen ist damit nicht nur Voraussetzung für Kommunikation, sondern zugleich auch deren Ergebnis: „Es entsteht erst im Kommunikationsprozess und bestimmt diesen zugleich maßgeblich, es ist Ergebnis einer gelungenen Interaktion und Basis für weitere gelingende Interaktionen" (Hubig 2014, S. 359).

Ob Ihr Gegenüber Ihnen vertraut oder nicht, hängt maßgeblich von folgenden fünf Faktoren ab (vgl. Stahl und Menz 2014, S. 70):

- **Offenheit** als Bereitschaft, Einblicke in Ihre eigenen Ziele, Mittel und Strukturen zu gewähren.
- **Ehrlichkeit,** dass Sie Mitteilungen nicht verfälschen, um Ihre eigenen Ziele durchzusetzen.
- **Toleranz,** die Meinung Ihres Gegenübers nicht nur zu dulden, sondern auch zu akzeptieren.
- **Gegenseitigkeit,** dass sich alle Beteiligten aktiv in die Kommunikation einbringen.
- **Fairness** in Bezug auf das Verhältnis von Leistung und Gegenleistung.

© Springer Fachmedien Wiesbaden GmbH, ein Teil von Springer Nature 2020
S. Pastoors und L. Meyer, *Das Konzept „Starke Sprache"*, essentials,
https://doi.org/10.1007/978-3-658-30692-2_4

Kommunizieren Sie deshalb offen und ehrlich. Dies beinhaltet unter anderem, dass Sie nichts bewusst verschleiern, verkürzen, beschönigen oder dramatisieren. Ob im Rahmen einer Kommunikation Vertrauen entsteht, hängt zudem davon ab, wie Sie das Gespräch gestalten und wie Ihr Gegenüber dies wahrnimmt und deutet. Es genügt nicht, sich gegenseitig Vertrauen zuzusichern. Alle Beteiligten müssen sich der Tragweite der damit verbundenen Verpflichtungen für die weitere Kommunikation bewusst sein:

- Vertrauen setzt voraus, dass die Beteiligten einseitige Vorteile, die sich zum Beispiel aus einem Mangel an Informationen, Kompetenz oder Macht ihres Gesprächspartners ergeben, nicht nutzen.
- Ihre Vertrauenswürdigkeit stabilisiert sich, wenn sich das Vertrauen als gerechtfertigt erwiesen hat. Sie führt außerdem dazu, dass andere Ihnen immer mehr vertrauen.
- Es ist rational, Vertrauensbeziehungen sofort zu kündigen, wenn jemand Sie sehr enttäuscht hat. Vertrauen ist ein hohes Gut. Es vermindert den Aufwand und die Transaktionskosten für die Zusammenarbeit. Setzen Sie es deshalb nicht leichtfertig aufs Spiel (vgl. Hubig 2014, S. 351–370).

Für starke Sprache und erfolgreiche Kommunikation spielt Vertrauen eine zentrale Rolle. Dieses können Sie auch bei bisher unbekannten Gesprächspartnern fördern, indem Sie offen kommunizieren, woher Sie Ihr Wissen haben. Zudem fördert es das Gesprächsklima, wenn Sie erst nachfragen, bevor Sie sich Ihre Meinung bilden oder den Beitrag Ihres Gegenübers kommentieren.

4.1 Bleiben Sie bei der Wahrheit

„Alles, was Du sagst, sollte wahr sein. Aber nicht alles, was wahr ist, solltest Du auch sagen." Voltaire (1694–1778)

Lügen bzw. Schwindeln gehört zur menschlichen Natur. Im Rahmen einer Studie, bei der sich zwei Versuchsteilnehmer einander vorstellen sollten, die sich vorher noch nie gesehen hatten, log jeder der Teilnehmer innerhalb von zehn Minuten im Schnitt dreimal (vgl. Feldmann 2012, S. 10). Aber warum lügen Menschen so häufig, selbst gegenüber Fremden, die sie wahrscheinlich nicht wiedersehen werden?

Nicht alle Lügen werden kalkuliert eingesetzt, um sich selbst einen Vorteil zu schaffen oder anderen zu schaden. Auch wenn solche Motive eine Rolle spielen, sind die Beweggründe für das Lügen vielschichtiger. Viele Menschen lügen aus Höflichkeit oder ihrem Verhältnis mit anderen Menschen zuliebe: Sie möchten eine neue Beziehung aufbauen, eine bestehende Beziehung nicht gefährden oder erreichen, dass andere sie als Teil ihrer Gemeinschaft akzeptieren.

Sie können Lügen außerdem dazu nutzen, ein Gespräch aufrechtzuerhalten. Sie können zum Beispiel vorgeben, sich besser mit dem Gegenstand der Diskussion auszukennen, als dies tatsächlich der Fall ist. Auf diese Weise verhindern Sie, dass das Gespräch abbricht oder sich in irrelevanten Details verliert. Das Gegenteil ist natürlich auch möglich: Sie stellen sich dümmer, um Ihrem Gesprächspartner mehr Fragen stellen zu können und ihm vielleicht auch ein gutes Gefühl zu vermitteln. Falsche Komplimente funktionieren auf dieselbe Weise. Manchmal machen Sie anderen Personen Komplimente zu Dingen, Handlungen oder Eigenschaften, die Sie vielleicht gar nicht so besonders an ihnen schätzen. Aber Sie hoffen, der anderen Person auf diese Weise zu gefallen (vgl. Feldmann 2012, S. 19–24).

Wie Sie Lügen moralisch bewerten, bleibt Ihnen selbst überlassen. Mit der Wahrheit fahren Sie in der Regel besser. Aber zumindest gesetzlich sind Bewerbern Notlügen im Vorstellungsgespräch oder auch bei der Wohnungssuche erlaubt – als eine Art Notwehr bei unzulässigen Fragen. Denn wer hier die Aussage verweigert, macht sich verdächtig – und die Traumstelle oder Traumwohnung wird dann an andere vergeben. Deshalb sind hier Notlügen grundsätzlich erlaubt.

Praxisbeispiel

Bei Bewerbungen auf eine neue Position müssen alle Inhalte in einem Bewerbungsprozess der Wahrheit entsprechen. Bleiben Sie bei der Wahrheit und sich treu, bevor Sie vollmundig mitteilen, Sie könnten verhandlungssicher spanisch sprechen, um die Stelle zu bekommen. Spätestens im Gespräch mit spanischen Kunden zeigt sich, wie gut Ihre Spanischkenntnisse wirklich sind. Dies gilt jedoch nicht, wenn andere Sie zum Beispiel nach Ihrer Religion oder Ihren sexuellen Vorlieben fragen. Solche Fragen haben in Vorstellungsgesprächen nichts zu suchen. Sie dürfen diese deshalb auch falsch beantworten. ◄

4.2 Nennen Sie Ihre Quellen

Manchmal verbreiten Sie Unwahrheiten, ohne sich dessen bewusst zu sein. Dies kann zum Beispiel passieren, wenn Sie davon überzeugt sind, die Wahrheit zu kennen, obwohl Ihnen nicht alle Details bekannt sind. Ihre eigene Wahrnehmung ist jedoch immer subjektiv. Seien Sie sich bewusst, dass Sie je nach Wahrnehmung, Gefühlen, Vorurteilen und früheren Erfahrungen ein und dieselbe Situation ganz anders wahrnehmen und bewerten. Überprüfen Sie deshalb gelegentlich, inwieweit Sie sich von Vorurteilen oder vorschnellen Annahmen blenden lassen. Wenn Sie Ihre eigene Wahrnehmung regelmäßig hinterfragen, vermindern Sie die Gefahr, andere unabsichtlich zu täuschen. Nicht alles, was auf den ersten Blick plausibel erscheint, muss auch wahr sein (vgl. Lay 1999, S. 25/64 f.).

Lassen Sie Ihre Zuhörer zudem wissen, woher Sie Ihr Wissen haben: Beruht es auf eigenen Erfahrungen? Haben Sie es im Internet oder einer Zeitung gelesen (falls ja, wo genau)? Oder haben Sie es von einem Bekannten gehört? Ihr Gegenüber kann Ihre Aussagen dann viel besser einschätzen und Sie gewinnen auf diese Weise an Glaubwürdigkeit (Tab. 4.1).

Tab. 4.1 Praxisbeispiele: Quellen benennen

Schwache Sprache	Starke Sprache
„Ich bin teamfähig!"	„Meine Teamfähigkeit konnte ich im Projekt xy unter Beweis stellen."
„Soziologisch betrachtet bedeutet dies…"	„Max Weber hat hierzu geschrieben, …"
„Mein Nachbar hat hierzu einen Artikel in der Zeitung gelesen."	„Mein Nachbar hat mich auf einen Artikel in der Frankfurter Rundschau aufmerksam gemacht, der darüber berichtet."
„Wie Sie sicherlich alle wissen, verfügt die Europäische Kommission über 43 Generaldirektionen."	„Die Europäische Kommission verfügt über 43 Generaldirektionen. Wenn gerne mehr über dieses Thema wissen möchten, finden Sie hierzu weitere Informationen auf der Webseite der Europäischen Kommission."

Quelle: eigene Zusammenstellung

4.3 Fragen Sie nach, bevor Sie sich eine Meinung bilden

„Solange man selbst redet, erfährt man nichts." (Marie von Ebner-Eschenbach, österreichische Schriftstellerin, 1830–1916)

Egal, wie gut Sie jemanden kennen, Sie können nicht erraten, was er denkt oder wie er etwas meint. Vermeiden Sie es deshalb, das Verhalten anderer über zu interpretieren. Dies kann schnell dazu führen, dass Sie das Verhalten anderer auf sich beziehen, ohne zu wissen, ob es tatsächlich so gemeint war. Versuchen Sie stattdessen, den anderen besser zu verstehen. Hierzu ist es notwendig, Fragen zu stellen. Nur wenn Sie anderen Fragen stellen und ihnen die Gelegenheit geben, ihr Verhalten, ihre Äußerungen oder ihre Entscheidungen zu erklären, lernen Sie andere besser kennen. So können Sie aktuelle Missverständnisse klären und ähnliche Missverständnisse in Zukunft vermeiden (vgl. Ebert und Pastoors 2017, S. 193 ff.).

Fragen Sie deshalb lieber nach, wenn Sie in einer Situation nicht weiterwissen (Tab. 4.2). Denn Fragen haben viele Vorteile:

- Mit Hilfe von Fragen zeigen Sie, dass Sie sich für den anderen interessieren und dass Ihnen seine Meinung wichtig ist. Auf diese Weise verbessern Fragen die Beziehung zu ihrem Gegenüber und verhindern, dass Sie aneinander vorbeireden.
- Fragen geben Anreize zum Nachdenken und beheben auf diese Weise Denkblockaden.
- Durch Fragen können Sie die Informationen des Gesprächspartners überprüfen und frühzeitig Missverständnisse erkennen.
- Sie erkennen frühzeitig Vorbehalte des anderen, bevor Sie ihn eventuell verärgern.
- Sie erfahren, welche Argumente Ihr Gegenüber noch in der Hinterhand hat, ehe Sie Ihre Karten offen gezeigt haben.
- Mit Hilfe von Fragen können Sie schnell erkennen, ob Ihr Angebot für Ihr Gegenüber attraktiv ist. Dies ermöglicht es Ihnen, aus verschiedenen möglichen Angeboten das passende auszuwählen.
- Mit Hilfe von Fragen führen Sie den anderen gedanklich dorthin, wo Sie ihn gerne haben möchten. Damit ersparen Sie sich lange Erklärungen, die oft nur schwer zu bremsen sind.
- Während der andere antwortet, können Sie in Ruhe nachdenken: Über das, was er sagt und darüber, was die Information in Bezug auf Ihr Angebot bedeutet (vgl. Birkenbihl 2007, S. 150 f.).

Tab. 4.2 Praxisbeispiele, wie Sie gute Nachfragen stellen

Schwache Sprache	Starke Sprache
„Da können Sie gerne die Stirn runzeln."	„Sie runzeln die Stirn. Kann ich Ihnen eventuell weiterhelfen?"
„Sie denken wohl, dass ich zu ungeschickt bin, um die Maschine zu bedienen."	„Warum erklären Sie mir das?"
„Sie lehnen den Vorschlag doch nur ab, weil er von mir kommt."	„Was genau stört Sie an dem Vorschlag? Vielleicht finden wir ja eine gemeinsame Lösung, wenn Sie mir Ihre Sicht darlegen."

Quelle: eigene Zusammenstellung

Stellen Sie auch in der schriftlichen Kommunikation keine Vermutungen an. Fragen Sie zum Beispiel bei Bewerbungsverfahren telefonisch nach, falls Sie noch offene Fragen haben. Auf diese Weise können Sie in Erfahrung bringen, wer der richtige Ansprechpartner für Ihr Anschreiben ist und welche Eigenschaften genau von einem Bewerber erwartet werden. Dies hat zudem den Vorteil, dass Sie bereits persönlich mit dem Unternehmen in Kontakt getreten sind.

In wissenschaftlichen Arbeiten sollten Sie ebenfalls noch einmal genauer nachforschen, wenn Sie sich nicht sicher sind. Falls Sie dann immer noch keine Antworten finden, macht es Sinn, dies schriftlich festzuhalten und entsprechend kritisch zu würdigen.

4.4   Checkliste

Die folgende Checkliste gibt Ihnen einen Überblick, wie Sie Vertrauen schaffen und glaubwürdig kommunizieren können (Tab. 4.3).

Tab. 4.3   Checkliste zu Kapitel 4: Schaffen Sie Vertrauen

Checkliste	
Schaffen Sie Vertrauen	√
Für starke Sprache und erfolgreiche Kommunikation spielt Vertrauen eine zentrale Rolle	
Kommunikation dient Ihnen einerseits dazu, Handlungen des anderen zu beeinflussen. Andererseits ermöglicht sie es Ihnen, Rückschlüsse auf die Emotionen des anderen zu ziehen	
Kommunizieren Sie offen und ehrlich. Dies beinhaltet unter anderem, dass Sie nichts bewusst verschleiern, verkürzen, beschönigen oder dramatisieren	
Es genügt nicht, sich gegenseitig Vertrauen zuzusichern. Alle Beteiligten müssen sich der Tragweite der damit verbundenen Verpflichtungen für die weitere Kommunikation bewusst sein	
Bleiben Sie bei der Wahrheit	
Alles, was Du sagst, sollte wahr sein. Aber nicht alles, was wahr ist, solltest Du auch sagen.	
Gesetzlich sind Bewerbern Notlügen im Vorstellungsgespräch oder auch bei der Wohnungssuche erlaubt – als eine Art Notwehr bei unzulässigen Fragen	
Nennen Sie Ihre Quellen	√
Sie können bei bisher unbekannten Gesprächspartnern Vertrauen fördern, indem Sie offen kommunizieren, woher Sie Ihr Wissen haben	
Seien Sie sich bewusst, dass Sie je nach Wahrnehmung, Gefühlen, Vorurteilen und früheren Erfahrungen ein und dieselbe Situation ganz anders wahrnehmen und bewerten	
Überprüfen Sie gelegentlich, inwieweit Sie sich von Vorurteilen oder vorschnellen Annahmen blenden lassen. Auf diese Weise vermindern Sie die Gefahr, andere unabsichtlich zu täuschen.	
Lassen Sie Ihre Zuhörer wissen, woher Sie Ihr Wissen haben. Ihr Gegenüber kann Ihre Aussagen auf diese Weise viel besser einschätzen und Sie gewinnen an Glaubwürdigkeit	
Fragen Sie nach, bevor Sie sich eine Meinung bilden	√
Fragen Sie nach, bevor Sie sich Ihre Meinung bilden oder den Beitrag Ihres Gegenübers kommentieren	
Vermeiden Sie es, das Verhalten anderer über zu interpretieren. Dies kann schnell dazu führen, dass Sie das Verhalten anderer auf sich beziehen, ohne zu wissen, ob es tatsächlich so gemeint war	
Wenn Sie anderen Fragen stellen und ihnen die Gelegenheit geben, ihr Verhalten oder ihre Entscheidungen zu erklären, lernen Sie andere besser kennen. So können Sie aktuelle Missverständnisse klären und ähnliche Missverständnisse in Zukunft vermeiden	

Stiften Sie Sinn

„Wir haben nicht nur das Recht, sondern die Pflicht, Sinn zu geben. Sinn ist nicht zu finden und braucht deswegen auch nicht gesucht zu werden. […] Er wird gegeben, gestiftet, von uns." Messner (2012, S. 84)

Ihre Mitmenschen erwarten von Ihnen, dass Sie Ihnen auch komplexe Entwicklungen und Sachverhalte gut verständlich erklären. Wie der Bergsteiger und Autor Reinhold Messner schreibt, erhoffen sich andere von Ihnen Sinn und Orientierung. Dies wird Ihnen nur gelingen, wenn Sie die Informationen im richtigen Kontext und mit anschaulichen Beispielen erläutern. Dazu ist es wichtig, dass Sie Ihren Mitmenschen erklären, was genau Sie bezwecken und was die Alternative zu Ihrem Vorschlag wäre.

So können zum Beispiel Führungskräfte ihre Mitarbeiter langfristig nur motivieren, wenn sie ihnen auch den Sinn ihrer Arbeit vermitteln. Materielle Anreize helfen zwar vielen Menschen, persönliche Hürden und Herausforderungen zu meistern, sie halten aber nur für kurze Zeit an. Deshalb entwickeln viele Unternehmen immer aufwendigere Anreizsysteme, deren Wirkung meist rasch verpufft. Anstatt sich mit Anreizsystemen zu beschäftigen, sollten sich Führungskräfte fragen, wie sie die Eigenmotivation der Mitarbeiter stärken können. Hierbei spielt die Sinn- und Wertefrage eine zentrale Rolle (vgl. Reusche 2015).

Sinn- und werteorientierte Führung sieht in Mitarbeitern verantwortliche Menschen (vgl. Berschneider 2003, S. 41). Eine sinn- und werteorientierte Führung bezieht die Mitarbeiter deshalb aktiv mit ein. So können Führungskräfte den Blick der Mitarbeiter zum Beispiel durch Informationen und eine frühe Diskussion über den Sinn geplanter Änderungen auf das große Ganze richten. Sinn entsteht erst, wenn die Mitarbeiter erkennen, inwieweit das Erreichen der

S. Pastoors und L. Meyer, *Das Konzept „Starke Sprache"*, essentials,
https://doi.org/10.1007/978-3-658-30692-2_5

Ziele den Unternehmenszweck unterstützt – also einen Beitrag zum Wohl eines
größeren Ganzen leistet. Etwas für das größere Ganze zu tun, unterstützt die
Sinnfindung. Dieses größere Ganze kann die eigene Abteilung oder Firma sein.
Hierbei kann es sich aber auch um die Kunden oder die Gesellschaft handeln
(vgl. Reusche 2015).

5.1   Erklären Sie anderen, was Sie genau bezwecken

Geben Sie immer an, was genau Sie damit bezwecken, wenn Sie Ihr Gegenüber etwas fragen, um etwas bitten oder einen Auftrag erteilen. Zum einen hilft
es Ihrem Gegenüber, Ihre Frage oder Ihren Auftrag richtig einzuordnen. Zum
anderen versteht Ihr Gegenüber auf diese Weise den Sinn Ihrer Aufforderung.

Der US-amerikanische Autor Simon Sinek Autor empfiehlt seinen Lesern und
Zuhörern, immer mit der Frage nach dem „Warum" zu beginnen. Vor allem bei
Appellen und Veränderungsprozessen ist es wichtig, diese gut zu begründen. Auf
diese Weise geben Sie eine Antwort, warum Ihr Gegenüber das tun soll, wozu
Sie ihn auffordern. Wenn dies nicht klar ist, wird er nicht dazu bereit sein, Ihnen
zu folgen (vgl. Sinek 2011) (Tab. 5.1). Achten Sie deshalb auf folgende Punkte,
wenn Sie andere zu etwas bewegen wollen:

- **Setzen Sie klare Ziele:** Jede Aufgabe braucht ein Ziel, auf das alle Beteiligten
gemeinsam hinarbeiten können. Wenn kein konkretes Ziel gesetzt oder dieses
nicht ausreichend kommuniziert wird, kommt es sonst immer wieder zu
Problemen. Wieso soll sich Ihr Gegenüber für etwas einsetzen, das er nicht
versteht und dessen späteren Nutzen er nicht erkennen kann?
- **Informieren Sie Ihr Gegenüber frühzeitig:** Viele informieren Ihre Mitmenschen erst dann, wenn es sich nicht mehr vermeiden lässt. Diese haben
dann keine Möglichkeit mehr, sich selbst in den Entscheidungsprozess ein-
zubringen. Binden Sie Ihre Mitmenschen bei wichtigen Entscheidungen von
Anfang an ein. Sie werden es Ihnen danken. Wenn Sie Ihre Mitmenschen
dagegen vor vollendete Tatsachen setzen, fühlen diese sich übergangen und
reagieren mit Ablehnung und Widerstand.
- **Bieten sie nachvollziehbare Erklärungen:** Nachvollziehbare Begründungen
machen es Ihrem Gegenüber leichter, undankbare Aufgaben zu übernehmen
oder Veränderungen zu akzeptieren. Vorgeschobene Argumente durchschauen
andere dagegen schnell. Sie führen deshalb nur zu Resignation und Widerstand (vgl. Ebert 2019, S. 232 f.).

Tab. 5.1   Praxisbeispiele, wie Sie Ihre Gründe darlegen können

Schwache Sprache	Starke Sprache
„Ihr Vorschlag ist leider nicht umsetzbar."	„Wir können Ihren Vorschlag leider nicht umsetzen, da wir vertraglich/rechtlich an andere Absprachen gebunden sind."
„Wir empfehlen, rechtzeitig zu buchen."	„Buchen Sie rechtzeitig. Im Augenblick ist die Nachfrage sehr groß und es kommt zu Terminengpässen."
„Sie sollten sich Ihre Gedanken aufschreiben."	„Schreiben Sie Ihre Gedanken auf. Dann können Sie sich diese später noch einmal vor Augen führen."
„Nehmen Sie Ihren Lebenslauf mit in das Bewerbungsgespräch."	„Wenn Sie Ihren Lebenslauf im Bewerbungsgespräch vor sich liegen haben, gibt dies Ihnen Sicherheit."
„Um die passende Preisstrategie für das Unternehmen zu finden, muss eine Primärforschung, sowie Sekundärforschung vorgenommen werden."	„Um die passende Preisstrategie für das Unternehmen zu finden, wird zuerst mithilfe einer Sekundärforschung das Preisniveau für vergleichbare Produkte untersucht. Anschließend wird eine Primärforschung durchgeführt, um herauszufinden, wie viel potentielle Kunden für das Produkt zahlen würden."

Quelle: eigene Zusammenstellung

5.2   Verwenden Sie konkrete Beispiele

Wenn Ihr Gegenüber Sie nicht versteht, obwohl Sie ihm etwas in einfachen, klaren Sätzen erklärt haben, kann dies daran liegen, dass ihm der Zusammenhang fehlt. In diesem Fall können Sie ihm das Gesagte noch einmal mithilfe eines Beispiels aus dem alltäglichen Leben Ihres Gegenübers oder bildhafter Sprache erklären.

Beispiele und Vergleiche (Analogien)

Beispiele und Vergleiche (Analogien) eignen sich gut, um ähnliche Prinzipien und Zusammenhänge zu erklären. Stellen Sie hierzu eine Verbindung zwischen zwei unterschiedlichen Situationen her. Auf diese Weise können Sie Ihren Zuhörern fremde Dinge anhand bekannter Situationen erklären. Vor allem fachspezifische Inhalte können Sie gut vermitteln, indem Sie diese mithilfe konkreter Beispiele veranschaulichen. Dazu stehen Ihnen unterschiedliche Möglichkeiten zur Verfügung:

- (Praxis-)Beispiele: Anhand konkreter Beispiele aus der Praxis Ihres Gegenübers können Sie gut Fachinhalte veranschaulichen und dessen Verständnis für neue Dinge fördern.

- Gegenstände oder Objekte: Mithilfe von Gegenständen können Sie Inhalte oder Prinzipien anschaulich erklären. Dieses Vorgehen eignet sich zum Beispiel sehr gut für technische Fragen.
- Bilder: Mit Bildern können Sie gut eine konkrete Situation oder einen konkreten Gegenstand veranschaulichen.
- Filme: Mithilfe von Filmen können Sie gut Prozesse und Reaktionen auf ein bestimmtes Ereignis veranschaulichen.

Praxisbeispiel

Mithilfe von Analogien können Sie komplizierte Zusammenhänge einfach und verständlich erklären. Sie kommen deshalb häufig im Unterricht, der Lehre und bei Veränderungsprozessen zum Einsatz:

- Im Chemieunterricht oder auch im Studium vermitteln Lehrer und Dozenten die Grundlagen der Atomtheorie mithilfe sogenannter Teilchenmodelle. Hierzu werden entweder die einzelnen Bestandteile eines Atoms oder von Molekülen anhand bunter Kugeln veranschaulicht. Auf diese Weise lassen sich nicht nur die Zusammensetzung von Atomen oder Molekülen, sondern auch unterschiedliche Aggregatzustände und der Ablauf chemischer Reaktionen anschaulich darstellen.
- Bei Veränderungsprozessen in Unternehmen vergleichen Führungskräfte den Wettbewerb am Markt gerne mit der Evolutionstheorie nach Darwin. Dabei wird gerne auf das folgende Darwin-Zitat zurückgegriffen: „Weder die stärkste noch die intelligenteste Spezies überlebt. Sondern jene, die sich am besten dem Wandel anpasst." Dieser Vergleich wird gerne genutzt, um die Mitarbeiter von der Notwendigkeit und der Dringlichkeit unbeliebter Maßnahmen zu überzeugen (vgl. Rettig 2014).
- Ein beliebtes Bild im Coaching ist das sogenannte Eisbergmodell. Dabei wird wahlweise die Psyche eines Menschen oder die Kommunikation zwischen zwei Menschen mit einem Eisberg verglichen. Genau wie bei einem Eisberg würden bei der menschlichen Psyche oder der zwischenmenschlichen Kommunikation nur ca. 20 %, bewusst wahrgenommen. Die anderen 80 %, also der weitaus größere Teil, befände sich dagegen unsichtbar unter der Oberfläche. Das Eisbergmodell soll auf diese Weise veranschaulichen, wie Menschen miteinander kommunizieren und was dabei unausgesprochen transportiert wird. ◄

Sprachbilder (Metaphern)
Wenn Sie einen komplizierten Sachverhalt bildhaft und einfach darstellen möchten, können Sie hierzu auch Sprachbilder (Metaphern) nutzen. Die Metapher ist eine besondere Form des Vergleichs. Dabei wird ein Wort oder eine Formulierung aus ihrem ursprünglichen Zusammenhang in eine andere Situation übertragen, um diese zu veranschaulichen. Hierzu verbinden Sie Begriffe aus zwei Bereichen, die im normalen Sprachgebrauch nichts miteinander zu tun haben. Beispiel hierfür sind Formulierungen wie „bärenstark", „sonnenklar", „Schneckentempo" oder „ein Tropfen auf dem heißen Stein".

Metaphern eignen sich gut, um Vorträge, Reden oder Geschichten aufzuwerten. Achten Sie jedoch darauf, dass Sie nur Bilder nutzen, die Ihre Zuhörer auch verstehen.

Praxisbeispiele

Besonders häufig kommen Metaphern bei Veränderungsprozessen und der Werbung zum Einsatz. Dies erleichtert es dem Leser oder Zuhörer, den Sachverhalt zu erfassen:

- Vor allem bei Veränderungsprozessen benutzen Manager gerne Metaphern, um die Notwendigkeit der geplanten Maßnahmen zu verdeutlichen. Mit dem Bild „Wir sitzen alle im gleichen Boot." wird das Unternehmen als Schicksalsgemeinschaft beschworen. Die Bilder vom Feuer, das immer weiter um sich greift, oder der schmelzenden Eisscholle helfen dem Management dagegen, die Dringlichkeit von Veränderungen zu betonen.
- Beim Coaching werden Teams oder sogar ganze Unternehmen mit Segelschiffen verglichen: Der Geschäftsführer wird dabei zum Kapitän und aus der Belegschaft wird die Mannschaft, die gemeinsam das Schiff durch eine stürmische See in ruhigere Gewässer lenken. Ziel dieses Bild ist es, den Teilnehmern des Coachings zu vermitteln, dass es im Unternehmen auf jeden einzelnen ankommt. Auch Vergleiche aus dem Sport sind im Coaching beliebt: „Das eigene Leben zu verändern, gelingt einem nicht im Sprint, sondern nur im Dauerlauf."
- Einer der erfolgreichsten Werbeslogans der letzten Jahre lautet „Red Bull verleiht Flügel". Damit will der Hersteller des Energy Drinks seine Kunden davon überzeugen, dass das Getränk nicht nur gut schmeckt, sondern diesen auch dank des Zusatzes von Koffein und Taurin zu Höchstleistungen verhilft. ◄

Im täglichen Sprachgebrauch fallen Metaphern vielen Menschen überhaupt nicht mehr auf. Das liegt daran, dass sich viele Metaphern bereits stark in die Alltagssprache integriert haben und so ihren Übertragungscharakter verloren haben.

Vorteile von Beispielen und Sprachbildern
Der Einsatz von Bildern (Metaphern) und Beispielen (Analogien) bietet Ihnen viele Vorteile:

- Wenn Sie ein Arbeitstreffen mit einem „Kindergarten" vergleichen, entsteht in den Köpfen Ihrer Zuhörer automatisch das Bild eines chaotischen Durcheinanders, das weder zielführend noch erfolgreich war. Wenn Sie diese Aussage noch mit konkreten Beispielen untermauern, wird es für andere schwer, dagegen zu argumentieren. Achten Sie jedoch darauf, den Einsatz von Bildern und Beispielen nicht zu übertreiben.
- Wenn Sie die Dinge anschaulich erläutern und mithilfe von Bildern und Beispielen Zusammenhänge erklären, erzeugen Sie lebhafte Bilder im Kopf Ihres Gegenübers. Dieses „Kopf-Kino" erlaubt es Ihren Lesern oder Zuhörern, in Ihre Welt einzusteigen.
- Zudem sprechen Sie mit deren Hilfe unterschiedliche Sinnesebenen Ihres Gegenübers an, wodurch sich andere besser an das Gesagte oder das Geschriebene erinnern.

Verwenden Sie die beiden Stilmittel trotzdem sparsam. Nur dann können sie ihre volle Wirkung entfalten. Es ist kontraproduktiv, wenn Sie diese in jedem zweiten Satz benutzen. Überlegen Sie sich zudem genau, was Sie erreichen wollen, damit Sie die passenden Bilder und Beispiele wählen (vgl. Englert 2014, S. 103 ff.).

5.3 Zeigen Sie anderen Lösungen und Alternativen auf

Verbote und negative Formulierungen wirken demotivierend. Häufig erreichen Sie damit genau das Gegenteil von dem, was Sie wollen. Wie oft haben Sie schon Dinge gehört oder gesagt wie: „Das schaffst du nicht." oder „Lernst Du es denn nie?". Mit solchen Formulierungen sabotieren Sie sich selbst und andere. Sie möchten ja, dass Ihr Kollege sich ändert oder dass er die Prüfung besteht (vgl. Ebert und Pastoors 2017, S. 128).

Zeigen Sie Ihrem Gegenüber deshalb Alternativen auf und liefern Sie ihm Anreize, sich zu ändern. Sprechen Sie über das, was Sie wollen, und nicht über das, was Sie nicht wollen, wenn Sie möchten, dass jemand sein Verhalten ändert (Tab. 5.2).

Tab. 5.2 Praxisbeispiele, wie Sie im persönlichen Gespräch Alternativen aufzeigen

Schwache Sprache	Starke Sprache
„Hör endlich auf zu jammern."	„Überlege dir, was du ändern kannst."
„Pass auf, dass du keinen Unfall baust."	„Konzentriere dich auf die Straße."
„Verschluck' dich nicht."	„Genieße das Essen."

vgl. Ebert und Pastoors (2017, S. 129)

Denn ein „Nein" oder ein „Nicht" kann das Gehirn nur schwer verarbeiten, weil es in Bildern denkt. Wenn Sie jemand auffordert, nicht an grüne Tomaten zu denken, konstruiert Ihr Gehirn genau das falsche Bild: Grüne Tomaten.

Solche Formulierungen sind psychologisch geschickt – nicht nur bei Kindern. Auch bei Erwachsenen erreichen Sie mehr, wenn Sie Ihre Botschaft positiv formulieren. Das Wort „nicht" ist als solches unbeliebt. Viele Menschen assoziieren es mit den vielen Verboten aus ihrer Kinderzeit. Zuhörer und Leser wollen erfahren, was ist, und nicht, was nicht ist. Je besser Sie dieses Bedürfnis erfüllen, desto mehr werden andere Ihr Wort schätzen. Das gilt auch für das Berufsleben (vgl. ebd., S. 128 ff.).

Ihre Kunden zeigen mehr Verständnis, wenn Sie Ihnen direkt Alternativen aufzeigen (Tab. 5.3):

Tab. 5.3 Praxisbeispiele, wie Sie Ihren Kunden Alternativen aufzeigen

Schwache Sprache	Starke Sprache
„Das kann ich Ihnen nicht sagen."	„Da muss ich mich kurz erkundigen. Darf ich Sie gleich zurückrufen?"
„Da bin ich nicht der richtige Ansprechpartner."	„Dafür ist Frau Busch zuständig. Ich stelle Sie zu meiner Kollegin durch."
„Frau Müller ist jetzt nicht zu sprechen."	„Frau Müller ist ab 15 Uhr wieder zu erreichen. Soll ich ihr etwas ausrichten?"
„Da kann ich Ihnen nichts versprechen."	„Das ist möglich, sobald das neue EDV-Programm fertig ist. Wann das sein wird, hängt davon ab, wie schnell es der EDV-Firma gelingt, unser System umzustellen. Ich halte Sie gerne auf dem Laufenden."

vgl. Ebert und Pastoors (2017, S. 129)

5.4   Checkliste

Die folgende Checkliste gibt Ihnen einen Überblick, wie Sie mit Ihren Aussagen
Sinn stiften können (Tab. 5.4).

Tab. 5.4 Checkliste zu Kap. 5: Stiften Sie Sinn

Checkliste	
Stiften Sie Sinn	✓
Ihre Mitmenschen erwarten von Ihnen, dass Sie Ihnen auch komplexe Entwicklungen und Sachverhalte gut verständlich erklären. Dies wird Ihnen nur gelingen, wenn Sie die Informationen im richtigen Kontext und mit anschaulichen Beispielen erläutern	
Führungskräfte können ihre Mitarbeiter langfristig nur motivieren, wenn sie ihnen auch die Ziele und den Sinn ihrer Arbeit vermitteln können	
Sinn entsteht erst, wenn die Mitarbeiter erkennen, inwieweit das Erreichen der Ziele den Unternehmenszweck unterstützt – also einen Beitrag zum Wohl eines größeren Ganzen leistet	
Erklären Sie anderen, was Sie genau bezwecken	✓
Geben Sie immer an, was genau Sie damit bezwecken, wenn Sie andere etwas fragen, um etwas bitten oder einen Auftrag erteilen. Zum einen hilft es Ihrem Gegenüber, Ihre Frage oder Ihren Auftrag richtig einzuordnen. Zum anderen versteht Ihr Gegenüber auf diese Weise den Sinn Ihrer Aufforderung	
Setzen Sie klare Ziele: Jede Aufgabe braucht ein Ziel, auf das alle Beteiligten gemeinsam hinarbeiten können	
Binden Sie Ihre Mitmenschen bei wichtigen Entscheidungen von Anfang an ein. Sie werden es Ihnen danken. Wenn Sie Ihre Mitmenschen vor vollendete Tatsachen setzen, fühlen diese sich übergangen und reagieren mit Ablehnung und Widerstand	
Nachvollziehbare Begründungen machen es Ihrem Gegenüber leichter, undankbare Aufgaben zu übernehmen oder Veränderungen zu akzeptieren	

(Fortsetzung)

Tab. 5.4 (Fortsetzung)

Checkliste	
Verwenden Sie konkrete Beispiele	√
Beispiele und Vergleiche (Analogien) eignen sich gut, um ähnliche Prinzipien und Zusammenhänge zu erklären. Stellen Sie hierzu eine Verbindung zwischen zwei unterschiedlichen Situationen her	
Vor allem fachspezifische Inhalte können Sie gut vermitteln, indem Sie diese mithilfe konkreter Beispiele veranschaulichen	
Wenn Sie einen komplizierten Sachverhalt bildhaft und einfach darstellen möchten, können Sie hierzu auch Sprachbilder (Metaphern) nutzen	
Die Metapher ist eine besondere Form des Vergleichs. Dabei wird ein Wort oder eine Formulierung aus ihrem ursprünglichen Zusammenhang in eine andere Situation übertragen, um diese zu veranschaulichen	
Metaphern eignen sich gut, um Vorträge, Reden oder Geschichten aufzuwerten. Achten Sie jedoch darauf, dass Sie nur Bilder nutzen, die Ihre Zuhörer auch verstehen	
Verwenden Sie die beiden Stilmittel zudem sparsam. Nur dann können sie ihre volle Wirkung entfalten	
Zeigen Sie anderen Lösungen und Alternativen auf	√
Zeigen Sie Ihrem Gegenüber Alternativen auf und liefern Sie ihm Anreize, sich zu ändern	
Sprechen Sie über das, was Sie wollen, wenn Sie möchten, dass jemand sein Verhalten ändert. Denn ein „Nein" oder ein „Nicht" versteht Ihr Gehirn nicht, weil es in Bildern denkt	

Sprechen Sie Klartext 6

„Ein Problem ist halb gelöst, wenn es klar formuliert ist." John Dewey, amerikanischer Philosoph, 1859–1952

Formulieren Sie Ihre Botschaft klar und deutlich, wenn Sie mit Ihrer Kommunikation etwas bewirken möchten. Hierzu ist es wichtig, den Interpretationsspielraum Ihrer Aussagen so gering wie möglich zu halten. Führungskräfte müssen zum Beispiel bei Veränderungsprozessen viele Fragen beantworten, zu denen es oft unterschiedliche Meinungen gibt: Wie schnell soll die Veränderung durchgeführt werden? Welcher Weg ist der Beste, um ans Ziel zu gelangen? Solche Fragen ergeben sich häufig erst dadurch, dass Führungskräfte Ihre Aussagen vage gehalten haben, um niemandem direkt vor den Kopf zu stoßen. Begreifen Sie solche Nachfragen und Diskussionen als Chance, die besten Entscheidungen zu finden. Arbeiten alle zusammen, werden aus unterschiedlichen Standpunkten schnell gemeinsame Interessen (vgl. Ebert 2019, S. 233).

Versuchen Sie deshalb, mehrdeutige Formulierungen zu vermeiden. Je allgemeiner Sie formulieren, desto größer ist die Gefahr, dass Ihr Gegenüber Sie falsch versteht. Deshalb sollten Ihre Angaben stets so präzise wie möglich und der Situation angemessen sein: Anstelle von „Ich besitze Berufserfahrung als IT-Berater" hilft Ihrem potenziellen Arbeitgeber die Aussage „Ich besitze vier Jahre Berufserfahrung als IT-Berater in der Finanzbranche" wesentlich weiter und erhöht so Ihre Chancen beim Bewerbungsgespräch. Neben vagen oder widersprüchlichen Aussagen, spielt häufig auch die Art, wie etwas gesagt wird, eine wichtige Rolle. So helfen zum Beispiel sogenannte „Ich"-Botschaften Ihrem Gegenüber, Ihre persönliche Meinung von Fakten zu unterscheiden.

© Springer Fachmedien Wiesbaden GmbH, ein Teil von Springer Nature 2020
S. Pastoors und L. Meyer, *Das Konzept „Starke Sprache"*, essentials,
https://doi.org/10.1007/978-3-658-30692-2_6

6.1   Vermeiden Sie widersprüchliche Aussagen

Ein noch größeres Problem sind widersprüchliche Aussagen. Widersprüchliche Botschaften führen zwangsläufig zu Missverständnissen, denn Ihr Gegenüber weiß dann nicht, auf welchen Aspekt der Nachricht es reagieren soll. Versteckte Botschaften sind besonders dann schwer zu verstehen, wenn sie nicht zur expliziten Botschaft passen. Wenn Sie vage Andeutungen machen, anstatt auf den Punkt zu kommen, ist der Empfänger gefordert, diese richtig zu deuten: Wollen Sie ihn über etwas informieren oder soll er etwas Bestimmtes tun? Oder wollen Sie ihm nur etwas über sich erzählen? Menschen senden aus unterschiedlichen Gründen indirekte Botschaften: Sie haben Angst andere zu verletzen, auf deren Ablehnung zu stoßen, sich festzulegen oder sie wissen selbst nicht, was sie wollen (vgl. Ebert und Pastoors 2017, S. 177).

Verwirrende Aussagen
Anhand einiger provokanter Fragen verdeutlichen wir Ihnen, was vage Formulierungen bei Ihrem Gegenüber bewirken:

- „Ich würde sagen, …" → Warum tun Sie es dann nicht?
- „Ich meine damit Folgendes: …" → Müssen Sie das zuvor Gesagte erklären?
- „An dieser Stelle …" → An welcher sonst?
- „Jetzt mal ganz ehrlich, …" → Haben Sie vorher gelogen?
- „Im Klartext: …" → Haben Sie zuvor nur drum herumgeredet?
- „Schlicht und einfach …" → War zuvor alles kompliziert und schwierig?

Auch das Zusammenspiel verbaler und nonverbaler Kommunikation ist wichtig, um eine Nachricht richtig zu verstehen. Wenn die nonverbalen Signale nicht mit dem Gesagten oder Geschriebenen übereinstimmen, verwirren Sie Ihr Gegenüber (vgl. Schulz von Thun 2007, S. 33 ff.).

6.2   Senden Sie „Ich"-Botschaften

Formulieren Sie Ihre eigenen Wahrnehmungen und Wünsche, aber auch Ihre eigene Meinung immer als „Ich"-Botschaften. Im Vergleich zu Du-Botschaften wirken gut formulierte Ich-Botschaften deutlich ansprechender und konstruktiver. Zudem erfährt Ihr Gesprächspartner, wie dessen Verhalten auf Sie wirkt und wo Ihre persönlichen Grenzen liegen. Diese Form der Konfrontation ist annehmbarer, da Sie den Empfänger weder verurteilen, noch zurechtweisen, angreifen oder beschuldigen. Sie bestimmen auch nicht, was er zu tun und zu unterlassen hat. Ich-Botschaften vermitteln, dass die eigene Wahrnehmung subjektiv ist (Tab. 6.1).

Tab. 6.1   Praxisbeispiele für „Ich"-Botschaften

Schwache Sprache	Starke Sprache
„Du bist schon wieder unpünktlich!" (Du-Botschaft + Feststellung)	„Ich habe hier eine halbe Stunde auf dich gewartet und mich total geärgert, weil ich viel zu tun habe. Ich fühle mich nicht ernstgenommen und nicht respektiert, wenn du unsere Termine nicht einhältst." (Ich-Botschaft + Sachaussage + eigene Bedürfnisse und Gefühle + Appell)
„Das wird man ja wohl noch sagen dürfen." (Man + vage Verallgemeinerung)	„Das ist meine Meinung und dazu stehe ich." (Ich-Botschaft + Übernahme von Verantwortung)
„Nun, da der Bericht erneut durchgesehen wurde, muss zugegeben werden, dass Fehler gemacht worden sind." (Passive Formulierung + keine Übernahme von Verantwortung)	„Ich habe den Bericht gelesen und muss zugeben, dass ich einen Fehler gemacht habe." (vgl. Clark 2015, S. 45) (Ich-Botschaft + Übernahme von Verantwortung)

Quelle: eigene Zusammenstellung

Sie geben Ihren Gesprächspartnern so die Möglichkeit zu entscheiden, ob sie Ihre Aufforderung oder Rückmeldung annehmen möchten oder nicht. Der Angesprochene ist deshalb eher dazu bereit, Ihnen entgegenzukommen. Teilen Sie Ihre Sichtweise einer Situation deshalb als Beobachtungen oder persönliche Meinung mit (vgl. Mai 2017).

Wünschen Sie sich, dass andere Ihre Meinung ernst nehmen und respektieren? Dann ist es wichtig, dass Sie diese als Ihre persönliche Meinung kenntlich machen. Dies geschieht mithilfe von Formulierungen, wie zum Beispiel „Meiner Meinung …" oder „Ich denke …". Mit deren Hilfe machen Sie deutlich, dass es sich beim Gesagten um Ihre persönliche Perspektive handelt. Zudem machen es Ihnen Ich-Botschaften leichter, Ihre eigene Meinung kritisch zu hinterfragen. Dies ist eine wichtige Voraussetzung, um bei Meinungsverschiedenheiten respektvoll und konstruktiv miteinander zu kommunizieren.

Anderen zuzuhören und offen auf deren Meinung einzugehen, sind wichtige Voraussetzungen für eine erfolgreiche Kommunikation. Dies ist nicht immer einfach, vor allem, wenn andere Sie mit Meinungen konfrontieren, die Ihrem eigenen Weltbild widersprechen.

Was ist eine Meinung?

Eine Meinung gibt ein persönliches Werturteil wieder. Jeder Mensch hat das Recht, seine Meinung frei zu äußern. Eine Meinung erkennen Sie daran, dass diese sich nicht überprüfen lässt. Es gibt somit weder „richtige" noch „falsche" Meinungen. Das unterscheidet die Meinung von Fakten. Die Feststellung „Der Himmel ist blau", lässt sich überprüfen. Es handelt sich also um eine Tatsachenbehauptung. Wer vermeintliche „Fakten" verbreitet, die eindeutig widerlegt werden können, kann sich somit nicht auf Meinungsfreiheit berufen.

Die Aussage „Das Verhalten Ihrer Kinder ist inakzeptabel", hängt dagegen von Ihrer eigenen Perspektive ab. Was andere für akzeptabel halten, beruht auf deren persönlichem Weltbild. Andere Menschen können zu einem anderen Urteil kommen. Es handelt sich somit um eine Meinungsäußerung. Doch auch die Meinungsfreiheit hat Grenzen. Wenn es einer Person nicht darum geht, einen Beitrag zur Diskussion zu leisten, sondern die Würde eines anderen Menschen zu verletzen, ist dies keine persönliche Meinung, sondern eine Beleidigung. Dies gilt nicht nur für einzelne Personen: Wer bewusst gegen eine Gruppe hetzt, um die Würde ihrer Mitglieder zu verletzen, macht sich der Diskriminierung oder sogar der Volksverhetzung schuldig. Dies ist zum Beispiel der Fall, wenn eine Person andere Menschen zu Gewalt gegen eine bestimmte Gruppe anstachelt (vgl. Kitz 2016).

6.3   Sagen Sie „Nein", wenn Sie etwas nicht möchten

Nein-Sagen ist eine Kunst, die Sie bei der Kommunikation mit Kollegen und Vorgesetzten ebenso weiterbringt wie im privaten Bereich. Dazu ist es wichtig, dass Sie Ihre Grenzen ziehen, ohne dem anderen gegenüber respektlos zu werden.

Wenn es Ihnen schwerfällt, nein zu sagen, hilft Ihnen vielleicht die folgende Überlegung: Für jedes Ja, beziehungsweise jedes Mal, wenn Sie sich bereit erklären, für jemand anderen etwas zu erledigen, zahlen Sie einen Preis: Sie zahlen mit Ihrer Zeit, Energie und Kraft. Diese Ressourcen hätten Sie vielleicht dringender für andere Dinge benötigt oder lieber in etwas Anderes investiert. Das Gleichgewicht von Geben und Nehmen spielt dabei eine wichtige Rolle: Müssen Sie langfristig mehr geben als Sie zurückbekommen, führt das zu Stress und Unzufriedenheit (vgl. Ebert und Pastoors 2017, S. 295 ff.).

Rufen Sie sich ins Gedächtnis, dass niemand immer verfügbar ist! Es lohnt sich deshalb, kurz abzuwägen, ob Sie einer Bitte entsprechen oder diese ausschlagen. Stellen Sie sich hierzu folgende Fragen:

- Was genau erwarten andere von Ihnen? Was sollen Sie tun?
- Möchten Sie das wirklich tun oder geben?
- Wie viel Zeit und Energie haben Sie?
- Steht die Bitte im Konflikt mit anderen Aufgaben, die Sie erledigen müssen? Was muss eventuell darunter leiden oder zurücktreten, wenn Sie der Bitte nachkommen?

- Wer bittet Sie um einen Gefallen? Was bedeutet dieser Mensch für Sie? In welchem Verhältnis stehen Sie zueinander?
- Wie oft hat diese Person schon etwas für Sie getan? Und wie oft haben Sie schon etwas für diese Person getan? Und – wenn das schon öfter der Fall war – möchten Sie es tatsächlich noch einmal tun?

Praxisbeispiel Es gibt verschiedene Möglichkeiten, respektvoll, aber gleichzeitig deutlich nein zu sagen (Ebd., S. 298 ff.):

- **Begründen:** Wenn Sie Ihre Absage begründen, zeigen Sie, dass Ihr „Nein" inhaltliche Gründe hat und nichts mit Ihrem Gegenüber zu tun hat. Eine Begründung ist nicht dasselbe wie eine Rechtfertigung. Sie sind nicht gezwungen, über die Verwendung Ihrer Zeit Rechenschaft abzulegen.
  Beispiel: „Ich kann diese Aufgabe leider nicht übernehmen, da mir sowohl Herr Müller als auch Frau Schmidt schon andere Aufgaben übertragen haben."
- **Mitgefühl zeigen:** Bringen Sie zum Ausdruck, dass Sie verstehen, dass es für den anderen unangenehm ist, dass Sie seine Bitte ablehnen.
  Beispiel: „Es tut mir leid, dass ich Ihrer Bitte nicht nachkommen kann."
- **Verständnis zeigen:** Zeigen Sie Verständnis dafür, dass Ihr Gegenüber diese Bitte äußert. Sie signalisieren damit, dass Ihre Ablehnung nicht persönlich gemeint ist. Außerdem versteht der Andere, dass Sie seine Bitte nicht ablehnen, weil Sie diese für unangebracht halten.
  Beispiel: „Ich verstehe, dass Sie zu viel zu tun haben, um diese Aufgabe auch noch zu erledigen, aber ich kann Ihnen im Moment nicht helfen."
- **Bedanken:** Wenn jemand Sie um etwas bittet, was Sie nicht annehmen können oder wollen, eignet sich auch der Dank für das gezeigte Vertrauen.
  Beispiel: „Es ehrt mich, dass Sie so viel Vertrauen in mich setzen, aber ich kann diese Aufgabe nicht übernehmen."
- **Mit Einschränkung annehmen:** Manchmal ist es gar nicht notwendig, eine Anfrage komplett abzulehnen, da Sie einem Teil der Bitte nachkommen können. Oder Sie können die Aufgabe zu einem späteren Zeitpunkt erledigen. Damit signalisieren Sie, dass Sie grundsätzlich bereit sind, zu helfen und das im Rahmen Ihrer Möglichkeiten auch zu tun.

Beispiel: „Heute schaffe ich das nicht mehr. Reicht es Ihnen, wenn ich diese Aufgabe morgen Vormittag erledige?"

- **Alternative:** Wenn Sie die Bitte nicht so ausführen können, wie sie an Sie gerichtet wurde, können Sie eventuell ein Gegenangebot machen, mit dem das gleiche Ziel auf andere Weise erreicht werden kann.
  Beispiel: „Es tut mir leid. Ich weiß, wie dringend diese Angelegenheit für Sie ist. Ich kann jedoch unmöglich diese Aufgabe übernehmen. Ich rufe aber gerne Herrn Schmidt an und frage ihn, ob er Ihnen helfen kann."
- **Interesse zeigen:** Überzeugen Sie sich, ob die von Ihnen vorgeschlagene Lösung für den anderen annehmbar ist. Damit beweisen Sie Respekt und Interesse für Ihr Gegenüber.

6.4   Checkliste

Die folgende Checkliste gibt Ihnen einen Überblick, wie Sie klare und eindeutige Botschaften senden (Tab. 6.2).

Tab. 6.2   Checkliste zu Kap. 6: Senden Sie klare Botschaften

Checkliste	
Senden Sie klare Botschaften	✓
Formulieren Sie Ihre Botschaft klar und deutlich. Hierzu ist es wichtig, den Interpretationsspielraum Ihrer Aussagen so klein wie möglich zu halten	
Vermeiden Sie mehrdeutige Formulierungen. Je allgemeiner Sie formulieren, desto größer ist die Gefahr, dass Ihr Gegenüber Sie falsch versteht. Deshalb sollten Ihre Angaben stets so präzise wie möglich und der Situation angemessen sein	
Vermeiden Sie widersprüchliche Aussagen	✓
Vermeiden Sie widersprüchliche Aussagen. Diese führen zwangsläufig zu Missverständnissen, da Ihr Gegenüber nicht weiß, auf welchen Aspekt der Nachricht es reagieren soll	
Auch das Zusammenspiel verbaler und nonverbaler Kommunikation ist für die Verständlichkeit einer Nachricht wichtig. Wenn die nonverbalen Signale nicht mit dem Gesagten oder Geschriebenen übereinstimmen, verwirren sie Ihr Gegenüber	

(Fortsetzung)

Tab. 6.2 (Fortsetzung)

Checkliste

Senden Sie „Ich"-Botschaften	√
Formulieren Sie Ihre eigenen Wahrnehmungen und Wünsche, aber auch Ihre eigene Meinung immer als „Ich"-Botschaften. Im Vergleich zu Du-Botschaften wirken Ich-Botschaften deutlich konstruktiver	
Machen Sie Ihre persönliche Meinung als solche kenntlich. Dies geschieht mithilfe von Formulierungen, wie zum Beispiel „Meiner Meinung …" oder „Ich denke …"	
Ich-Botschaften vermitteln, dass die eigene Wahrnehmung subjektiv ist. Sie geben Ihren Gesprächspartnern so die Möglichkeit zu entscheiden, ob sie Ihre Aufforderung oder Rückmeldung annehmen möchten oder nicht	
Es gibt somit weder „richtige" noch „falsche" Meinungen. Das unterscheidet Meinungen von Fakten. Wer vermeintliche „Fakten" verbreitet, die eindeutig widerlegt werden können, kann sich somit nicht auf Meinungsfreiheit berufen	
Sagen Sie „Nein", wenn Sie etwas nicht möchten	√
Ziehen Sie Ihre Grenzen, ohne dem anderen gegenüber respektlos zu werden.	
Rufen Sie sich ins Gedächtnis, dass niemand immer verfügbar ist! Es lohnt sich deshalb, kurz abzuwägen, ob Sie einer Bitte entsprechen oder diese ausschlagen.	

Befreien Sie Ihre Sprache von Ballast 7

„Vollkommenheit entsteht nicht, wenn man nichts mehr hinzufügen kann, sondern dann, wenn man nichts mehr wegnehmen kann." (de Saint-Exupéry 1939, S. 60)

Kennen Sie die Redewendung, dass jemand den Wald vor lauter Bäumen nicht sieht? Die Redewendung beschreibt Situationen, in denen Menschen sich so sehr in Details verlieren, dass sie das Offensichtliche bzw. die Kernbotschaft nicht mehr sehen.

Mit der Sprache ist es oft genauso. Häufig belasten Menschen Ihre Sprache mit unnötigen Botschaften, Wörtern oder Floskeln. Dies führt nicht nur dazu, dass andere nicht verstehen, was Sie eigentlich sagen wollen, sondern dass Sie am Ende selbst nicht mehr wissen, worauf Sie eigentlich hinauswollten. Deswegen ist es wichtig, dass Sie Ihre Sprache von unnötigem Ballast befreien. Hierzu zählen zum Beispiel Füllwörter, Weichmacher, Wiederholungen, Verallgemeinerungen, doppelte Verneinungen oder überholte Redewendungen. Was sich genau hinter den einzelnen Begriffen verbirgt, erfahren Sie in diesem Kapitel.

Versuchen Sie, sich solche Wörter und Formulierungen bewusst zu machen und schrittweise abzugewöhnen. Denn wie de Saint-Exupery gesagt hat, ist Ihr Beitrag erst dann vollkommen, wenn Sie nichts mehr weglassen können.

7.1 Vermeiden Sie abschwächende Formulierungen und Weichmacher

Einschränkungen und Weichmacher sind kleine Worte oder Floskeln, die das, was Sie gerade gesagt haben, zurücknehmen, verniedlichen oder abschwächen. Die Autoren Roy Clark und Sylvia Englert benennen eine Reihe Begriffe

© Springer Fachmedien Wiesbaden GmbH, ein Teil von Springer Nature 2020
S. Pastoors und L. Meyer, *Das Konzept „Starke Sprache"*, essentials,
https://doi.org/10.1007/978-3-658-30692-2_7

oder Formulierungen, die das Verb in einem Satz und somit auch Ihre Aussage relativieren oder abschwächen (vgl. Clark 2015, S. 37–39, 76):

- **Abschwächende oder verstärkende Wörter und Formulierungen,** die Ihre Aussage unnötig relativieren. Hierzu zählen Wörter und Formulierungen wie zum Beispiel eigentlich, etwa, ungefähr, irgendwie, relativ, im Prinzip, vielleicht, sicherlich, selbstverständlich, gänzlich, sehr, überaus etc.
- **Vorrausgehende Weichmacher,** mit denen Sie die folgende Aussage vorweg infrage stellen. Hierzu zählen Wörter und Formulierungen wie zum Beispiel „im Großen und Ganzen", „normalerweise", „im Prinzip" oder „generell". Auch unnötige Entschuldigungen, wie „Ich bin ja nur…" oder „Ich bin ja kein Fachmann/keine Fachfrau" führen dazu, dass Ihre Aussage infrage gestellt wird.
- **Verniedlichungen,** mit denen Sie Probleme oder Leistungen klein reden. Hierzu zählen Wörter und Formulierungen wie zum Beispiel „Gar nicht mal so schlecht", „unklug", „nicht so ganz glücklich", „Ich bin ja nur …", „Ich habe von dem Thema ja keine Ahnung, aber …" (vgl. ebd., S. 37–39)
- **Überflüssige Konjunktive,** mit denen Sie das Gesagte abschwächen. Hierzu zählen Wörter wie zum Beispiel möchte, könnte, wollte, sollte, müsste oder hätte.
- **Doppelte Umschreibung:** Hierzu zählen Formulierungen wie zum Beispiel ein tauber, schwerhöriger Mann (wenn er taub ist, kann er nicht mehr schwerhörig sein), ein weißer Schimmel (ein Schimmel ist ein weißes Pferd, daher reicht Schimmel), kreisrund (rund – ein Kreis ist immer rund), alter Greis (Greis), auseinanderdividieren (teilen, dividieren), das einzelne Individuum (Individuum), persönlich anwesend (anwesend – niemand kann „unpersönlich" anwesend sein) (vgl. ebd., S. 76).
- **Überflüssige und nichtssagende Adjektive,** die Ihre Aussagen kitschig klingen lassen und auf diese Weise abwerten. Dies gilt für Formulierungen wie knisternde Spannung, ein tragischer Todesfall, markerschütternde Schreie oder erfolgsverwöhnter Manager (vgl. Englert 2014, S. 100 f.)

In einzelnen Situationen sind Wörter wie „vielleicht", „eigentlich", „könnte", „sollte", „müsste" durchaus sinnvoll. Sie drücken Unsicherheit aus und geben Ihrem Gegenüber zu verstehen, dass Sie sich selbst nicht sicher sind oder andere nicht bedrängen wollen. Wenn Sie diese Formulierungen ersatzlos aus Ihrem Wortschatz verbannen, wirken Sie ruppig, dominant und unhöflich. Verwenden Sie sprachliche Weichmacher deshalb mit Bedacht und versuchen Sie, diese falls möglich zu vermeiden:

- Ihre Sprache wird dadurch klarer, einfacher und nachvollziehbarer.
- Ihre Zuhörer verarbeiten Ihre Informationen leichter und handeln dementsprechend schneller.
- Sie stärken Ihre Glaubwürdigkeit und Überzeugungsstärke durch eine nachvollziehbare Logik.

7.2   Vermeiden Sie Verallgemeinerungen

Viele Missverständnisse basieren auf Verallgemeinerungen, unter denen Ihr Gegenüber etwas Anderes versteht als Sie. Das passiert oft schon bei der Kommunikation zwischen Menschen mit derselben Muttersprache. Wie viel schwieriger ist es dann für Menschen, die Ihre Sprache erst in der Schule oder später gelernt haben? Drücken Sie sich daher konkret aus, wenn Sie mit anderen kommunizieren (vgl. Ebert und Pastoors 2017, S. 257).

Durch Verallgemeinerungen entstehen schnell peinliche Missverständnisse. Sprechen Sie deshalb zum Beispiel von den Vereinigten Staaten und nicht von Amerika, wenn Sie die USA meinen. Dies erleichtert die Gespräche mit rund 600 Mio. anderen Amerikanern, die in Brasilien, Kanada, Mexiko oder einem der anderen amerikanischen Länder leben. Gleiches gilt für Verallgemeinerungen über bestimmte Länder, Gruppen oder Kulturen. Verzichten Sie auf Stereotype wie „die Lehrer", „die Politiker" oder „die Deutschen". Es gibt keine homogenen Gruppen, die Sie problemlos „über einen Kamm scheren" können.

Eine weitere Ursache für Missverständnisse ist das Wort „man". Viele Menschen verwenden das Wort „man" in Texten und Reden. Wenn Sie „Man könnte …" anstatt „Ich möchte …" sagen, haben Sie nur nicht den Mut, für Ihren Standpunkt einzustehen. Sie signalisieren auf diese Weise, dass Ihnen die Angelegenheit oder das Thema nicht so wichtig ist, dass Sie dafür einen Konflikt oder Widerspruch riskieren. Wenn Sie solche Weichmacher zu oft verwenden, werden Sie unglaubwürdig und können andere nur schwer von Ihrem Standpunkt überzeugen. Zudem enthalten Sie anderen vor, wen genau Sie meinen, wenn Sie das Wort „man" benutzen. In heiklen Situationen kann es die Beziehung zu Ihrem Gegenüber gefährden, wenn Sie sich hinter „man" verstecken. Dies gilt besonders für Reden. Wenn Sie zu häufig das Wort „man" verwenden, wird Ihr Publikum hellhörig und durchschaut Ihr Manöver.

Machen Sie die Dinge und Menschen hinter „man" sichtbar (Tab. 7.1): zum Beispiel Sie selbst, Ihre Freunde, Unternehmerinnen, Touristen oder Delegierte

Tab. 7.1 Praxisbeispiele, wie Sie Verallgemeinerungen vermeiden

Schwache Sprache	Starke Sprache
„Man sollte die Situation wie folgt lösen…"	„Lösen Sie die Situation bitte wie folgt…"
„Man müsste mal was dagegen machen…"	„Ich ergreife die Initiative. Wer macht mit?"
„In dem Zusammenhang sagt man ja gerne…"	„In diesem Zusammenhang sagt der Kunde gerne…"
„Viele Klienten wünschen sich eine maßgeschneiderte Beratung…"	„Sie wünschen sich eine Beratung nach Maß? Wir bieten Ihnen…"

Quelle: eigene Zusammenstellung

auf einem Parteitag. Beim Reden kostet es ein wenig Übung, auf dieses Wort zu verzichten. Bei Texten können Sie dagegen am Rechner einfach die Suchfunktion benutzen.

7.3   Nutzen Sie positive Formulierungen

Vermeiden Sie Verneinungen. Das Gehirn kann ein „Nicht" nur auf Umwegen verarbeiten. Seien Sie deshalb mit negativ besetzten Begriffen vorsichtig. Wenn Sie zum Beispiel „Es besteht kein Risiko" sagen, rufen Sie Ihrem Zuhörer eben dieses Risiko ins Bewusstsein. Versichern Sie ihnen stattdessen besser: „Sie können sich sicher sein, dass …". Verneinungen sind zudem oft missverständlich, ihre Aussage ist unklar. Prüfen Sie deshalb, ob Sie negative Begriffe durch passende positive Formulierungen ersetzen können: Unverhofft ($\rightarrow$ überraschend, plötzlich), unvorsichtig ($\rightarrow$ leichtfertig, risikofreudig), unbewusst ($\rightarrow$ instinktiv), nicht glauben ($\rightarrow$ zweifeln), nicht erinnern ($\rightarrow$ vergessen) oder nicht zulassen ($\rightarrow$ verhindern) (siehe auch Tab. 7.2).

Tab. 7.2 Praxisbeispiele für positive Formulierungen

Schwache Sprache	Starke Sprache
„Unser Geschäft schließt täglich um 19.00 Uhr."	„Wir haben täglich bis 19.00 Uhr für Sie geöffnet."
„Da Sie nicht alle Voraussetzungen für die ausgeschriebene Stelle erfüllen, haben wir diese anderweitig vergeben."	„Wir haben uns für einen anderen Bewerber entschieden, der die Voraussetzungen noch besser erfüllt als Sie."

Quelle: eigene Zusammenstellung

7.4   Checkliste

Die folgende Checkliste gibt Ihnen einen Überblick, wie Sie Ihre Sprache von
Ballast befreien können (Tab. 7.3).

Tab. 7.3   Checkliste zu Kap. 7: Befreien Sie Ihre Sprache von Ballast

Checkliste	
Befreien Sie Ihre Sprache von Ballast	√
Befreien Sie Ihre Sprache von unnötigem Ballast. Hierzu zählen zum Beispiel Füllwörter, Weichmacher, Wiederholungen, Verallgemeinerungen, doppelte Verneinungen oder überholte Redewendungen	
Versuchen Sie, sich solche Wörter und Formulierungen bewusst zu machen und schrittweise abzugewöhnen	
Vermeiden Sie abschwächende Formulierungen und Weichmacher	√
Vermeiden Sie abschwächende Formulierungen, Weichmacher und Redewendungen	
Einschränkungen und Weichmacher sind kleine Worte oder Floskeln, die das, was Sie gerade gesagt haben, zurücknehmen, verniedlichen oder abschwächen: – Abschwächende oder verstärkende Wörter und Formulierungen, die Ihre Aussage unnötig relativieren – Vorrausgehende Weichmacher, mit denen Sie die folgende Aussage vorweg infrage stellen – Verniedlichungen, mit denen Sie Probleme oder Leistungen klein reden – Überflüssige Konjunktive, mit denen Sie das Gesagte abschwächen – Doppelte Umschreibung – Überflüssige und nichtssagende Adjektive, die Ihre Aussagen kitschig klingen lassen und auf diese Weise abwerten	
Wenn Sie diese Formulierungen ersatzlos aus Ihrem Wortschatz verbannen, wirken Sie ruppig, dominant und unhöflich. Verwenden Sie sprachliche Weichmacher deshalb mit Bedacht und versuchen Sie, diese falls möglich zu vermeiden	

(Fortsetzung)

Tab. 7.3 (Fortsetzung)

Checkliste	
Vermeiden Sie Verallgemeinerungen	✓
Viele Missverständnisse basieren auf Verallgemeinerungen, unter denen Ihr Gegenüber etwas Anderes versteht als Sie	
Eine weitere Ursache für Missverständnisse ist das Wort „man". Wenn Sie „Man könnte …" anstatt „Ich möchte …" sagen, haben Sie nur nicht den Mut, für Ihren Standpunkt einzustehen. Sie signalisieren auf diese Weise, dass Ihnen die Angelegenheit oder das Thema nicht so wichtig ist, dass Sie dafür einen Konflikt oder Widerspruch riskieren	
Machen Sie die Dinge und Menschen hinter „man" sichtbar	
Nutzen Sie positive Formulierungen	✓
Vermeiden Sie Verneinungen. Das Gehirn kann ein „Nicht" nur auf Umwegen verarbeiten. Seien Sie deshalb mit negativ besetzten Begriffen vorsichtig	
Prüfen Sie, ob Sie negative Begriffe durch passende positive Formulierungen ersetzen können	

Zum Abschluss

Der Erfolg Ihrer Kommunikation hängt maßgeblich davon ab, ob Ihr Gegenüber Sie verstehen (bzw. mit Ihnen kooperieren) möchte oder nicht. Um erfolgreich mit anderen zu kommunizieren, müssen Sie deshalb sprachlich aktiv mit diesen zusammenarbeiten. Dabei kommen Sie mit drei einfachen Schritten zu Ihrem Ziel:

- Kommunizieren Sie so, dass Ihr Gegenüber Sie versteht: Hierzu müssen Sie Ihre Gedanken ordnen, so einfach wie möglich formulieren, Sinn stiften, Klartext sprechen und Ihre Sprache von Ballast befreien (Maxime der Quantität, der Relevanz und der Modalität).
- Investieren Sie in die Beziehung mit Ihrem Gesprächspartner: Hierzu ist es wichtig, Vertrauen zu schaffen, ehrlich zu kommunizieren, Ihre Quellen zu nennen und nachzufragen, bevor Sie sich eine Meinung bilden (Maxime der Qualität).
- Falls es anschließend immer noch zu Missverständnissen kommt, sollten Sie mit Ihrem Gesprächspartner klären, ob Sie eventuell aneinander vorbeireden.

In den letzten sechs Kapiteln haben wir Ihnen die Grundsätze einer ausdrucksstarken und wirksamen Sprache vorgestellt. Selbst wenn Sie alle Punkte beachten, kann es zu Missverständnissen kommen. In diesem Fall empfiehlt es sich zu klären, ob die Gesprächspartner eventuell aneinander vorbeireden. Sie haben vielleicht etwas übersehen oder überhört, verstehen Dinge falsch oder interpretieren sie anders als andere. Solche Missverständnisse können Sie durch gezielte Rückfragen verhindern.

Bitten Sie Ihr Gegenüber, seine Aussage zu wiederholen oder kurz zusammen zu fassen, wenn Sie das Gefühl haben, nicht verstanden zu haben, was der andere

© Springer Fachmedien Wiesbaden GmbH, ein Teil von Springer Nature 2020
S. Pastoors und L. Meyer, *Das Konzept „Starke Sprache"*, essentials,
https://doi.org/10.1007/978-3-658-30692-2_8

gemeint hat. Wahlweise können Sie das Gesagte wiederholen, um zu überprüfen, ob Sie Ihr Gegenüber richtig verstanden haben („Heißt das, dass…?", „Habe ich richtig verstanden, dass …?"). Beobachten Sie das Verhalten des anderen: Lässt die Reaktion Ihrer Gesprächspartner darauf schließen, dass diese Ihre Mitteilung richtig verstanden haben (vgl. Flammer 1996, S. 105)?

Manchmal droht ein Gespräch zu scheitern, weil Sie falsche Annahmen äußern und erwarten, dass Ihr Gegenüber diese teilt. Oder alle Beteiligten haben unterschiedliche Annahmen im Hinterkopf. Bitten Sie in diesen Fällen um eine genauere Darstellung, weisen Sie auf Fragwürdiges hin und hinterfragen Sie die getroffenen Annahmen. Dies verbessert nicht nur den Gesprächsverlauf, sondern motiviert auch andere dazu, ihre eigenen Annahmen zu hinterfragen. Fragen Sie nach den Umständen der Situation, über die der andere spricht, damit Sie ihn besser verstehen und sich besser in dessen Situation hineinversetzen können (vgl. Flammer 1996, S. 164 ff.). Wenn Sie verstehen, wie der andere „tickt", können Sie die Situation neu bewerten und Ihre Ziele, Ihre Sprache und Ihre Argumente entsprechend anpassen.

Das Prinzip der starken Sprache hilft Ihnen, sprachlich auf Ihr Gegenüber zuzugehen, ohne sich dabei zu verrenken. Es ist ganz einfach: Überlegen Sie sich, was Sie erreichen möchten und machen Sie selbst sprachlich den ersten Schritt.

Was Sie aus diesem *essential* mitnehmen können

- Bevor Sie mit anderen kommunizieren, müssen Sie sich erst selbst bewusst werden, was Sie überhaupt erreichen wollen.
- Eine gute Struktur und ein klarer Fokus auf wenige zentrale Punkte helfen Ihrem Gegenüber, das Gesagte besser zu verstehen.
- Verzichten Sie auf unnötige Fremdwörter oder Abkürzungen, wenn Sie möchten, dass Ihr Gegenüber Sie als kompetent und gebildet wahrnimmt.
- Vermeiden Sie mehrdeutige Formulierungen. Je allgemeiner Sie formulieren, desto größer ist die Gefahr, dass Ihr Gegenüber Sie falsch versteht. Deshalb sollten Ihre Angaben stets so präzise wie möglich und der Situation angemessen sein.
- Formulieren Sie Ihre eigenen Wahrnehmungen, Ihre Wünsche und Ihre eigene Meinung immer als „Ich"-Botschaften. Im Vergleich zu „Du"-Botschaften wirken „Ich"-Botschaften deutlich konstruktiver.
- Vertrauen spielt für erfolgreiche Kommunikation eine zentrale Rolle.

© Springer Fachmedien Wiesbaden GmbH, ein Teil von Springer Nature 2020   53
S. Pastoors und L. Meyer, *Das Konzept „Starke Sprache"*, essentials,
https://doi.org/10.1007/978-3-658-30692-2

Literatur

Berschneider W (2003) Sinnzentrierte Unternehmensführung. Orthaus, Lindau

Birkenbihl V (2007) Psycho-logisch richtig verhandeln. Professionelle Verhandlungstechniken mit Experimenten und Übungen. mvg, Heidelberg

Clark RP (2015) Die 50 Werkzeuge für gutes Schreiben. Handbuch für Autoren, Journalisten und Texter. Autorenhaus Verlag, Berlin

de Saint-Exupéry A (1939) Wind, Sand und Sterne. Gallimard, Paris

Duden (Hrsg) (2016) Das Wörterbuch der sprachlichen Zweifelsfälle. Richtiges und gutes Deutsch, vol 9, 8. Aufl. Dudenverlag, Mannheim

Ebert H (2019) Veränderungen gestalten. In: Pastoors S et al (Hrsg) Praxishandbuch werteorientierte Führung. Kompetenzen erfolgreicher Führungskräfte im 21. Jahrhundert. Springer Nature, Düsseldorf, S 219–239

Ebert H, Fisiak I (2018) Bürgerkommunikation auf Augenhöhe. Wie Behörden und öffentliche Verwaltung verständlich kommunizieren können, 3. Aufl. Springer, Bochum

Ebert H, Pastoors S (2017) Respekt: Wie wir durch Empathie und wertschätzende Kommunikation im Leben gewinnen. Springer, Wiesbaden

Einstein A (1957) On Israeli-Arab Relations. New Outlook: Middle East Mon 1(1):5

Englert S (2014) So lektorieren Sie Ihre Texte. Verbessern durch überarbeiten. Autorenhaus Verlag, Berlin

Feldmann R (2012) Lügner – die Wahrheit übers Lügen. Springer Spectrum, Berlin

Flammer A (1996) Einführung in die Gesprächspsychologie. Huber, Bern

Glass L (2005) Sprich doch einfach Klartext! Wie man selbstbewusst kommuniziert und die Initiative ergreift. Goldmann, München

Grice P (1967) Logic and Conversation. In: Cole P, Morgan J (Hrsg) Speech Acts, Syntax and Semantics, vol 12. Academic Press, New York

Hesse N (2019) Wirtschaftsthemen verständlich vermitteln: Wie Sie mit ökonomischen Texten in Wissenschaft, Verwaltung und Unternehmen überzeugen. Schäffer-Poeschel, Berlin

Hölscher L (2012) Mit der Fünf-Satz-Technik zur perfekten Rede – Wie Sie mit der Fünf-Satz-Technik rhetorisch glänzen und Ihre Zuhörer begeistern. Beitrag vom 5. März 2012. https://www.akademie.de/wissen/5-satz-technik-rede-vortrag. Zugegriffen: 14. März 2020

© Springer Fachmedien Wiesbaden GmbH, ein Teil von Springer Nature 2020   55
S. Pastoors und L. Meyer, *Das Konzept „Starke Sprache",* essentials,
https://doi.org/10.1007/978-3-658-30692-2

Hubig C (2014) Vertrauen und Glaubwürdigkeit als konstituierende Elemente der Unternehmenskommunikation. In: Zerfaß A, Piwinger M (Hrsg) Handbuch Unternehmenskommunikation, 2. Aufl. Springer Gabler, Wiesbaden, S 351–370

Kitz V (2016) Meinungsfreiheit. Das wird man doch wohl mal sagen dürfen – oder? Online-Artikel vom 03.02.2016. http://www.spiegel.de/panorama/meinungsfreiheitwasdarf-ich-sagen-und-was-nicht-a-1074146.html. Zugegriffen: 7. Febr. 2019

Lay R (1999) Führen durch das Wort, 7. Aufl. Ullstein, Frankfurt a. M.

Lorenzoni B, Bernhard W (2001) Professional Politeness. Die Anti-Ellbogen-Strategie für Ihren persönlichen Auftritt im Beruf und im Privatleben. Metropolitan, Düsseldorf

Mai J (2008) Das ABC der Präsentationstipps. http://karrierebibel.de/praesentationstipps/. Zugegriffen: 23. Sept. 2016

Mai J (2017) Stichwort „Feedback geben: Regeln, Beispiele, Tipps". https://karrierebibel.de/feedback-geben/. Zugegriffen: 12. Nov. 2017

Messner R (2012) Berge versetzen: Das Credo eines Grenzgängers. GU, München

Pastoors S (2017) Präsentieren und Visualisieren. In: Becker JH, Ebert H, Pastoors S (Hrsg) Praxishandbuch berufliche Schlüsselkompetenzen. 50 Handlungskompetenzen für Ausbildung, Studium und Beruf. Springer, Heidelberg, S 59–67

Priebe M (2020) Die Substantivierung ist der Lebendigkeit ihr Tod. Warum zu viele Substantive jeden Text versauen, https://mathias-priebe.de/substantivierung-vermeiden/. Zugegriffen: 14. März 2020

Rettig D (2014) Change-Management. Wie der Wandel in Unternehmen gelingt. Artikel in der Wirtschaftswoche vom 02.04.2014. https://www.wiwo.de/erfolg/management/change-management-wie-der-wandel-in-unternehmen-gelingt/9680978.html. Zugegriffen: 14. März 2020

Reusche U (2015) Sinn stiften – fünf Thesen, Beitrag vom am 6. Juli 2015. https://www.hcc-magazin.com/sinn-stiften-fuenf-thesen/14649. Zugegriffen: 08. Okt. 2018

Scheel K (2018) Die Fünf-Satz-Methode erfolgreich anwenden: Nicht Überreden – Argumentieren! https://zeitsprung-c2.de/blog/5-Satz-Methode-argumentieren. Zugegriffen: 14. März 2020

Schneider W (2001) Deutsch für Profis. Wege zu gutem Stil. Goldmann, München

Schulz von Thun F (2007) Miteinander Reden 1. Störungen und Klärungen. Psychologie der zwischenmenschlichen Kommunikation. rororo, Reinbek bei Hamburg

Sinek S (2011) Start with why: how great leaders inspire everyone to take action. Portfolio Penguin, New York

Stahl HK, Menz F (2014) Handbuch Stakeholder-Kommunikation. Überzeugende Sprache in der Unternehmenspraxis. ESV, Berlin

Strunk W, White EB (2000) The elements of style, 4. Aufl. Allyn & Bacon, Boston Erstveröffentlichung 1935

Wöss F (2004) Der souveräne Vortrag: Informieren – Überzeugen – Begeistern. Linde, Wien

Printed in the United States
By Bookmasters

DALRIADA
THE DAWN OF A KING

DALRIADA
THE DAWN OF A KING

A Novel of Love, Honor, and Fury

CHRISTOPHER H. CONNOR

ARCHWAY
PUBLISHING

Interior Image Credit: Susan Curtis

Archway Publishing books may be ordered
through booksellers or by contacting:

Archway Publishing
1663 Liberty Drive
Bloomington, IN 47403
www.archwaypublishing.com
844-669-3957

ISBN: 978-1-4808-5807-7 (sc)
ISBN: 978-1-4808-5808-4 (e)

Library of Congress Control Number: 2018905549

Print information available on the last page.

Archway Publishing rev. date: 01/25/2024

*This book is dedicated to my father,
Michael F. Connor, who taught me right
from wrong and has always loved me.*

ACKNOWLEDGMENT

Six people have been key to getting this book into its final form, for that, I am indebted. Thank you, Austin Kimbrell, for working tirelessly in reviewing the original manuscript and painstakingly documenting the weaknesses in the story and characters and for offering sage guidance in clearing those hurdles. Thank you, Mike and Brent, for reading the raw first-cut and for encouraging me to "keep it coming." Thank you, Cathie Robbins and Allison Denny, for enduring the arduous task of inserting my red line edits, catching all my blunders, and adding spice where it was needed. Thank you, Susan Curtis, for your endless patience and fantastic work in producing Dalriada's map.

I want to thank my wife, Gina, and my kids, Colton, Casen, Cassidy, and Caryss for being my constant cheerleaders and forever asking, "How's it coming?" Your eagerness to read the book was a perpetual spark that lit my fire. Gina, thanks for enduring all the book hubbub and for giving up all those late nights so that I could complete this work, you're the best!

Also, every new author needs a special person to come along and say, with confidence, "Hey, you can write a book. Tell me your story. Okay, now write it." For me, that was Ray Vogel. Thanks, Ray, for giving me the courage to take the leap!

Finally, I lift my praise to the Lord God Almighty, Jesus Christ my Savior. Without you Lord, I would have neither the wit, nor breath, to put words to paper. You've always been there, in the sunshine and the storms of *my* story, for that, I am eternally grateful. I look forward to smiling at You face to face, and to seeing Your radiant smile in return. Thank you for the opportunity to pen this work—may Your glory shine through it.

Soli Deo Gloria.

Hooah!

PREFACE. 824 A.D.

LONG BEFORE SCOTLAND HAD A NAME, BEFORE Scotland had a people, before Scotland had a king, the people of northwest Britannia lived not as a nation, but as a patchwork of clans. These northwestern clans, boasting a Gaelic descent, held bloodlines tracing back to Ireland. They were a people who aspired to recapture the simple lives of their early Irish ancestry. They hoped to regain what was lost when prior generations veered from simplicity and squandered their God-given freedom.

In times past, their ancestors in Ireland had led simple lives tending to daily needs. Yet as successive generations grew in strength and prosperity, need gave way to want, and the more brazen among them laid claim to stature and power and sought to subjugate their fellow clansmen to servitude. These rapacious men looked to expand their domain, and in so doing, found an ever-growing taste for both wealth and might. Fueled by desire, such men crowned themselves king as a means of establishing their titles and fortifying their authority. As the Ireland kings focused the light of sovereignty upon themselves, Ireland's hope of peace was lost in darkness.

Many sought freedom from the dominion of these burgeoning provincial kingships. Yet freedom was only found in flight. Hundreds fled Ireland and ventured across the Northern Channel of the Irish Sea to the northwestern shores of Britannia. The untainted lands of Britannia offered an idyllic landscape of lush fields and rolling hills, etched with great structures of rock and granite and dense woodlands of oak and pine. As clans settled the land, they built homes of stone and wood and thatch. These immigrants named their land Dalriada, after the Dál Riata clan, who were among the first to migrate from Ireland.

In leaving their Irish homeland for Britannia, the Dalriadans brought with them their wives, their children, and their rudimentary Christian faith. Many settled along Britannia's western shores, while others migrated inland to the east. Settling clans formed villages and towns and erected meeting halls, markets, and trade shops. As they grew in number, the Dalriadans moved deeper into Britannia, boasting a livelihood of farming, shepherding, and raising families. They pursued peace with God, grateful for life, land, and freedom—these were esteemed highest among their possessions. Their faith obliged them to build places of refuge and repentance, lest their hearts wander. Abbeys and monasteries were constructed to suit such needs. For at times, they found need, even want, of the things offered in their Christ—things beyond births and weddings and burials.

Alpin, son of Eochaid and a fifth generation Dalriadan, was among these people. Like his fellow clansmen, Alpin and his family counted themselves blessed for the seasons of peace in their land. And though peaceful, Alpin and his sons bore a fighting spirit, necessary for protecting their beloved Dalriada, for even Dalriada had its rivals. The Picts to the northeast and the Britons to the south were adversarial and at times threatened the Dalriadan way of life. Commonly, these adversaries would seek peace with one hand while fighting with the other, twining a web of veiled truths and double-talk parlayed to protect self-interests.

Diplomacy was difficult and rare. Where diplomacy failed, the Dalriadans found use of the sword. Though civil, the Dalriadans were not docile. They were a valiant and passionate people, particularly when called to defend their land.

Indeed, Alpin and his sons were proud of their Dalriadan heritage. And though, in this era, the Dalriadans ceased to formalize their leaders as kings—preferring to live in deference to freedom rather than security—in troublesome times they rallied behind men worthy of leading their people. As with Alpin's father before him, Alpin was admired as a leader among the Dalriadans. His heritage was a calling passed down to his sons, a destiny to unfold with time. This calling flowed within their blood, it was who they were— men willing to live and die for such a calling. And in time, they would be asked to do both.

Britannia, 820 A. D.

PROLOGUE

DEEP DOWN, EVERY MAN HOLDS SOMETHING sacred, a piece of who he is, sewn into the fabric of his being, so essential that he may never reckon its presence, yet at the same time, a thing he dare not live without. Take this from him and you will crush his heart, though blood continues in his veins. Yet beware, a heartless man is a dangerous man. In losing what he holds sacred, he may find himself at life's razor-sharp edge, where he holds no regard for what remains—and thus, he becomes a man far more dangerous than ever before.

CHAPTER 1

CORIC AND KENNETH STOOD SIDE BY SIDE. BY every measure, they were ready—ready to give what was asked of them. Bearing the wanting wisdom of youth, yet the courage of warriors, they stood anxious to test their strength. They were prepared with swords, not to sway the battle, but to show proof they were men—able to give as men give and fight as men fight. Their hearts were unfettered by the shackles that bind the souls of weak men. They pursued this day in the same manner they pursued every day, unconstrained, even passionate in their calling. This they acquired from their father.

The two stood side by side, waiting for the others. Soon they'd be coming.

Aiden ran. His steps were light and nimble. His heart beat with anticipation. On this day, he was free and innocent, knowing not danger but rather excitement. Surely, one day much would be asked of him, yet on this day he would remain a boy. And as a boy, he would only dream of the great deeds men dare to pursue.

The cool autumn smell of moist earth and fertile fields

fueled his steps, while the distant mountains offered his soul adventure. He bounded forward in a youthful gait, running through the wide, sunken valley that awaited the barley harvest. A breeze blew over his flushed red cheeks, seemingly lifting his feet from the field as he ran toward the figures.

Barley tops as soft as feathers wisped under his small hands. The tiny seeds stemming with grain tickled his palms as he parted them. Like a sea, the golden brown stalks swayed in the gusting wind, performing their dance across the valley.

Being a lad of but eleven, Aiden had no cares, no concerns—he owned nothing but the world as his journey carried him across the field of gold.

Aiden slowed. He drew close to the once distant figures. A grin of excitement formed on his face.

He eased down at the edge of the field, hiding behind the last row of barley stalks. From there, he could spy the two conversing back and forth. Aiden lifted his head. He glanced down the length of the pebble path—no one was coming. Like a pouncing cat, Aiden leapt from the sea of barley.

The two brothers stood beside the path, anxiously awaiting the band of men. As the stalks crackled behind them, Coric spun on his heels. The blow landed before he caught sight of his assailant.

Aiden's hurling body crashed into the backside of the two boys, landing hard against Coric's frame and whipping Kenneth's legs. The three twisted frames tumbled onto the pitted pebble path.

Kenneth hit the ground with a thud and his cheek pressed against the dirt. A moment passed before he realized what had happened. "You fool!" he yelped. He wrapped his forearm around Aiden's neck and wedged it under his brother's chin. Leveraging his arm against Aiden's head, he lifted himself. Then he pounded his brother's ribcage with half-hearted thumps. Satisfied, he wiggled free from his eleven-year-old attacker, positioned himself on top, and pinned his knees on either side of Aiden's head.

Aiden giggled and squirmed.

At fourteen, Kenneth was a light-hearted boy. Smart, and even handsome, he was the expressive one. "You little rogue. You dare to sneak up on two of Dalriada's mightiest warriors? Did you really think you had a chance?"

"I am the fox and you are my prey," Aiden blurted out, laughing and fighting to loosen his brother's hold.

Coric wasn't as pleased. The blow of the smaller boy had knocked him to the ground. After pushing away from the two, he lifted to his knees and watched them tussle.

Coric's annoyance showed in his expression. In truth, the days had not long passed since he was the young juvenile, often even the instigator of such pranks against his older brother, Drostan. Those days were fading from his heart. He missed them at times, not wanting to let them go, but having to. And on this day, he certainly found no such pleasure in the childish mischief.

Coric rose to his feet and brushed off his dirty brown kilt. He peered at Aiden, still pinned beneath Kenneth's knees. "You devil, why did you follow us? I told you to stay at home with Mother. You know that Kenneth and I must go with the others. We are no longer children. We must help the men."

Coric, the oldest of the three, was a rugged, gritty,

sixteen-year-old boy who saw himself as a warrior, though he bore neither scars in his flesh nor dents on his shield. If listening to legends of gallantry and battles, and practicing the demolition of wooden barrels with a short sword qualified as combat, then indeed, Coric was a warrior. But truth knows warriors are not made in training, yet rather in the living and breathing of life and death as it is mixed and twisted on the battlefield. However, on this morning such truth did not dissuade Coric from standing tall and brave for his father and family—and the honor of both.

"You two gather yourselves and end this mess," Coric barked. "The men will be coming soon."

Kenneth paused from his wrestling foray and gazed down between his knees at Aiden, whose cheeks and forehead were dusted with grime. Then their eyes locked. Villainous smiles appeared on their faces as a silent plan formed in their minds.

Coric stepped toward the two as they unraveled their intertwined knot. "Stop this. Get up. Get up, I said." Coric bent to grab Kenneth.

Alone neither could take him, but together they had a chance.

Kenneth leapt from Aiden's chest and grabbed Coric's waist.

Aiden rolled his body and constricted around the calves of the unsuspecting sixteen-year-old.

The attack came quickly. Coric struggled to hold his ground and free himself from Kenneth. He kicked with his legs to free his feet, and he extended his arms and pushed away from the two. Shuffling from side to side, he torqued his body to shift his weight, but Kenneth and Aiden tightened around him. Slowly, he teetered and then fell, twisting the three into a heap of limbs and torsos.

The two swelled with excitement in bringing down the bigger buck. They leapt on top of Coric like rabid dogs. Rarely had they held such an advantage, yet they quickly realized their plan was ill-conceived. Grabbing him and knocking him down was clever, but without a next step to the plan, their advantage soon eroded.

"Aaarrrrhhh!" Coric roared.

Kenneth and Aiden peered at one another. It had seemed like a good idea at first. The momentum was shifting, yet their laughter grew uncontrollably. Even Coric found a smile as he flexed his arms and brought a surge of strength beyond that of his brothers.

Coric twisted and turned and wrestled like an angry bear. He would show the two who was the dominant man in the fight. Grabbing Aiden's shoulder with one hand and securing Kenneth's waist with the other, he pressed the two together on the ground and jumped on top. Spit ran from the corner of his mouth and his chest heaved as he caught his breath. He glared down at the two. "Boys, did you really think you could?"

Kenneth wrestled to free himself as Coric mocked.

"You're not going anywhere," Coric said.

Kenneth's playfulness faded in the clutches of his older brother. His joy turned to frustration—humiliation often has a way of changing the heart. He remembered why he and Coric had come to stand beside the path early that autumn morning.

"Get off Coric! Let us up!" Kenneth fumed as he pried at Coric's grip.

Kenneth was strong for a boy of fourteen, but he could not match the strength of his older brother, nor could he match his aggression. Though angered from the fracas, Kenneth was typically calm in nature. He was less combative than Coric, but it would be wrong to mistake him as being devoid of a warrior's heart. It was simply hidden a little deeper within.

The commotion of the scuffle masked the sound of the approaching horses and the chatter of steel against steel. The riders were coming.

Kenneth's ire grew and his determination surged. He mustered his strength and tried once again to break free, but suddenly Coric's grip relented.

And then, Kenneth heard *his* voice.

"Boys!" The roar of the voice paralyzed the three. "That's enough!" The echoing words hit the boys like a flaming arrow and brought a piercing of the heart that only a father could deliver.

Coric melted. He had so desired to be there for his father. Knowing the war party would pass, he had purposed to show himself able. He had donned his short sword and the wooden shield passed down from Drostan in preparation to meet the men. He was to prove to his father that he was ready to fight. Crossing the field early that autumn morning, Coric knew in his soul that he was capable of standing alongside them. And at his stance along the path, he was to meet the men and convince them he was ready. Instead, he now appeared as a foolish child. Coric cursed himself for letting his father find him like this.

Alpin, a man familiar with battle, understood the

difference between a warrior and a boy. He carried his lean, tall frame with an upright posture. His dark hair matched his dark eyes and fell just above his shoulders. His jaw was narrow and rigid like his father's. His years and scars testified of his bravery. As a leader, his mind was sharp and his words were few. As a warrior, his fierce courage had garnered the respect of those who had fought beside him in battle.

Considering Alpin a monger would be to miss much of the man. He was no lover of war. War had steeled his fortitude but hadn't hardened his heart. He pursued life earnestly. Hardship had taught him an awareness of a God beyond him—One bigger than he, and even life itself. Occasionally, he found profit in giving ear to the Christian clerics, though his time was sparse for such extras. Above all, Alpin was a man of honor, not a pretentious honor as the pompous foster, but rather an honor bestowed over time to those whose actions and character merit such. Within Renton, he was a leader, a man who poured himself into others, pushing them to rise above the common throngs of life and press on to take hold of their purpose and destiny. This stirring overflowed to those around him, particularly his sons. He was a well from which they drew vigor. One may say his greatest strength—family honor—was his greatest weakness. He would die for them, one and all, should it be asked of him.

Alpin's courage had provided a semblance of peace for the surrounding clans of Dalriada in recent years. Yet on this day, their way of life was in danger, and Alpin and over a hundred other men had assembled to protect their land and safeguard the precious freedom they treasured. And Coric, a mere boy of sixteen, had dared to join them.

"Boys, return home. You must help your mother with the harvest and the animals," Alpin ordered, his tone even and firm.

Coric separated from his brothers. He lifted and worked to right himself. "Father, I will join you and Drostan and help push back the Britons." The words exited his mouth with hollow confidence. His younger brothers, working to untangle themselves, only betrayed his message, making him to appear wanting.

"You will not be joining us, Coric. You will stay at Renton. Drostan and the men and I will handle matters with the Britons," Alpin said. His horse fidgeted below him. "Your mother needs—"

"But Father, I'm ready. My sword is quick and my feet are swift," Coric interrupted, hoping to convince his father without finding the end of his patience. "I assure you, my sword will be counted an aid."

"You're but a boy. You're of no use to us," Gormal groused, sitting on a horse not far from Alpin. Gormal was a sordid man who spoke more often than he should. He did the things a man must do, but little beyond finding the bottom of his mug in Renton's tavern. He was not a habitual drunk, but he contributed his share to the sampling of Dalriada's ales. And though Gormal saw that his son, Searc, was not with Alpin's boys, he didn't care. His son, the same age as Aiden, shared many of Gormal's flaws.

"Go home with the women and tend to the things there," Gormal said. He glanced at the other men. "Let's go ... what are we waiting for?"

"Pay no attention to him, Coric," Luag remarked. Luag was a noble man and Alpin's right hand in battle. He respected Coric's bravery and wanted to encourage the boy, "You are eager to join the men, Coric. That is admirable. But you are needed here to protect Renton."

"There's nothing in Renton to protect, besides a few maidens and a handful of sheep," Gormal rebuffed with a loud laugh.

"Gormal, enough!" Alpin demanded, without turning his eyes from Coric. "Son, your passion and courage are unquestioned, yet your time is not here, not now. You still have much to learn, and in time you will."

"But Drostan has fought many times and is but a few years older than me. I am ready."

"Indeed, your brother has fought with the men, but his sword was needed. I needn't remind you that Drostan was not a boy when he joined our battles."

"I, too, shall fight! Father, you have told us to act like men! I am doing as you say!"

"Coric, I am not asking you to act like a man. I am asking you to be one!"

His father's words cut like a razor. They carried a weight that landed like a boulder shot into Coric's gut. *What was left to say? What words could be spoken to convince his father, or even himself?* Having so intently assured himself that he would capture the confidence of the men and his father, he lost hope. He was undone. Only silence remained.

Coric stood still, motionless before his father.

The sun peered over the distant mountains. Morning promised to come. The light hit the backside of the men and filled Coric's eyes. His two brothers were now beside him, standing upright before the men. Dawn's silence was only interrupted by the impatient grumbling of the horses, the antsy clip-clop of their hooves, and the cool September morning breeze skirting through the pack of men.

Drostan, twenty-two and battle-tested, gazed down at his demoralized younger brother. He broke the silence, "Coric, your sword is sharp. I await your presence on the battlefield, and soon you shall join us. I will gladly stand alongside you, trusting you, my brother, with my backside. Your zeal and strength will make your blade my friend … in time we will serve as one."

Coric remained despondent. He struggled to find words. Finally, he spoke, "Drostan, you're going now, as you have gone before. You will surely bring back stories more valiant than my ears can bear. How I wish I could ride with you and fight at your side." Coric's concession carried a mixture of admiration and regret, while his jealousy was hardly discernable. He bit his lip and turned, staring at the distant mountains.

Drostan gazed at the other two. "Kenneth, keep your sword sharp, for you will be needed soon as well. And Aiden, we will surely have to retire your weapons of wood and replace them with something more weighty for your strengthening arms." The wind blew Drostan's long hair from his face, and a grin formed across his narrow jaw.

In the eyes of Aiden, Drostan was a hero, larger than life. As a small boy, Aiden often suited himself in his brother's garments and boots. He would grab his brother's heavy shield and sword and jab back and forth into the air, slaying would-be foes, pretending to be Drostan in the midst of battle. Though none of the brothers knew for sure if Drostan had killed a man in combat, they had heard stories of how he defended himself bravely and even cut off a man's hand when he was nearly stabbed.

Kenneth, too, highly esteemed his oldest brother. In times past, Drostan and Kenneth would wade through the cool creeks of Renton in the summers of Dalriada, offering their tired feet relief from the day's chores. It was during these times that Drostan would tell tales of death-defying feats of the battlefield, feats of Dalriada's warriors. His stories would grab Kenneth's heart, inspiring him with tales of bravery, yet at times nauseating him with awful and bloody accounts of war. Drostan never glorified war, rather he told of the uncertainty and misery of the battlefield. Kenneth was convinced that at such times, boys had no choice but to become men.

Drostan spoke again, "Brothers, it is your task to defend our home. Should the Britons separate, seeking to elude us, you shall be our rear guard to protect the families of Renton." He paused and studied the three. "Tell Mother and Nessa I love them, and tell young Donald that I shall see him soon."

Drostan's words softened Coric's angry spirit. There was no more to be said. Coric would honor his father's wishes and return home with his brothers. He would help the women and children of the village, watching over the animals and tending to the barley harvest, should the men not return in time.

The sun faded from Coric's eyes as he stood in the shadow of his brother. Coric turned to his father. "Father, I shall go home with my brothers. Promise me that you will return and that you will call for my sword the next time you gather the men for battle. I will prove to you that I have what it takes to fight."

Alpin gazed down from his horse, staring at Coric. "My son, I am proud to be your father. You do not need to fight to prove yourself to me. War is not the friend you presume it to be. Death is not the friend of any man—though you are right to see that certain times require a man to fight. Trials beyond ourselves demand of us to protect those we love."

Alpin paused, shifting his gaze to his two younger sons and then back to Coric. He continued, "Coric, for every man there comes a day when his life will be asked of him, and he must be willing to give his life on that day. My son, the times grow ill. Enemies threaten our land and our way of life. In the days ahead I fear that peace may be fleeting, stolen from our hands if we are not vigilant. Your sword and shield will see more blood than your eyes desire, and I am not eager to cast you ahead so quickly. I am content to watch you grow into the man you are destined to be. The day will come when you are called to commit your life to the fight, but today shall not be that day."

Alpin looked upon his son as if peering into his soul. Coric stood solemn under his father's gaze, absorbing his words. For a moment, time stood still.

Coric swallowed and slowly lowered his head. He could not help but wonder the fate of his father. *Would he ever look upon his father again?* He knew his father loved him. Though often hidden in his words, his actions had always convinced Coric of such.

Alpin's horse twisted beneath him. The animal was eager to ride and the time to depart had come. Alpin faced his three sons. "Be of good courage! Defend Renton!" Snapping the reigns of his horse, he turned and steered the animal south to Dumbarton.

"Return with their heads, Father!" Aiden shouted. He made a slashing wisp through the air with his hand, pretending to slice his opponent.

Kenneth smiled at Drostan, "Return soon, you know how Mother and Nessa worry." Searching for something more, he finished, "… be swift and show them how Dalriadans fight!"

"And bring back a dagger from the fallen Britons," Aiden yelled, still caught up in his make-believe battle and working to gain the upper hand over his enemy.

The men followed Alpin, riding past Drostan as he shifted on his horse. Drostan tightened the grip on his reigns, turned, and gazed down at Coric. "Smile my brother, our day shall come. Let not your sword grow dull. It is up to you, for now, to keep these mischievous rogues in line. I shall return soon and we shall spar again." He nodded and sized Coric. "Don't grow weak," he playfully prodded and trotted forward to catch the others.

"It is not I whom I fear will grow weak … I look forward to matching skills when you return," Coric called out, refusing to smile.

Drostan glanced back and smirked.

The gesture unarmed Coric and his mouth formed a youthful grin. Drostan was everything Coric wanted to be.

Drostan lifted his hand into the air and gave a final wave before turning to catch the men.

Coric, Kenneth, and Aiden fixed their gaze on the fading silhouette of their brother, longing for the day when they could be him.

As Drostan finally disappeared from sight, the mountains of Renton already seemed eager to beckon him home.

CHAPTER 2

A SOUTHERN WIND BLEW STEADILY AGAINST THE riders, but Alpin's thoughts were elsewhere. The image of Coric standing on the path burned in his mind. The boy had been broken and left like an arrow snapped in two and cast aside. Alpin's gut wrenched for his son, but he would not permit him to enter battle—for war was hell for a man and no place for a boy. Coric was not ready for battle, but convincing him otherwise was no simple matter. At sixteen, his reasoning was his own and words of wisdom were seldom received.

Memories of Coric tossed in Alpin's mind. His son was stubborn, but being his father, he was proud of the lad. The boy had grown up quickly. The years of innocence and questioning had passed. Gone were the days when his son would point to the moon sitting in the night sky, or at the distant mountains resting like sleeping giants under a sunrise, and ask the questions of a child. Together, he would marvel with his son as to how such things were made by a Hand more magnificent than the hands of men. Alpin recalled how he would tell his children stories of the Dalriadans of old, how they fought against adversity and, at times, tragedy. How he would tell of the legend of the distant princess Scotia, of her coming to the land of Ireland with her many sons a thousand years prior, and how they carried her namesake through the centuries, bearing the name, *Scots*. These were the stories Alpin's father had passed down to him as a boy, and in turn, Alpin passed them on to his sons.

Stories and tales kindled pride and passion, but Alpin knew that more than stories were needed to shape a young boy. Times of grueling chores and lean meals when harvests failed were a suitable means for molding and shaping a young heart. Indeed, hardship does much good, but hardship alone can quench a young heart, or any heart for that matter. As a father, Alpin knew the befitting benefits of praise were also needed for growing the heart of a lad.

Alpin's thoughts remained afar. The drumming of the horses' hooves against the path produced a monotone ambiance, keeping his mind on distant memories. He recalled the days spent with Drostan and Coric at the river running east of Renton, a river rich with grayling and trout. He remembered their rides through the valleys of Dalriada and the beauty of the countryside. His sons thrived in Dalriada's freedom, freedom found in the unbounded thrill of riding bareback hard and fast with the wind gusting against their faces. Those were times when his sons dreamed of daring adventures, conquering lands, and pretending to be kings—if only for a day.

Drostan rode amid the pack of men, with riders behind and in front. The sun sat overhead and shined its light down on him. His long locks swayed on his shoulders to the rhythmic motion of his horse's gait.

Drostan lifted in his saddle and peered above the men riding near him, searching for his father. Seeing him, he maneuvered his horse and rode alongside. He glanced at his father, lost in thought. "Father?"

Alpin gave no response.

"Father, what is it?"

Alpin gazed at Drostan with a blank expression.

"Father?" Drostan repeated. "What is it?"

A small grin emerged on Alpin's face, his left cheek lifting higher than his right, forming a crooked smile. "What is what?"

"What has you so occupied?" Drostan asked.

"The mind is always occupied, but for now it is occupied with simple things," Alpin replied. "I was thinking of Coric, and the rest of you … you were all so young not long ago. It passes so quickly." His smile faded, and he straightened his gaze toward the distant hills.

With hours remaining on the journey south, Drostan emptied his mind. His thoughts wandered to the barley field where Coric, Kenneth, and Aiden had stood early that morning.

Drostan already missed Coric. The two had spent their days growing up together. Drostan had taught Coric how to use a shovel as well as a sword. They had labored together in sun and rain for hours measuring in days performing their chores, including ditch digging to irrigate the barley fields and ignoble chores, too, such as digging latrines and graves. They had plowed fields and harvested crops and tended sheep too many times to recount. But their time away from chores was far more glorious—riding horses, fishing the river, and donning wooden swords and shields in their imagined fights to the death. Drostan rarely lost, though Coric would argue the matter if asked.

Looking back, Drostan had known that Coric was desperate to join the men in battle. For days Coric had begged Drostan to convince their father he was old enough to fight the Britons. Drostan knew Coric was a strong fighter, but he loved his brother too much to advocate for him to join the men.

Drostan recalled Coric's foolhardy plan a day prior:

"Drostan," Coric had said, "I'll hide in the stables overnight and ride out with the men in the morning. Father won't know I'm with you."

"Coric, do you think Father is going to ride into battle wearing a blindfold? Even if that were so, he would smell you!" Drostan had responded.

Coric had not been amused, and though he admitted the plan was poor, he was determined to find a way to join the men.

Drostan missed his brother. He would have enjoyed their conversations on the ride south. He would be sure to remember the events of his journey so that he could regale his brothers with suitable tales upon his return.

He thought long of his family and home as he and his father rode far away from both.

Large, distended clouds napped in the midafternoon sky above Dalriada. They were accompanied by a bright yellow sun that would soon begin its descent.

Alpin and the men pressed southward. They were pensive and dour, silence held their tongues. Alpin knew such a thing was not uncommon when heading to battle.

Reflection upon those most loved often filled one's thoughts in that lonely time between looking for war and finding it. Only once the madness of battle had passed, in those long hours returning home, did a man dare to carry the happy expectation of holding those awaiting him.

Alpin gazed over his men, knowing the fresh scars they would soon bear—scars on their bodies and souls. How their minds would grow jaded in war, scarred from its sights, sights better left unseen. What man desires to fight a war when so much stands to be lost? But a man's motive for battle is always a fine line, cherishing the things that stand to be lost while risking one's life to protect them. Alpin knew these things. He'd lived these things.

Alpin said a silent prayer for his men. By appearances, their spirits seemed ready for the days ahead. Their morale had been lifted when the Dalriadans of Cashel had joined the men of Renton the evening prior. The clan of Cashel was led by Constantine, Alpin's cousin on his father's side. Constantine was respected by his men, yet when the two clans united, the men looked to Alpin to lead.

Attaining the aid of Cashel had been vital. As with any battle, numbers were needed to defeat the Britons. The Britons were fighters, yet unlike the savage Vikings, the Britons were known for their calculated attacks, uncommon among the clans. Alpin knew if the Britons were bold enough to attack the Dalriadans in the south, then they must have been confident they had the numbers to succeed. Alpin wanted—and needed—the additional men of Cashel and from elsewhere, but he would only have Dalriadan men. No others were to be trusted. When asked of the Picts, Alpin had insisted that the Dalriadans not seek their aid. He wanted nothing from the Picts—neither their men nor their aid against the Britons.

In times past, the Picts had sought the allegiance of the Dalriadans when the Britons contested Pict lands in the northeast. But such unsavory alliances were temporal and unstable. The previous summer had washed away any semblance of truce with the Picts. A dispute over bordering Dalriadan lands with the Pict lord, Oengus, had broken all ties of diplomacy, and skirmishes had ignited between the Dalriadans and Picts. With the Briton threat now looming to the south, Alpin had settled that they would face the Britons alone.

Dumbarton lay just beyond the distant hills. As the men approached, the gusting wind grew stronger, carrying an autumn chill and bringing a swath of dark clouds in the western sky. Alpin felt the cool moisture of his horse's sweat seeping through his kilt. He lifted his arm and signaled the men. "Slow the horses. Dumbarton is not far ahead," Alpin said, and then he turned his gaze toward Constantine and Luag who rode beside him.

"We need Guaire's men, yes?" Constantine said, confirming more than inquiring.

"Yes, we need the men of Dumbarton," Alpin replied. He peered at Constantine and then at Luag. "We need them, but if they turn their backs again, I will hunt them down myself."

"They are Dalriadans, and we'll need the additional warriors," Constantine said.

"Perth is not easy to forget. Guaire's desertion was a coward's way out," Luag muttered.

"He'll contend the shortage of food forced his men to leave," Alpin replied.

"All of us were suffering, starving in that miserable cold," Luag said and then leaned away from his horse and spat a wad of phlegm. "When an enemy attacks, a man doesn't abandon his countrymen ... not with lives at stake!"

"Guaire was foolish ... you are right, Luag," Alpin said. "His actions were regrettable. I suppose without the men from Milton joining us, we may not be here today. Without their resupplies and their archers, we may have found our graves in Perth."

"The man still makes me sick," Luag said. "He never should have left us."

"Peace," Constantine replied. "You're going to have to let it go, Luag."

Alpin glanced at Constantine with a subtle leeriness. He pulled the reigns of his horse and craned his head back toward his men. He lifted his hand again, this time motioning them to halt.

As the men slowed to a stop, Alpin continued to stare down the path behind them. He hoped he would see the slower horse-drawn carts trailing.

Nothing.

The carts aided in the march to Dumbarton, carrying men and supplies, but they also slowed the pace. The pace would be slower still when leaving Dumbarton with more men and supplies to haul.

After several moments, the carts crested the hill and the Dalriadans from Renton and Cashel continued south toward Dumbarton.

They would be expected.

"Greetings," shouted Guaire, surrounded by a dozen men on horseback and dozens more on foot. His eyes fixed on Alpin. Guaire was flanked by his son, Taran, and the other leading men of Dumbarton. They sat tall and straight, even arrogant, on their horses.

Alpin, Constantine, Luag, and Drostan approached while the others watched from the distance.

The four stopped ten feet from Guaire's steed.

Alpin surveyed the men of Dumbarton before landing his gaze upon Guaire.

Neither man spoke a word. The shifting swords and shields of the standing soldiers were the only sounds to be heard.

Guaire remained silent. He was a stout man, heavy but not obese. His dark hair was lightened by the gray that speckled his temples and beard. He had a proud demeanor, evidenced by his upright posture and dignified dress for a warrior. Though most men wore thick leather into battle, Guaire's battle leather was studded with small metal beads along the arms and chest as an extra measure against the edge of a blade.

Alpin broke the silence, "Guaire, by appearances you are ready for battle … is your heart ready as well?"

Guaire's wince was hardly discernable. He had half expected a token reminder of Perth the moment he saw the Scots from the north enter his village. Still, Guaire had long convinced himself that withdrawing from Alpin at Perth was the best strategy at the time. It was his departure that allowed the men of Renton to keep what little supplies remained. "Alpin, worry not about the condition of my heart but rather the strength of my sword. It is my blade and my men who are needed to help stop the Britons."

Taran spoke up and added to his father's words, "Men of Renton, men of Cashel, you can see our hearts are more than eager to engage the Britons. We've been awaiting your arrival, preparing our swords and bows. We are quite glad you have finally reached Dumbarton."

Taran didn't mind that his comments were smug, he liked them that way. He was a peppery young man with ice blue eyes and fiery red hair, and he boasted a temper to match. He continued, "We are eager to fight, but we did not want to leave without you."

"Leave without us! Son, that was your trickery at Perth," Luag replied, inflamed at the youth's prattle.

"Gentlemen! We are all Scots here. We share a common enemy. Let's focus on the matters at hand," Constantine insisted, searching for diplomacy. He turned his attention to Guaire. "We have brought over a hundred and fifty men, many on horseback. We need somewhere to bed for the night and a place for the horses. Certainly, you have gathered many men as well. Together we look to be roughly three hundred strong. You agree, Guaire?"

Guaire begrudgingly nodded in agreement. "We have more than a hundred and thirty able men. We are ready to fight the Britons and defend Dumbarton." Guaire paused and looked at Alpin, then continued, "Alpin, my sword, and that of my son and my men, are yours. We are prepared to defend all of Dalriada."

Had Guaire pressed the issue of Perth, he would have lost the fight. Though his retreat at Perth had reason in the world of waging war and fighting battles, his actions were not acceptable. Moving on was a wise decision, and offering his sword to Alpin was wiser still. Guaire had aspirations of leading—both his men and all of Dalriada—but he could not do so with Dalriada's high regard for Alpin. Somewhat blinded by his ambition, Guaire was not so blind as to overlook Alpin's standing among the men, even his own. Though his men had followed him to—and from—Perth, withdrawing at Perth had not been well received. Some of his men had disappeared during the retreat. Weeks later, Guaire had learned that they returned to fight with Alpin and their fellow Scots.

Guaire's son, Taran, wasn't so ready to concede. He grew agitated with the dialogue. As the son of the Dumbarton leader, and being slightly older than Drostan, Taran considered himself superior in both strength and status to Alpin's son. His youth provided vigor, yet his mind reasoned like a child, rash and impetuous. He was capable with the bow and the sword, yet his time in battle had been primarily from a distance with the archers. He had yet to encounter the rage and fury of a man wielding a sword against him. Such an encounter was often sobering, if not debilitating. And Taran could have benefited from a dose of sobriety to round the edges of his foolish pride.

Taran mulled his father's concession and then attempted to regain ground. "Indeed we will fight, and fight well. So know that you have our swords ... but understand that our bows may shoot quickly at the Britons," he said, suggesting he and the Dumbartons would deliver the first blows to the enemy.

Alpin ignored the boy. He spoke directly to Guaire. "I

am pleased to have your swordsmen, your bowmen, and all those fighting for Dalriada. I am certain the Scots here today will again prove their cunning and courage." He continued, "Let's release the men for the night, then the few of us can gather to discuss the Britons. Time is passing and we must leave at dawn."

Guaire nodded. He turned his horse and rode back to his men.

Drostan and Taran remained motionless on their horses, peering at one another. No words were exchanged, only the silent measuring of one another. Drostan ended the encounter with a nod and then turned his horse to follow his father.

A hush settled among the men as the groups disbanded, and the sun found a home on the far side of the mountains. Darkness entered and the chill of the air dispelled the day's lingering warmth.

The leaders would plan and the men would sleep on this night. Tomorrow was yet another day.

A dreary rain fell and intensified the chill of the coming dawn. The men prayed for sunshine as they marched into the emerging light of the wet morning. The journey south could take four to five days, depending on the rains and the movement of the Britons. Alpin sent scouts ahead to spy and report the enemy's advances.

The drizzling rains had subsided by late afternoon, though a sky of clouds remained. The road proved difficult as the poorly formed paths pooled with puddles and thick mud, encumbering the Scots' progress.

Conditions over the next two days offered little

improvement. Then, at dusk on the third day, the sun emerged from behind the clouds. The departure of the foul weather lifted the men's spirits, as did the sight of Milton, now sitting on the horizon. Milton would offer a good night's sleep and the addition of capable warriors. The southern Dalriadan village, known for its archers, was the last opportunity to add to the Dalriadan numbers before reaching the Britons.

Cheers burst forth in Milton when Alpin and his men arrived. Latharn, the leader of the clans of Milton, greeted Alpin with an embrace. It was Latharn who'd brought reinforcements at Perth in the Dalriadan clash against the Picts. His archers had helped stave off defeat, and for that, Alpin was grateful.

As the sun descended, the men settled by their campfires and prepared for a night of rest. Little was discussed concerning the days ahead. Most often the men spoke of times past. Some spoke of the woman they loved or the children they had raised. Stories were told of battles fought and heroes remembered. The younger men, including Drostan, fancied the stories, often wondering if one day such stories would be told of their deeds.

As the evening grew late, the fires fell dim. Luag, who'd been silent most of the evening, rose from his seat and stirred the fire with a stick he'd been whittling. He gazed across the flames and peered at Alpin. "Brother, you should tell the story of your grandfather and how he cast off the Vikings, sending them away with neither booty nor pride."

Alpin shook his head back and forth, dismissing the idea. "Story? With so many years passed, Luag, I am sure it should rather be called a tale," he replied. "Besides, these men don't want to hear of wit and trickery. They want to hear of legend and lore."

"Your years have turned you into a lout, Alpin. I'd say fire and rocks and knives make for good lore." Luag chuckled and hooted to rouse the men and tempt his friend.

"Well then," Alpin replied, "you tell the story."

"You stogger, tell your tale—"

"I'll tell the tale," a voice came from somewhere in the dark.

The men glanced from the fire, searching the shadows to find the mystery voice.

"I'll tell it," Constantine said a second time and appeared behind Luag. Drostan and the others spun on their stumps to face Constantine as he ambled from the darkness and sat on a log next to Alpin. Constantine then eased his arm to the ground and selected a stick of his own. He took a moment to inspect the slender twig and then stared into the fire as the illumination of the flickering flames danced on his brow.

"In days past," Constantine began, "when our fathers first settled this land we now call Dalriada, the Britons were not the only threat to the Scots. Another threat came, not by land, but by sea. In the far northwest, an enemy entered our land and pushed their way through the West Isles. They were vile men, more ruthless than Britons or Picts. They were Vikings, Norsemen." Constantine paused and gazed at his now captive audience.

"The Vikings didn't stop after their destruction in the West Isles. They moved south and brought a horrific attack on Lindisfarne, decimating villages and monasteries and anyone, or anything, standing in their path. They plundered as they pleased. Our people tried to hide their relics and gold in the monasteries, believing they'd be protected from the Vikings." Constantine finished his thought and glanced across the fire at the younger men.

"This was rather foolish," he continued, "for the Vikings had no regard for God—they had gods of their own. They burned and destroyed the monasteries and robbed them of their treasures. But make no mistake, these were not simple thieves. These were brutal men in conquest for land and slaves. Stories tell of their taking women and children by boat and carrying them back to their motherland. After Lindisfarne, they later attacked Iona and even closer to our homelands in the Isle of Skye, not far from the coast of Dalriada."

"So how were they stopped?" a young man from Milton asked.

"Patience, boy," Luag said.

"Patience is right," Constantine began again. "It was patience that stopped their advance, the patience of my grandfather and the men that fought at his side. It was my grandfather, Malcolm, who saw that he and his men were outnumbered and stood little chance against the Viking savages. The Vikings were big, husky men. They carried large double-bladed axes and could wield them as swift as a short sword.

"Late one evening, on a night much like tonight, my grandfather and his men snuck up on the Vikings as they sat beside their fires, boasting of their battles. They paid little attention to the shadows moving about them.

"My grandfather had contested the Vikings several days before, but his men suffered severely in the battle. With the handful of men that remained, he patiently waited for his moment ... and on that night, he found it. He sent a handful of men to the ridge above the Viking camp. Then he and those remaining crept through a small gap in the rocks below. After moving through the rocks, he found himself twenty feet from the Viking leader ... the man the Vikings called Ulrich the Large. He was a monster of a man, from what is told."

"What did your grandfather do?" the man sitting next to Drostan asked.

"He waited," Constantine said. "He waited until the Vikings had had their fill ... he waited until they bedded down to sleep. That is when they struck. The men below, with only their knives, burst into the Viking camp and cut down Ulrich the Large and the men around him. The fighting roused the others, and all hell broke loose. The Vikings watched as Ulrich fell, and a dozen men charged my grandfather and the Scots. The Scots turned and slipped back through the gap in the rocks. As the Vikings rushed forward, the Scots on the ridge sent man-sized boulders over the edge, jarring rocks loose and raining down the wrath of God on the Vikings below. Those that escaped rushed to their boats along the shore of the camp."

"Did they get away, or did they come back attacking?" the young man from Milton asked.

"Some got away. But most didn't. Remember, the Scots were enraged at the Vikings. They wanted them all dead. My grandfather and the others pursued the Vikings to the shore. And from there, they launched their arrows." Constantine pulled his stick from the campfire and stared at its glowing red tip. "Their arrows were lit with fire," he said with great relish and smiled. "When the arrows hit those Viking devils, their boats burst into flames, lighting them all ablaze."

"They killed them all?" the young man asked, gazing at the older men for confirmation.

They were smiling and smirking and nodding their heads.

The young man peered back at Constantine. "You're lying!"

Constantine grinned at the young man. "You asked for a story, I am simply telling you what I was told as a boy."

Luag burst out a lung full of laughter, "Boy, you better believe it. Every word is true." He stood and brushed off his rear, and then he peered at the young man. "That should teach you. That should teach you to think long and hard before you contend with a Scot. They'll getcha. One way or another, they'll getcha."

The men at the fire hooted and cheered.

Luag continued to chuckle to himself as he stepped away and walked into the darkness to find sleep.

Morning came early when the scouts returned with news. They rode into camp and quickly found Alpin.

"Alpin," the lead scout shouted.

Alpin, standing outside his makeshift tent, lowered the bedroll he was folding and approached the two riders. "What have you learned?"

"The Britons have continued their advance. They raided and overtook both Annan and Lockerbie and have now pushed well north of Hadrian's Wall," the lead scout said, gasping to gain his breath after the hard ride.

"Presently, the Britons occupy the village of Ae," the scout continued. "It seems they brought the fight to the people of Ae, killing all who resisted. The Britons appear to be roughly three to four hundred in number, and we saw others on the trail south of Ae heading north with more supplies. Their numbers could swell to five hundred with the reinforcements coming from the south. We're guessing the Britons have occupied Ae for a couple of weeks, based on the waste holes and paths to and from the tents and horse corral."

Ae remained a day's journey from the Scots' present location south of Cumnock. The Forest of Ae, a forest dense with thick pine timber, bounded the village of Ae to the north. With Ae taken, the Britons would likely not wait long before pressing north to Milton.

"Good work," Alpin said to the scout. "Get some food and tend to your horses. We'll need your eyes and ears ahead of us again soon." Alpin dropped his bedroll and left his tent to find the others.

"Constantine," Alpin shouted. "Find Guaire, I'll get Luag and Latharn. The scouts report that the Britons are at Ae. We need to gather the men and head out."

Constantine dropped his morning meal of boiled oats and lifted to his feet. "Did they say how many?"

"Maybe four hundred, with up to a hundred more moving north to join them. Find Guaire," Alpin said, departing in a rush. He leapt over a man waking from his slumber and hurried toward the pond where others had bedded for the night.

"I suppose I won't be finishing breakfast," Constantine muttered to himself.

The Dalriadan men set out for Ae. Their mission was clear—advance to Ae, establish positions for battle during the night, and prepare for war at daybreak.

Drostan's mind wandered over the peaks and valleys of his memories as he rode the path to Ae. The sun offered warmth to his unshaven face. The days were not easy, but it was good to be alive. He recalled the milky white skin and soft blue eyes of his mother, Ena. She was gentle and he missed her.

Drostan's horse slowed, and his attention turned to the men in front of him as the group stopped beside a small creek. The men dismounted and let their horses drink the cold running water. Drostan dismounted behind them and stepped to the creek.

After refreshing his steed and filling his water sack, Drostan returned to his horse. There he noticed a four-and-a-half-foot bow strapped to the horse beside him and a quiver of arrows measuring nearly three feet long. The owner of the horse was a tall man who appeared to be roughly five years older than Drostan.

"Drostan, son of Alpin," Drostan introduced himself, looking up into the man's eyes. Then he extended his arm to greet the man.

"Laise, son of Latharn," replied the tall, strapping warrior boasting the long bow and standing nearly a head taller than Drostan. He gripped Drostan's arm. "I saw you with your father when the men arrived in Milton yesterday."

Drostan shook his head. "I'm not sure how I missed seeing you," he said, lifting his eyebrows to take in Laise's expanded height.

Laise laughed. "I was leaving as you were coming. I returned to my home for a special gift," he said, and he lifted the flap of his saddlebag, revealing two golden-brown loaves of bread. "My sister made these for me."

"Sisters make the best bread," Drostan replied with a grin. "Now I know who to come to when I'm hungry."

"I'll share if there's any left," Laise said, smiling.

Drostan nodded, and then his eyes wandered to the long bow tied beside Laise's saddlebag. It was much larger than the common three-foot bow. "You men of Milton are known for your archery. But why do you carry such a large bow?"

A proud grin spread across Laise's face. "This is a longbow. It's called a longbow because of its length and range. The Britons have been using it for several years now, though not all of them use it well. The draw is a challenge for most men, but the return gives good distance."

"And the accuracy?" Drostan asked.

"Well, you can hit an army at over three hundred yards," he boasted, "and with a little luck and a dead wind you can hit a horse at two hundred yards … if he's standing still."

"Laise, remind me to have you cover my back when the enemy is rushing me from a distance," Drostan said and grinned.

Laise gave a tooth-filled smile as he chuckled and nodded.

Drostan mounted his horse and coaxed the animal forward through the creek.

"Drostan, son of Alpin," Laise yelled, "Godspeed."

Drostan tugged the reigns of his horse and glanced back. "Godspeed … Laise, son of Latharn."

Not all Scots had taken to the Christ and the Father, but many had.

CHAPTER 3

AUTUMN HAD GROWN COLD IN RENTON SINCE the day the men had left for battle. The trees had lost their beauty. Their colors of red, orange, and gold had faded. The withered leaves had dropped and blown away, far from where they had once blossomed. And the cold autumn rains of the hill country had now forced the barley harvest. Renton could no longer wait for her men to return. The barley needed to be cut and bound into stooks to dry for threshing.

Coric hunched and tied the twine around the stook in front of him. He lifted and peered across the landscape at the severed stalks covering the ground like so many fallen soldiers. A dozen bound stooks dotted the field where the once ripe golden barley had stood. Coric glanced at Aiden who was fumbling with several stalks of his own, fighting to form another stook.

"Where's Kenneth?" Coric shouted.

Aiden cursed and threw down the stalks in his hands. "What?" Aiden asked, frustrated and tired.

Coric turned to his right and then his left. "Where's Kenneth? He needs to be out here helping with the barley." He shook his head in disgust. "Where did he go?"

"I don't know. He said he needed something from the barn," Aiden replied, "the hoe, maybe." He put his hands on his hips and spat.

"Dammit," Coric grumbled, "I am not going to spend the day out here while he's playing games! Finish gathering those stalks … I'll find Kenneth." He tossed his twine to the ground and stormed from the field.

Aiden eyed the barley strewn about his feet and kicked at the stalks. He muttered something, but Coric didn't bother with trying to understand him.

"Kenneth?" Coric called as he moved toward the barn.

"Kenneth, you need to get out here," Coric repeated, this time in a louder voice. He passed the corner of the barn and stepped sideways to avoid a mud puddle. Then he pulled open the barn door and walked inside.

"Kenneth?" Coric called again, standing in the middle of the barn. His head swiveled about, and he spotted the hoe in the corner, standing next to the shovel. "That lazy oaf!" Coric grabbed the hoe and marched from the barn to the house. Reaching the house, he swung open the door and stepped inside. "There you are!" he said, eyeing Kenneth in his father's large wooden chair with a lambskin pillow by his side. "What are you doing in here?"

"I had to get the hoe … and I came to get water to bring to the field," Kenneth replied.

Coric stepped toward Kenneth, his chest bowed like a gamecock. "You need to get out there and help," he said in a gruff voice and then stopped when he heard his mother. He took another step and peered around the corner. His mother and Arabella were rolling dough on the counter.

Ena abruptly ended her conversation with Arabella, and she turned her eyes to Coric. He stood halfway between her and Kenneth. "Coric, is there something you need?" she asked.

Coric didn't respond.

Arabella spun and faced the boys, her hands covered with flour from the dough. She glanced at Kenneth and pushed her hair from her face, leaving a thin trail of white dust on her cheek.

Coric grimaced and peered long at Kenneth. "Now I know why you're in here, sitting there in Father's chair. It's Arabella, isn't it?"

Arabella was a lovely girl. Her frame was slender and shapely, and her eyes were green with an upward shape, unusual for her Pict bloodline. Her lips were prominent and carried a teetering smile, and her nose was small with a slight dimple where it curved. Though barely fifteen, her beauty was in blossom.

"I can't believe you," Coric muttered.

Kenneth tried to restrain his boyish smile. "I was just getting the pail to fetch some water for the three of us."

"Just getting the pail. Right ... you were simply getting water for us." Coric wiped the grime from his brow and stared down at the floor, shaking his head and stoking his bitterness.

"Coric, what's the matter?" his mother asked.

"What's the matter?" Coric's tone elevated. "Aiden and I are out in the field, working ourselves to death to try to feed this family, and Kenneth is loafing in here, sitting in Father's chair and chatting with Arabella!"

"Coric!" his mother scolded.

"Mother, this is wrong, he should be helping. When Father gets back—"

"Your father is not back, and until he is …" Ena stopped and held her words.

Kenneth lifted from his seat. "When Father gets back, he'll know that I've helped. Because I came in to get water doesn't mean I am not working as hard as you, Coric."

"Don't tell me what Father would suppose. If he were here, he'd backhand you into the field himself!" Coric turned, marched to the door, and then paused. "Don't bother with bringing water … Aiden and I have work to do." He hastened out the door, slamming it with a bang as he departed.

Kenneth turned to face Arabella, yet didn't speak a word. She stood silently next to his mother with her head tilted down, then she glanced at Kenneth and offered a sympathetic smile.

Kenneth responded with a disappointed frown— disappointed with himself as much as his brother. Then he turned to his mother, "I'm sorry, Mother. Don't worry about the water pail." Without waiting for a response, he walked toward the entryway. He pressed his shoulder against the door, pushed, and stepped outside.

It was nine years prior that Constantine and his wife, Senga, took in a small orphan girl of five. Constantine found the orphan when he and his men were returning to Cashel after a skirmish with the Picts. On their return, they came across an unsettling sight, a horrific sight—a Pict family waylaid, slaughtered, and left for dead. The killings were not typical of a clash amongst clans. By appearances, it was not the work of the Scots or the Picts. One of the older men swore it held the marks of a Viking attack, though the Vikings had not been in Britannia for decades. The only survivor was the young girl who had been hidden by her father. The child was nearly dead from starvation when Constantine found her. He brought the young girl home to his wife, Senga, to care for her. The two raised the girl as their daughter. She would be there only child.

Her name was Arabella.

At Senga's passing six years later, it was Constantine who kept Arabella from utterly closing off her world. Having lost her father and two mothers, Arabella had grown familiar with loss, a familiarity she didn't care to know again.

Outside, Kenneth ran to catch his brother. "Coric, I'll take the hoe. I left the field to get it, I'll take it now," Kenneth hollered as he drew closer to Coric.

Coric continued toward the field as though he hadn't heard a word. He let the head of the hoe sway in front of him and hit the ground, pushing off of it with each step like a walking stick.

Kenneth caught Coric and remained a step behind. "Coric, let me have the hoe." He tapped his brother's shoulder, "Coric."

Coric turned. "Don't push me, Kenneth!" he snapped.

"I need the hoe, Coric," Kenneth said as he grasped the shaft of the hoe with his hand.

Coric gripped the hoe with both hands and yanked it

back. "Well you don't need it anymore. Go back inside with the women and rest up and get your water," he said, his breathing heavy and accelerated.

"Coric, why do you have to get so angry? I was only trying to get some water for us. I know Aiden was thirsty. I was thirsty. What are you so mad about?"

Coric stepped close and edged his chin towards Kenneth's face. "Why am I mad," Coric said, his lips barely moving, "because I should be out with the men and instead I'm here with you ... and your God-forsaken laziness. Father would have your hide if he knew you weren't helping ... at least Aiden is willing to work. Can't you at least do that?"

"I have been cutting barley all morning. I stop for one moment and you're furious." Kenneth's heart thumped in his chest, guessing what may happen next. "Why do you have such a problem with it, Coric?"

"Problem? Problem!" Coric's eyes narrowed. "You want a problem!"

In a blink, the staff of the hoe thumped Kenneth's chest, knocking him backward and off balance. Coric threw the hoe to the ground and rushed forward. Coric's fist met Kenneth's eye like a mallet hitting a sack of meat.

Kenneth's head snapped sideways, and he tumbled downward. He quickly caught himself, his palms flexing flat upon the ground. Turning his gaze, he eyed Coric's legs and kicked his heel into his brother's knee.

The blow hit hard. Coric came down, leaping onto Kenneth as he fell. Their bodies tangled, with Coric on top. Coric freed his hands and punched Kenneth square in the mouth. Again, he punched. He raised his fist once more—

"Coric!" Ena yelled.

"Kenneth!" Arabella screamed, running behind Ena.

"Stop this, stop right now!" Ena yelled again, rushing toward the two.

Coric stood and stared down at his brother. His head slowly cocked and he faced his mother. He held her gaze for a moment, took a deep breath, and then turned and walked away.

"What is this all about? Is it about that silly drink of water? Is that why you needed to fight your brother? Answer me, young man!" Ena demanded, marching behind her son.

Coric stooped and picked up the hoe. He held the tool in one hand while shaking the bloody fingers of the other, trying to dispel the sting of his punches. He gazed at his mother. "Mother, he sits inside and refuses to work ... and then he runs out and yanks the hoe from my hands. He had it coming."

Ena stared at Coric, studying the angry boy. She tried to speak calmly, "He's been in that field all morning with you and Aiden. The three of you have worked tirelessly to cut the barley. Why can't you take a rest? The barley can wait."

Coric said nothing. He struggled to look her in the eyes. Then he turned and gazed across the field as if watching for someone in the distance.

"Coric ... they're coming back," Ena said, her voice gentle and kind. "Coric, don't do this to yourself ... don't do this to us."

A breeze blew across Coric's cheeks. He stood still and closed his eyes as the locks of his hair blew against his face. He glanced at Kenneth. Arabella was kneeling beside him, pressing her fingers against his swollen eye.

"Coric," Ena said.

He looked at his mother. His eyes were heavy and moist. He turned, with hoe in hand, and slowly headed back into the field of fallen barley.

"Arabella, go get Nessa and have her bring a strip of red meat for Kenneth," Ena said. "We'll need it to get the swelling down."

Arabella rose and hurried to find Nessa.

"Get some water for them, too," Ena hollered as Arabella rushed away. She knelt down next to Kenneth. "Are you alright?"

Kenneth rubbed his cheek and shifted his jaw from side to side, checking that it was still in one piece. "Yes, I'm alright … don't know why he came at me like that."

"He's struggling, Kenneth." Ena gazed over her shoulder at Coric. Her heart broke as she watched him thrust the hoe into the ground and rake it back and forth as though he was punishing the earth for some grave injustice. She turned back to Kenneth, "It's not you, Son. He's looking for someone, or something, to be angry at."

Kenneth rubbed his eyes to clear his sight. "Maybe Father should have taken him with him … and let Coric take it out on the Britons."

CHAPTER 4

ALPIN GAVE THE SIGNAL TO HALT. THE MEN HAD reached the north face of the fabled forest of Ae. The dense pines stood tall before them, like giants with strange intertwined arms. If the scouts' reports were correct, the Britons remained a half mile ahead in the village of Ae, and their reinforcements from the south had recently arrived.

Darkness was coming. Alpin stared into the sky at the western sunset. The glowing orb sat on the horizon, radiating its brilliant pink tones against the bellies of the distant gray clouds. The sight was there and then gone, disappearing as quickly as it came, fleeing like a startled doe.

Alpin joined Luag and Constantine and sent a man to gather the scouts and the other leaders.

Once assembled, the handful of men rode forward into the dark forest.

Inside the forest, Ae's dense foliage enveloped the small band of Scots. Only the spotty glow of light penetrated the treetop openings where a random giant pine had fallen to rest. The forest was thick indeed. The trees were sizeable, allowing but a scant amount of underbrush to grow up under the canopy of branches.

The men pushed through the forest and reached the south edge of the tree line. Shrouded in the woods, they surveyed the campfires of Ae. Distant figures walked back and forth in front of the fires, moving about randomly and showing no sense of urgency.

Luag turned to Alpin and the men beside him. "We will attack from here?" he asked.

Alpin scanned left and then right, noting the thickness of the trees in all directions. The sun had descended, but the occasional sliver of moonlight allowed sufficient light to see. "This is a suitable spot. We will gather here, but we'll spread wide. At dawn, the foot soldiers will charge from the center. The men on horseback will hold the sides."

"And what of the archers?" Guaire asked.

"Father, I have an idea for the archers," Drostan interrupted. He edged his way between the men and faced the group. "Rushing the Britons across the field will let our men spread out like a wall, but now with their reinforcements, they could outnumber us by a hundred or more." Drostan glanced at Luag and the men and then his eyes returned to his father. "I think there's another way."

"Drostan, the men are ready to fight. Do not fear that our smaller numbers will be outmatched by the Britons," Alpin said. "We will win this battle."

"I'm not questioning the men's courage. I'm saying we can strengthen our attack if we split them—"

"Split our forces?" Guaire said. "I don't like that."

"But we can hit them with distraction and surprise," Drostan replied. "By splitting the men in two groups, we can send our best fighters toward the Britons. They will rush Ae on foot from the edge of the forest. After we have hit them, the Britons will rally. Our men will retreat back to the forest."

"It's both dangerous and unwise to turn your back in a fight, Drostan," Luag responded.

"The retreat is a distraction … to pull the Britons out of Ae. We want them to pursue our men to the forest. We'll have our longbows launch their arrows over our men into the Britons!" Drostan exclaimed, standing in the middle of the group and gesturing with his hands as he spoke. "Our foot soldiers will be protected once back in the forest while the crossbowmen and archers take down the Britons as they charge after us. If any Briton reaches the trees, our swordsmen will cut them down where they stand."

Alpin crossed his arms. His chin tilted down in thought. He rehearsed the plan in his mind. "I hear you, Drostan," Alpin said. "The plan is reasonable, but having the longbows shoot over our men is too risky. I won't lose a man to a Dalriadan arrow."

Alpin began to pace.

He stopped and peered at Guaire and Luag. "We will station the longbowmen to the east of the advancing men. When our men retreat to the forest, our longbows will deliver their arrows from the flank."

"I suggest our men on horseback take a position beside the longbows. See there, see those trees to the east," Constantine said as he pointed in the moonlight to a cluster of pines protruding from the forest like an enlarged thumb from a palm. "That location, tucked behind those trees, would allow the horsemen to enter the field without notice, attacking the remaining Britons while the others are fighting in the forest. Once the horses take the open area, our men in the forest can reenter the field and finish the Britons."

"It could work, Father," Drostan said.

"It could," Alpin replied. He allowed his thoughts to linger on the plan several moments longer. Then he glanced about the group. A pensive, contemplative look filled his gaze. He nodded, satisfied that he had seen enough. Without a word, he signaled the men to head back. He left only his scouts to remain in the forest of Ae. They would be his eyes throughout the night.

The band of Scots weaved their way back through the thick trees and rejoined the encamped men. The sun would rise in eight hours. The Scot warriors would rest to regain their strength for the day ahead. They would rotate shifts, sleeping and serving as posts until dawn.

On that night, sleep was elusive. Slumber kept its distance from the Scots like a king from a beggar. The darkness had riches to offer the men's tired bodies, but they found no such mercy. Scenes of war filled their minds, playing over and over its unquenchable fury. If respite did come, it lasted but a moment, only to be interrupted by a muscle spasm or a hooting owl, stirring them in the night's cold darkness.

Two hours before dawn, the men were up and assembled. Sleeplessness had stolen the night.

Alpin addressed the Scots, detailing the battle plan and assigning roles commensurate with each man's experience and ability. Some men—those rare men steeped in courage— volunteered to serve on the front line. They would be the first to engage the Britons.

Upon breaking camp, the men moved in groups through the forest. They reached Ae's southern tree line and found their positions. The crossbowmen climbed the trees and filled the treetops. The archers advanced to the edge of the woods with the swordsmen and axemen lined in front.

An older man from Milton, sporting a mane of white hair and a wrinkled, weathered face, proudly toted the Scots' war pipes. The man remained deep in the thick forest. His task was singular—he would play an elegy of lament, replete with descending keys and hanging notes, designed to stoke the warriors' souls as they stepped into the battlefield.

As those on the north edge of Ae found roosts among the trees, the longbows moved on foot to the eastern edge, following the horsemen to the flank position. When the horsemen took their stance, Latharn signaled Alpin that the horses and longbowmen were ready.

Alpin, sitting horseback along the northern timberline, eyed the trees. He was hardly able to spot the hidden warriors, woven among the pines like clandestine shadows at the forest's edge. He nodded to Constantine and the two turned their horses toward the village.

Though the sun had yet to show, its illumination was already pushing back the darkness. The large field of Ae lay between the Scots and the Britons. The field was empty except for the two riders that morning. The Dalriadan men, cloaked in the forest, gazed ahead as the two rode forward.

A young Briton gathering wood was the first to see the two Scots. The young man dropped his bundle and ran to the Briton tents scattered through the village.

Alpin and Constantine stopped their horses in the

middle of the field, eyeing the young Briton as he searched for his leader. In the distance, the young man stopped beside a tall, sturdy Briton and quickly pointed toward the two.

The tall Briton shouted to a group of men. Then he mounted a horse, along with three others, and advanced into the field.

The four Britons rode toward Alpin and Constantine as the two waited on horseback in the middle of Ae's open field. Two of the Britons wore dark brown overcoat-like coverings that buckled across the chest, common for Briton warriors. The tall man wore garb of deep red, almost blood red, distinguishing himself from the others. The forth Briton's outfit was different. It was black, and not only did it cover his arms and chest, but it also wrapped close to his neck and up over his ears and head.

The tall Briton leader stopped his horse twenty feet from the two Scots. The man in black stopped next to him, and the two in brown split off and slowly began to circle the Scots.

"I am Alpin of Renton, son of Eochaid. This is Constantine of Cashel, son of Duncan. We are sons of Dalriada," Alpin said and then paused. "You and your men are on land that belongs to Dalriada. You must remove your men from Ae and return south," Alpin insisted, ignoring the two circling behind him.

"My men are settling quite well here in our new village," the Briton leader replied, peering out over the field and motioning with his arms as he spoke. "They are enjoying themselves and the plenty of this land."

"I have no care for your interest in the land," Alpin responded. "I'm stating that it is not yours."

The Briton relinquished with his pretense of cheer and

peered at Alpin. He spoke in a deliberate tone, "Scot, if you wish to reclaim this land, you'll have to be willing to take it."

"I trust, in due time, you'll find the Scot blade quite willing."

The two circling Britons completed their course and trotted beside the others, forming a line of four.

"You're a fool to think we'd turn and flee. Your villages are pitiful and your men are weak. They run scared at the sight of a dagger." The Briton grinned and glanced at the man to his right. Then he gazed back at Alpin. "I believe my men have found a new home."

Alpin adjusted his reigns and shifted his weight in his saddle. He stared at the four men and then beyond them to the hundreds of men watching from the village.

Alpin's eyes returned to the Briton leader. He glared at the man for a long moment. "We shall see … we shall see." He tugged his reigns and made a clicking sound to cue his horse. The two Scots turned and rode swiftly across the field, back to the tall thick forest.

Alpin sat high on his horse at the edge of the tree line and called out to the eager ears awaiting him, "Men of Milton, Dumbarton, Cashel, and Renton—men of Dalriada. You have come here today to show the Britons, and all of Britannia, that this land is not Briton land. This land is our land. It belongs to Dalriada!"

The angry forest echoed back the furious shouts of the men.

"Our fathers before us bought this land with blood— their blood and the blood of their brothers and sons. They bought this land, and with it they gave us freedom and the opportunity to live as free men. You, too, have fought for this land. You bear the scars on your flesh and on your hearts—with many of you having lost your own fathers and brothers in battle—a costly price indeed. The day of battle has returned once again, and as our fathers before us fought, so too shall we fight!"

Alpin's horse began to dance beneath him. He turned the animal and trotted beside the forest edge. "Know this—life hangs in the balance today … as does freedom and tyranny. Men, recognize that we fight as one, brave and sure. And our fight is noble and right!" Alpin spun his horse and returned along the tree line. "Death shall soon visit this field of Ae. Make no mistake, Death will come this day! … And should my life be asked of me, then I shall give it!"

The trees thundered with a roaring fury.

Alpin's voice grew louder, "A man must know what he is willing to live for—and what he is willing to die for! If called of us, we shall give our blood at Ae … we shall ensure the blood of our sons flows with freedom in their veins! We will give up neither our land, nor our sons, nor our daughters, nor our sacred honor. We will fight!"

Alpin drew his sword and held it high above his head. He shouted to the men of Dalriada, "Do not submit your honor to another. Let it be known to all! Here! Today!"

The forest of Ae ignited in a fiery furor.

Alpin's long metal sword dropped and a great horn of war sounded. The heart of every Scot pounded and the men released their cry. It was loud and awful. As the great horn faded, the haunting sound of bagpipes emerged from deep within the woods. The swiftest led as nearly two hundred

Dalriadan men broke into the clearing, charging with an angry passion as if hurled from a sling.

Taran and Drostan were among the warriors storming Ae. They were side by side, screaming in rage as they rushed forward.

All of life seemed to be brought to this single moment as the men charged across the green grass of Ae. The white clover blossoms bloomed harmlessly in the field, yielding as the torrent of warriors rushed forward and stomped the tiny flowers beneath their feet. Although the blossoms bloomed to glorify life, the men rushed to take it.

Chaos erupted in the village as the Britons armed themselves. Soon the flood of Scots would hit. Briton soldiers found their swords and axes and hastened to form a battle line in the field. The Briton archers gathered behind the foot soldiers, setting arrows in their bows. In moments, the bows were lifted. A shout came, "Release!" In a single fluid motion, the strings pushed, the arrows lifted, and an arsenal of steel-tipped shafts soared into the sky toward the rushing Scots.

Bodies fell as the arrows hit. Yet the fearless Scots stormed headlong across the field.

Alpin readied himself with the horsemen, anchored along the eastern stretch of trees. He was accompanied by the longbows. The men would wait as planned, as long as the battle moved in their favor.

Alpin watched the field swell with the fury of men and fought the urge to charge forward and join Drostan and the foot soldiers. Then he glanced at Constantine and the others on horseback beside him. He wasn't the only one anxious to move. He resisted. He would wait for the counterattack as planned.

Alpin watched life and death unfold before his eyes.

The warriors of Dalriada crossed the field like a tidal wave. The loud clanking of metal weapons was an ominous sound. Three warriors leading the charge reached the Britons first, they were the tip of the spear. The three appeared as a single mass of flesh when they reached the Briton fighters, and then they split into three men divided, each searching for worthy prey.

The Scot in the center continued straight, piercing through the Britons, spinning and stabbing as he engaged his enemy. He danced in a destructive rhythm, knowing instinctively where to place each step as though rehearsed a hundred times before. Each step and spin ended with a penetrating slice, severing flesh and finding bone. Several Britons fell to the mad Scot's blade, while others fled to save themselves.

The Scot on the right, a short man from Dumbarton, was less nimble and more brutish in his attacks. After wrestling his bloody blade free from the belly of his first victim, he lunged shoulder first into the chin of a surging Briton, knocking the man from his feet. The Briton thumped to the ground unconscious, with missing teeth and a broken jaw. The Dumbarton man pressed forward like a charging bull, barreling into two more men. The two stumbled sideways and the Scot tumbled to the ground. Then he lifted and leg-whipped a third man charging him. The Briton's knees buckled, dropping him to the ground, and the Scot buried his dagger in the man's throat.

The Scots' attack continued against the Briton soldiers. Their advancing front pummeled and pounded the overconfident, less-spirited Britons.

Drostan was not far behind the lead row of men. He could hear the sound of swords crashing across metal and flesh. His heart thumped hard in his chest. His breath seemed to flee his lungs and not return. His anxiety intensified with every step. In moments, the Britons would break through the front line. He could hear their voices, see their eyes, smell their sweat. The emotions of battle seized him—emotions known by all men: anger, fear, surprise, rage; yet, they were magnified a thousand times over in the throes of war. Every fiber in his soul pulsated with amplified arousal. Drostan clenched his teeth. His nostrils flared to take in air. He summoned his courage and charged forward.

A Briton instantly materialized, coming straight at Drostan and locking eyes with the young Scot. The man slowed, then coaxed Drostan, daring him to move first.

A sudden rage burst inside Drostan and he leapt toward the man. Their blades collided with a clang. The weight of the larger man's blade pressed heavy against Drostan's. Another swing came. Drostan lifted his shield and twisted to avoid the sharp steel. With his sword he pushed back the man's weapon. Quickly shifting his feet, he prepared to strike. In a blur, he swung his blade hard and sliced deep into the Briton's side.

The man shuttered and crumpled to his knees. The cut was fatal.

Drostan withdrew his sword and peered down into the glossy eyes of the fallen Briton. The man stared back, and his lifeless gaze slowly faded.

Drostan stood stone-still, mesmerized.

A loud noise pierced the air. The horn of the Scots!

Drostan sprung from his daze and glanced back at the forest. The Scots were in retreat.

He ran to join them, but a sudden blow struck his shoulder and sent him reeling. His body twisted. Again, a cruel force pounded his backside. The blow knocked him off balance, and he tumbled to the ground. Peering up, he saw the cold iron trim of a large wooden shield descending toward his neck like a guillotine. Drostan rolled to the side and jumped to his feet.

The Briton, large and round, turned and charged Drostan. The man carried no sword, yet his shield alone was sufficiently deadly. The man dove at Drostan. Drostan side-stepped the man and hit him with the butt of his sword.

The round man grunted in anger and spun. He recoiled and swung his shield, hitting the side of Drostan's head and knocking him back to the ground.

Drostan's vision blurred. He tried to refocus. A shadow loomed over him. Glancing up, he saw the guillotine rising.

The shadow left as the Briton's guillotine peaked in its ascent, ready for its fall.

Drostan slid left and shoved his sword upward. The Briton never saw the blade that pierced his chest.

The man slowly lowered his arms. His eyes widened and blood oozed from his lips. It dripped and splattered on Drostan's neck.

Drostan pulled his sword from the man's chest and rolled from beneath the sweaty, bloody mass of flesh as it faded to the ground. The man would never swing a shield again.

Alpin's heart raced, beating and pounding in his body. The horses beside him kneaded the ground, their riders set to charge. Yet, for the moment, they could only watch.

Alpin's hand tightened around his sword as the Scots retreated to the forest. A gap formed between the withdrawing Scots and the Britons, who appeared momentarily baffled by the retreat. The opening in the field lay rife with carnage— bodies, swords, and shields lay strewn across the bloody green divide.

Alpin spotted Drostan, not far from the muddled mass of Britons. He watched as Drostan pushed aside the large, rotund Briton and lifted to his feet. "Hurry, Son," he whispered.

The Britons had not anticipated the Scots' retreat. Loud voices lofted from among the Britons, encouraging their men to pursue, and the Briton warriors charged toward the forest, chasing the fleeing Scots.

Alpin peered to his left and scanned the standing row of longbowmen. "Ready your bows!"

Laise and the archers of Milton lifted their great weapons.

Alpin's eyes swept back to the field. Drostan trailed the retreating Scots. "Son, run, run," he muttered, not at all eager to have the longbowmen release their arrows while Drostan remained on the field.

Alpin turned toward the longbow archers, watching them press their bodies into their flexing bows and draw back their heavy cords. The muscles in their arms rippled and strained against their skin. Anxiety coursed through Alpin's body. He would have to give the command.

"Release!"

The silent, thirty-inch, steel-tipped killers soared from the eastern flank toward their victims two hundred yards ahead. Within seconds the killers reached the north-charging Britons. Several men stopped abruptly and then sunk into the bloody field. The remaining Britons pushed forward, pursuing the retreating Scots to the forest.

A second round of long arrows released. At these distances, the longbow was rarely good for hitting a single man, yet it was highly suitable for hitting an army. The second round of arrows sailed and found new victims. More Britons fell and littered the field.

Ae reeked with the madness of battle, saturating the air and clouding the mind. Desperation and fury wove tangled knots of angst in the hearts of the men, Scots and Britons alike.

The surging Britons rushed headlong across the field. A handful led the charge, and a great many more swept behind them like an army of predators hungry for prey—wounded prey.

The slower, injured Scots were the first to be overtaken. And the slaughter began.

Drostan headed toward the north edge of the field where the Britons were fighting at the timberline. With several Britons in front of him and many more behind, he found himself pinned between the two. Continuing forward would take him to the heat of the battle at the forest's edge, but he'd be trapped by the Britons coming behind.

Then he turned east and spotted his father and the Dalriadan horsemen in the distance. He dropped his shield and sprinted, carrying only a sword.

He ran hard and fast. His lungs burned with fire, as if flames filled his chest.

The retreating Scots at the forest's edge took cover in the trees. The Britons closed on their heels. To the south, the Briton horsemen poured onto the battlefield. The galloping horses rushed across the divide, toward the northern tree line.

Silhouettes darted in the shadows of the forest. Scots, armed with short bows, suddenly emerged from the underbrush, while the crossbowmen shifted among the branches in the pines.

The Britons hesitated as the forest awakened.

A single arrow exited the trees and dropped a charging Briton. The lone arrow was followed by a hundred more, flying like a swarm of bees and riddling the bodies of the ambushed Britons. Limbs, torsos, and skulls caught the arrows indiscriminately.

A second round of arrows released.

Over half the Britons died where they stood beside the trees of Ae. Others were injured and maimed, while still others retreated. The bravest of the Britons rushed into the forest.

Their bravery was short-lived. The Scot foot soldiers surrounded and attacked their enemy as they entered. The best a Briton could hope to find in the forest of Ae was a quick, decisive death, by sword or bow, rather than a slow painful death, delivered one miserable cut at a time.

Drostan continued his sprint toward the horsemen to the east. He saw Taran, who had reached the horses and was mounting beside the other riders. A moment of relief came when he saw his father lift and drop his arm, the signal for the horsemen to charge. A hundred yards separated Drostan from his people. His sprint never slowed.

Drostan suddenly heard the faint sound of hoofbeats coming from behind. He glanced over his shoulder. *Where was the rider, left or right? How close?*

He felt fear and tried to suppress it. The rider was coming quickly. Drostan's foot twisted below him. He stumbled and caught himself. *Keep moving, keep moving,* he told himself.

The rider closed on Drostan and was now twenty feet to the rear. The Briton slowed and peered down the narrow plank of his crossbow to target his victim.

Drostan ran in disarray, sprinting and stumbling, fighting to fill his lungs with air. He wished he could fly and soar into the sky.

The Briton sighted his target. He steadied his weapon and pressed against the trigger.

A single long arrow released from the east.

It soared and thumped with deadly impact.

The Briton on the horse gasped for breath but found none. The palm of the man's hand turned limp, and the crossbow fell from his grip. The lifeless rider slid from his galloping horse and hit the ground.

Drostan had heard the wisp of an arrow as it flew overhead. He glanced back and saw the rider crumple in a mound. The thirty-inch longbow arrow had flown past Drostan and found the soft chest of the Briton rider.

A hundred yards away, Laise grinned. He had seen the rider coming and waited for his moment. When the rider had paused, Laise had not. A direct kill at that distance was not typical of longbow accuracy, but Laise was not a typical longbowman.

Alpin was halfway to Drostan when the first rider fell. But his fear was not the first rider with the bow. It was the second Briton rider behind him—the rider with the sword. The second rider was closing quickly on Drostan.

Laise drew another arrow.

It fumbled in his hands.

He seated the arrow and pressed hard into his constricted longbow.

He drew back the bowstring.

Continuing his sprint, Drostan heard a second set of pounding hooves. *Had the horse kept running without a rider?* His mind whirled.

The rider drew closer.

The hoofbeats grew louder.

Drostan's heart jolted. *Something's wrong.* Confusion hit. *Why was the horse still coming?*

He glanced back. It was then he realized there was a second rider—and the rider was ten feet behind him.

The Briton lifted his sword into the air.

Laise released his arrow.

A north wind blew across his brow—and a chill ran down his spine.

He watched his arrow soar and twist in the wind, praying it would find its mark.

The second arrow flew past Drostan—and past the rider with the sword.

Drostan's eyes fixed on the rider's face, a face etched with hatred.

There was no time.

Drostan lifted his sword, but the rider's blade crashed down like a lightning bolt.

The cut ran down Drostan's shoulder and across his chest to the bottom of his ribs.

Drostan's eyes fell to his chest. He stared at the crown of his sternum. It protruded out from his open skin.

The pain severed his thoughts. He lost his breath and dropped to the ground. Blood oozed from the wound, slowly painting the surrounding white clover blossoms a deep crimson.

"DROSTAN!"

Alpin's glare locked on the second rider. His horse raced forward. He closed the distance between him and the Briton and leapt from his horse, lunging into the man and driving his long steel blade into the heart of the Briton. The two tumbled from the Briton's horse.

The Briton was dead before he hit the ground.

Alpin jumped to his feet and ran to his son. Reaching Drostan, he dropped to his knees beside him. He lifted his son's head and gazed into his eyes, his body shadowing

Drostan's face from the morning sunlight that brought no warmth.

"Drostan, can you hear me?"

Drostan smiled a faint smile. "Father, it is good to see you." His eyes blinked several times and then slowly began to close.

"Drostan, stay with me," Alpin pleaded. He fought for words. "I watched you on the battlefield. Son, you were a mighty warrior today."

"Father, I thought I was done when that big fellow ..." Drostan tried to laugh, but the blood in his throat made him cough. He struggled to speak, "... when the big fellow struck me with his shield." He coughed and spat a thick red film from his tongue.

Alpin scanned his flanks. No Britons near.

"How is he?" Constantine asked as he approached and moved his horse in a circle around the two like a protective mother hawk.

Alpin didn't speak, he only shook his head. Nothing needed to be said. His eyes combed across the field toward the forest. In the distance, Luag, Gormal, and the others on horseback were fighting hard and overwhelming the struggling Britons. His eyes passed over the piles of tattered bodies twisted across the field. The Scots had suffered losses, but the battle was theirs. To Alpin, the sweetness of the victory tasted harshly bitter.

He gazed down at his son. The boy's face was a pale whitish-blue. Alpin placed his hand on Drostan's cheek. "Son. Son, listen to me. You've done well today. The Britons needed more than a shield to fight you. You were too quick for them," Alpin said, groping for words.

Drostan's eyes cracked open, and a smile eased upon his lips.

Alpin studied his face. His son's eyebrows were dark and thick. His eyelashes were long with a slight curl. The boy's nose was thin with a circular curvature, much like his mother's. His bottom lip was full and his chin bore a slight cleft in the center. Flashbacks flooded in, memories of holding Drostan as a newborn baby while the boy's mother cried with joy, how he had given Drostan his first sword as a young lad, how he had wrestled with his son as a boy in Renton, how they had worked together every hour of sunlight during the harvest season. His son was a gift—of that, he was certain.

"Drostan." Alpin shook the boy. "Coric is going to be mad with envy to hear how you ran against a hundred charging Britons." He tried, with much desperation, to give his son something to cling to.

Drostan's eyes flickered. He lifted his arm and clasped his father's hand as it rested on his cheek. "Father, I thank God for you." Drostan wheezed for breath. "I fear I will not see Mother or Nessa with my own eyes again. I will not see Coric either. And Kenneth and Aiden ... and Donald, he is but a boy." His grip suddenly tightened, and he convulsed and coughed. "I miss them, Father."

"Drostan ... Son! Look around." Alpin lifted his son's head. "Your plan for battle was our strongest weapon. The Britons could not match your wit. Son, Dalriada is victorious." Alpin smiled for his son.

"Father, I hope that someday ...," Drostan fought for breath, "someday ... when time has passed and you are older ... I hope that you will still remember me, Father."

The words paralyzed Alpin. He had not known tears since he himself was but a boy. This day was different. This day was a day he would forever remember. And, despite its misery, it was a day he would never desire to forget. Tears dripped from his nose and fell to Drostan's pale, clammy skin.

Drostan blinked at the soft tickle on his cheek. He stared up at the sky of crystal blue and shivered at the chill running through his body. A gentle wind blew back his hair as he rested his head in his father's lap.

Drostan turned his gaze to the distant western mountains and then to the grassy field, dotted with tiny white blossoms. The colors radiated with brilliance. He took in his last breaths of the cool fresh air of the free land of Dalriada.

Alpin held the boy gently and spoke in a quiet voice, "Drostan, my son, in whom I am well pleased. You have honored your father, your family, and your countrymen, even giving your life to do so. As my son, I will always remember you, I will always hold you close in my heart … and as a man, you shall never be forgotten in the land of Dalriada."

Drostan whispered to his father, "Father, will you take me home?"

"Yes, Son, I'll take you home," Alpin promised.

Drostan's gaze turned from his father to Dalriada's blue sky above, and then his eyes closed forever.

Other Scots had died that morning, though none as dear as Drostan. Alpin never left Drostan's side. He watched as the Scots pushed back the last of the Britons, sitting in a silence all his own and holding his son in the midst of that awful field of Ae.

The Britons lost over two hundred and fifty men at Ae, nearly six to one of what the Scots lost. Yet the Scots' losses were costly. They lost Drostan. They lost nearly forty others, including Gormal. Telling Searc of the loss of his father would be painful for the boy.

On that cold, bloody, autumn morning, the Dalriadans proved much—that a passionate heart and a brave spirit made for a mighty foe, a foe not simply made of men, but of courageous men, men willing to give what was asked of them.

Death had stolen much from Alpin that day. It was a day that would scar him forever. A day etched with loss and pride, honor and pain.

Alpin would take his son home now.

CHAPTER 5

THE BARLEY FIELD LAY BARREN OF ITS ONCE proud stalks. All that remained were three soggy stooks that stood on the far side of the field, slumped over from the storms. Though the rain had departed Renton, blanketing clouds and thick moist air hovered above the small village, leaving an overcast gray sky that veiled the setting sun. The remnants of the rain pooled into puddles across the field—a field that refused to dry.

Coric, Kenneth, and Aiden had finished cutting the barley and had moved most of the crop into the barn. The time for threshing had arrived. In threshing, the grain was to be separated from the stalk, a tedious task without the proper tool. To hasten the task, a flail often proved useful. The simple tool consisted of two wooden shafts connected loosely together with a short leather strap. One shaft of wood was held and used to sling the free shaft. When slung, the free shaft carried a great force, suitable for beating grain and separating it from the stalk.

With the day of chores nearly past, the evening was much like any other evening. The fading light of day grew dim, and darkness crept in to replace it. Coric and Kenneth were in the barn, finishing their day of threshing. Taking turns with the flail, they beat the last of the dry stalks. As with each prior evening of threshing, the two again found themselves warring against their aching muscles as they beat the stalks and gathered the grain.

Aiden and Donald had escaped the evening chores and had fled to a nearby copse of willow trees to complete their makeshift fort. They had promised themselves that they would finish their fortress before their father and brother returned. What had started as a few broken sticks now stood as a walled stronghold of branches, twine, and stone footings.

Nessa and Arabella labored inside, working to prepare the evening meal. Ena had them tend to the meal while she brought the final stalks into the barn to be dried for threshing. The extra chores brought Ena contentment in the men's absence. The work kept her from dwelling on things far away. She saw to it that the boys' chores were plentiful as well, wanting them busy rather than have their young minds wandering. Though her thoughts of the men frequently nagged her, the chores brought relief, and in her relief, she found hope.

The men on horseback were the first to crest the hill. The hollow clip-clops of the horses and the cracking of pebbles under the wheels of the heavy carts broke the silence of the evening air. The horses toiled and tugged as they pulled their carts over the hill. But their carts no longer carried supplies, rather they carried a cargo much more precious.

Ena dragged the last of the barley stalks toward the barn

in the dim light of dusk. It was then that she heard the horses approaching. She glanced into the distance and gasped when she saw the men. A gush of excitement flushed over her, and she dropped the stalks and rushed along the path toward the returning riders.

"They're home!" she shouted, calling back to the barn.

Alpin's horse rode lead.

Ena ran to her husband. Reaching his horse, she grabbed Alpin's leg and peered up into his tired eyes. "Alpin, you're home," she said and smiled while her eyes glimpsed past him to locate her son. "Drostan," she called her son's name and lifted her head to see past the other riders.

Something was wrong.

She glanced at Alpin and released his leg. Slowly stepping back from the horse, she tensed. Her small frame shifted left and then right, still searching for her child. "Drostan?"

No one spoke.

Her gaze fell to Alpin, and her heart sank as her husband's eyes conveyed the awful words that her ears could not bear to hear.

"Where is he?" she asked. "Where is he!" she screamed.

Silence.

Then the words came as Alpin spoke—"He fell in battle."

Her lungs heaved to take in a breath, and she pressed her head against Alpin's horse. She stood motionless for a moment and then began to pound the apathetic animal with her fists. "No, no, no!" she cried. Her husband's words had crushed down upon her like a falling mountain.

Alpin slid from his horse and stood beside his wife. He took Ena in his arms and held her. She buried her face in his chest, her body shuddering as she wept. Alpin eased his hand to her head and gently pushed her hair away from her brow. He gazed into her eyes. "I have carried him back to you, to his home."

Coric hustled up the path. "Mother," he called from the distance.

Kenneth followed behind.

Ena lifted her head and stared at Coric in a daze.

"Father, you're home!" Coric called as he neared—then he saw his mother, teary-eyed and broken. "Mother!" He dropped his flail and rushed to her. A raw, bitter pain seeped from her gaze. He turned to his father, slowly shaking his head. "No … no!"

He hurried past his father to the carts. Reaching the first cart, he grabbed the side panel and peered into its dark belly. There, under the dull moonlight, he found his brother.

"No. Drostan, no!"

His frame fell limp and he staggered, staring at his mother and father. Tears of rage streamed down his cheeks. "My brother … my brother." His lip turned under and his face tightened in a scowl. "Drostan is dead. He's dead!"

Coric froze in a heartbroken stance like a defeated statue, his disbelieving mind weaving thoughts and memories in and out, trying to grasp the weight of losing Drostan.

When Kenneth reached the cart he stopped a few steps behind his crestfallen brother, unsure if he truly wanted to peer inside the cart's wooden belly. He hesitated and then stepped forward. Slowly, he peered into the cart and gazed down at his brother. The cold pale face and blanket-covered body of the brother he loved lay before him—lifeless.

Without warning, Coric shoved Kenneth aside and

pulled a knife from his belt. He buried his blade over and over into the sidewall of the weathered cart, cursing it with every blow. When his storm of anger was spent, he gave into grief and leaned against the mutilated wood, sobbing with a ruined heart.

Alpin stood stoic, allowing the boy's rage to run its course. Then he stepped to his son and gazed over him. "Coric," was the only word he said, and he waited for his son to come back to him.

Coric lowered his knife while leaving the crown of his head still pressed against the side of the cart. He stared down at the scarred wood he'd left behind. "Why, Father … why?"

Alpin removed the knife from his son's grip and slipped it into the side of his belt. Then he placed his hand on Coric's shoulder. "We're not always given answers, Coric," he said. "Your pain will not easily be relieved, but you should know that your brother gave his life fighting with courage for those he loved."

Coric said nothing.

Kenneth stood silently at Coric's side—sad for him, sad for himself. The loss of Drostan was great. Kenneth drew a deep breath and then let his eyes ease upward to his father.

Alpin's heavy gaze found Kenneth. "Drostan is home now," he said.

The rain fell hard the next morning as the old horse drudgingly pulled the cart forward. Its destination— Renton's small abbey. Alpin walked the procession alongside the cart that carried his son. He would not remove his hand from its wooden side. The drizzling rain soaked his skin and clothes. The wet chill of the rain mattered little.

Alpin's thoughts wandered back to Ae and how he had watched his son die in his arms. The same thoughts had haunted him for the past two days and nights as the men had pushed hard to return to Renton to let his son rest as he had asked. The thought of having his son, and now having him no longer, tore at him with every step.

He had dreaded telling Ena and the children that Drostan had died. How could he look her in the eyes while he ripped a hole in her heart? He had devastated his family with the loss he'd brought upon them. He was a crushed, defeated man, with little life remaining in his soul.

He'd brought loss not only to his family, but to many families in Renton. His mind replayed the hour when he had told Searc of the death of his father, Gormal. The boy took the news bitterly. He knew the young twelve-year-old would. With his mother having died during his birth, Searc's life had already been hard enough. Growing up, Searc had only Gormal and a deaf aunt to call family. And it didn't help that his father had always been a harsh man, a man plagued with fits of drunkenness and rage. Still, Alpin pitied the boy— though Gormal was no noble man, he was the boy's father.

Alpin cringed as he recalled the boy's words and how he had blamed Alpin for his father's death, "Those murderers, they're animals! I'll kill those Britons, I'll kill them, every last one of them! He never should have died. It's because of you, he died. You wanted to go and fight. You wanted this!" Searc had even threatened Alpin with a knife, and had Luag not been present to stop the boy, he may have followed through on his threat.

Alpin dismissed his thoughts of the troubled lad and stared down at the soggy ground in front of him. The drizzle persisted as he walked beside the cart. The rain dripped from his nose and chin as the procession moved along the muddy path to the abbey.

Though Alpin's son lay within his grasp, the finality of Drostan's death gnawed at him like a dagger serrating his gut. He took another step forward as the rain continued to fall.

The cleric lifted his arms and the abbey quieted. The cleric's name was Gilchrist, a taken name meaning, "servant of Christ." He was a middle-aged man in his late thirties. He had become Renton's cleric when he arrived six years prior. He was quiet, but considered wise, and the people of the village trusted him.

Gilchrist surveyed the family, lowered his head, and recited a ritualistic Latin prayer, leaning over Drostan's body as he prayed.

Alpin struggled with the cleric's foreign words. He was sure the words were a sort of blessing or mystic chant that would open the doors of Heaven, but he could guess little more beyond that. Though he didn't understand many of the rituals, he believed the power of the cleric's words provided a passage between this life and the next. As a younger father, Alpin had acknowledged the message of the Christ as a truth given by God to men and had even granted Kenneth his Christian name to complement his Dalriadan birth name, Ciniodh.

Kenneth stared at his father as Gilchrist spoke. His father appeared almost like a stone, gazing listlessly at Drostan's body. It was then that Kenneth realized that a piece of his father had died on the battlefield with his brother—not the piece that fights, or protects, nor the piece that gives or provides, but rather the piece that enables one's eyes to warm and one's countenance to flow forth. For his father, it was a loss that could never be regained but only remembered.

In the midst of the prayers, Aiden too silently surveyed the small abbey and its attendants—and felt alone. Aiden had no Drostan left to wrestle, except in his memories of a past now gone. Though eleven, he understood enough of the world to see that death had a way of stealing the goodness of life. Once carefree, his exuberance had suddenly been robbed of him, only now to be replaced with a painful, hollow bitterness.

Aiden tried to listen to the cleric. He yearned to hear some sort of answer to his unanswerable questions. Yet the cleric's words only brought madness, and nothing made sense. *This shouldn't be happening!* he thought, struggling with anger. He wanted his brother, not promises and prayers.

Aiden broke his silence, "Where is this Christ?" he demanded. He stood to his feet, staring at Gilchrist. "Where is He? Everything is lost!"

"Aiden!" Ena exclaimed.

Angst filled the cold air of the small abbey.

Gilchrist lifted his hands to quiet the boy. "Christ is with us, Aiden. He receives Drostan. He receives him even as we speak, to a place where death and misery cannot be."

"Then why is my brother dead?"

Gilchrist paused, and then, with a patient tone, he spoke, "Be sure of this Aiden, we will know loss in this life. Do not be surprised that death comes and takes the ones we hold dear. But be sure of this as well, suffering is devised by God to loosen our hold on this world. Sorrow is often that one great means by which God awakens our heart, confronting our mind and capturing our soul. We do not wish for pain or loss, but you must know that God is not far from either. And though we do not see it at present, the Lord shall use Drostan's death to His glory, just as He did through Drostan's life among us. It is hard now, but in time, I pray you will grow to understand."

Aiden eased down onto the wooden bench beside his mother. He lowered his head and placed his forehead in his hands. "It's not right," he muttered to himself, "it's not right."

The men carried Drostan outside and laid his body in the ground. The grave had been dug early that rainy morning by the three brothers. They had insisted they would be the ones to dig Drostan's final place of rest.

Ena stood beside Alpin and clutched his hand. Nessa, Coric, Kenneth, Aiden, and Donald watched in mourning as their oldest brother was lowered into the earth.

Alpin spoke, "This is my son, my first son. He is an honorable son who proved to be a brave and valiant warrior. He gave all that could be asked of him, and did so with courage." Alpin stared down into the wet grave at his boy. "Drostan, you shall not be forgotten in Dalriada, and you shall never leave my heart."

A dirge was sung, a dirge of remembrance.

Men with shovels returned dirt to the grave while the sullen sound of bagpipes lamented from the abbey's rear steps.

Arabella leaned close and whispered to Kenneth. Her tears remained on his cheek as she pulled away. She hoped her words would somehow assuage his sorrow, but even a kind word offers little solace for such a deep wound. She tightened her grip on his hand and smiled, wanting to comfort him on this day, the saddest of days.

CHAPTER 6

SEVEN WINTERS HAD PASSED. THE PAIN HAD subsided, but the memories remained.

"Steady your aim. Breathe out. Hold. Release!" Kenneth gave the command.

The arrow flew straight but missed the mark by a good four feet.

"How did I do?" Donald, now ten, asked his older brother, hoping for approval.

"You did well, quite well for a young lad," Kenneth replied. "Every large barn in Dalriada now has good right to fear you."

The others laughed. They enjoyed watching young Donald attempt his skill with the bow. The bow Donald held was smaller than a common bow, but it could still harm a man if ever its arrow found its mark. Donald reveled in the attention. He enjoyed being with his older brothers. He enjoyed laughing with them.

The warmth of the sun felt good that morning. It was a good day for being with family and friends. It was good to be

outdoors again, shooting arrows and taking in life. Winter
had passed and spring had come. The daffodils had burst
forth, displaying their gentle yellow petals. They speckled
the landscape here and there, finding a home beneath the
cool shade of the budding black elders. The reed buntings,
sporting their handsome black caps, flittered among the
treetops. The spring season had brought hope and warmth
and life. The red-breasted robins joined the chatter, soaking
in the new morning and calling to one another with clicks
and chirps. Yet it was the pyramidal orchids that made the
grandest announcement, declaring to all their presence. The
orchids' pastel blooms glimmered with a palette of pinks and
purples as they nestled among the rolling green plains of
Renton. Their odiferous scent boldly heralded their arrival.

The spring season offered a new hope for those who
would receive it. It was the dawning of the seventh spring
since Drostan's death. Time had passed, and though scars
had formed, the cuts weren't as tender as in the early years
since losing Drostan, when a memory could strike the heart
with a sudden sadness and rob the soul of joy. Yes, the spring
offered a new hope to press on with life and look ahead to
the seasons to come.

The three older boys had grown into men. They were
boys no longer. The loss had broken them and the healing
had reshaped them, each into his own man. And though
each walked with a limp all their own, at least they were
walking.

For Alpin it was different. His mountains were giants
and his valleys devils. Life was a struggle in the season
following Drostan's death. Were it not for Luag, Alpin
may have remained despondent. It was Luag who regularly

coaxed Alpin and their older sons to escape Renton and do what men were supposed to do—hunt. The hunts were not simply good for providing food, they were also good for clearing the mind and healing the soul.

"Drostan would be proud of you, Donald," Coric hollered to his little brother. Then he jumped down from his sunny perch atop a jagged rock and ambled across the grass to Donald and the others.

"Indeed, he would be proud," Alpin said, sitting on a fallen log that he shared with Luag. The two men sat rightly, like judges in a contest, heckling the boys whenever an arrow missed its mark.

The boys took turns with the bow, each trying to prove his worth. They were shooting at more than targets—they were shooting for posture, shooting for manhood.

"Donald, if you come that close at thirty feet, you'll be dropping deer from a galloping horse before you're twelve. I pity the poor critters," Coric said.

Kenneth chuckled. "That's right Donald, quite right."

"I'm next," Coric said as he bent over and pulled an arrow from the quiver.

"In just a moment," Aiden uttered in an even, measured voice as he pulled back his bowstring and aimed. He pointed the arrow's iron tip at the small, half-eaten apple perched beside the wooden shield Donald had targeted.

Searc hovered behind Aiden, watching over his shoulder. Searc aligned the arrow and the apple in his own line of sight and closed one eye. "Imagine the apple is the throat of a Briton," he muttered and then snickered with a tinge of spite.

"I'm trying to focus," Aiden replied, his voice remaining

steady. He leveled his arrow and aimed at the top half of the distant apple.

"Come Aiden, take down them blokes!" Searc groused.

"Let it rest, Searc," Aiden replied.

The release came quick and smooth. The arrow flew high, sailing inches over the fleshy brown apple core.

"Not bad," Coric said with a nod. Aiden moved aside, and Coric stepped forward to take a turn. "Mind if I have a go?"

Coric seated the arrow in the cord of his bow and lifted his arms to aim. "I'm going for the shield … but keep your eyes on the center, because that's where she'll land." He drew back the cord, flexing the bow with a steadied aim, exhaled, and released.

Thunk.

His arrow clipped the edge of the shield and buried itself in the dead log behind it. "Breeze took it," he exclaimed before the others could begin their hazing.

"Coric, were your eyes closed?" Luag asked, spurring a round of laughter.

"Maybe you could take a few lessons from Donald," Alpin noted. The young boy peered at his father, wearing a smile from ear to ear.

"Ronan, why don't you give it a try," Luag called to his son and waved him forward.

Ronan glanced at his father and then at the two targets in the distance. "It would be my pleasure."

Ronan, Luag's only son, was twenty-three. He was a few months younger than Coric. Having no brothers of his own, Ronan had always considered Coric and Kenneth his closest companions. Ronan was particularly close to Coric, as the two commonly ventured off together to hunt. Ronan was a quick-witted, competitive young man, and he was also very good with his hands. He could whittle a bow from a crooked stick and could skin a deer before its heart stopped beating, though he never did. Indeed, he made for a fine hunting partner.

Ronan picked up his bow and strode to where Coric was standing.

"Nice bow," Alpin said.

Ronan scanned the lean wooden bow he held and admired it for himself. "Yew wood, made it with my own two hands." He set his arrow and pulled back the bowstring. He gazed at the backdrop of trees and then focused on his target. The arrow released.

Thunk.

The arrow burrowed into the wooden shield, eight inches from the center mark.

Ronan lowered the bow and turned to his audience. "Now you know where to come for help."

"Lucky shot," Coric moaned. "Pure luck."

"Jealousy is unbecoming," Alpin chided.

"Jealousy! That was nothing but luck, a friendly wind."

"May I?" the tall man from Milton interrupted. It was Laise. He had come with his father, mother, and sister to Renton for the wedding. "Nice bow. Mind if I try?" he said with a smile and extended his hands.

"Sure." Ronan handed Laise the bow and stepped back to his seat.

Laise took a moment to inspect the bow. He plucked the string delicately and then pulled it to test the draw, each time pulling it back farther. Satisfied, he knelt beside the quiver and withdrew the remaining arrows, aligning them next to one another in a single row. One by one, he began sifting through the arrows, testing each for weight and balance. Holding the last arrow, he paused and measured it a bit longer. Then he clasped it in his fist, smiled, and stood.

The others gazed in anticipation, mesmerized by the respected archer's meticulous process.

Laise assumed a bowman's stance, back straight and feet separated with the fore foot pointed slightly outward. He drew back the arrow in a single graceful motion, like a master musician strumming an instrument before an eager audience.

The veins in Laise's forearms bulged as he held the readied arrow in a frozen pose. No one spoke. Every eye remained fixed on the tall bowman from Milton. He marked his target, the small one. Then, drawing a deep breath, he exhaled and released. The arrow vanished in a blur.

Gone.

The apple was gone.

Claps sounded and cheers erupted. Alpin and Luag rose from their seats to join the applause.

Laise nodded his head and bowed. "That's how we do it in Milton."

"You need to come hunting with us more often," Luag said above the cheers.

"Then you wouldn't have to return empty-handed so often, Luag," Alpin said with a generous smile. He turned to Coric, "I hope you were taking notes, Son. Since you'll be spending more time with Laise, maybe he could give you some lessons."

"If he'll teach me how to use a bow, then I'll teach him how to use a sword," Coric replied.

"So I suppose that's the real reason you wanted to marry his sister ... to improve on the bow. You could have asked for lessons and spared yourself a lot of trouble," Alpin teased.

"Father, Coric's interest in the bow pales to his interest in Ceana," Kenneth said. "I think his shot is so poor because his vision is so clouded."

"You're a fine one to talk, Kenneth," Coric rebutted. "I'm surprised you're here with the men ... thought you'd be doting on Arabella rather than joining us for sport."

Kenneth's face reddened. "Well ... someone needed to come and make a good showing for the family," Kenneth stammered, groping for a suitable response.

Alpin lifted his hands to catch the attention of the younger men. "That was good shooting, especially from you Laise. I'm glad our families are uniting. Coric has made a wise decision ... and I won't mind having you on my side with that kind of shooting." He glanced up at the midday sun sitting high in the spring sky. "Let's gather our things. It's time to head back ... I'm certain the women are getting anxious."

"Hold still, hold still," Sorcha fussed at Ceana as she fastened the last button on her daughter's dress.

Ceana took a deep breath. She stopped fidgeting long enough to let her mother finish the button and fluff the ruffle that circled her waist.

Arabella stood in the doorway, watching Sorcha and

Nessa adorn the bride. "You are beautiful, absolutely beautiful! Coric is fortunate to have such a lovely bride," Arabella said, entranced by Ceana and the thought of marriage.

"I don't feel beautiful. I feel as if I'm a mess," Ceana replied, never more conscious of her appearance than now, on her wedding day. She had always been self-conscious, ever since she was a young girl when she had fallen on the rocks at the river in Milton. The fall had left a jagged scar below her right eye. It was a raised scar, roughly an inch in length. It had always made her feel less than beautiful.

"It's true. You're radiant! Coric will faint when he sees you," Nessa said. She stood behind Ceana, brushing the bride's soft, sandy-brown hair.

"Excuse me, Arabella," Ena said, moving past Arabella and stepping into the room. "The stew is done and—well don't you look like a princess!" Ena exclaimed. "I don't recall seeing a more beautiful bride in all of Dalriada."

Ceana blushed and turned her cheek to one side, a habit of hers when others took notice.

The women stepped back to inspect Ceana. Their eyes combed the young lady, hunting for imperfections. Sorcha stooped beside Ceana's feet and straightened her daughter's dress, fixing the last wrinkle in the delicate fabric.

The others watched with critical eyes to ensure the wrinkle was properly addressed.

Ceana fiddled with her top button for a moment, then released the button and gazed at her mother. "Mother," she asked, "will I make Coric happy?"

Sorcha stood and spun her daughter to face her.

"Young lady. You are beautiful. Your beauty surpasses

that of the rose, your heart is as kind as a child's, and your mind is more clever than any man's!" Sorcha said and smiled at her daughter. "If you do not capture his heart with your beauty or charm, then you will outwit him into believing you have."

The women burst into laughter.

Arabella laughed the hardest. She enjoyed being with the women. She enjoyed seeing Ceana in her wedding gown and fussing over every detail. Her mind began to stir with visions of marriage and being a bride of her own. She thought of Kenneth. They had played together often as children and she had taken note of how he had always shown a fondness toward her. She enjoyed the attention he paid her and how he would often make much of her. Her thoughts carried her away.

Knock, Knock.

"Someone's at the door," Nessa exclaimed. Her eyes widened with excitement.

"Well, lassie, see who it is," Ena fussed, and she shooed Arabella toward the door.

Arabella hurried from the room. When she reached the door, she opened it to find Feragus, the blacksmith, dangling two corded necklaces from his lofted hand. Each necklace held a cross, one of gold, one of silver.

"Here you are ma'am, the necklaces for your wedding," Feragus said between his crooked, yellow teeth.

"Oh, no, not my wedding." Arabella blushed at the thought. "But yes, for the family wedding, thank you." She extended her hand and took the necklaces from the blacksmith. She smiled and shut the door. Holding the two crosses, one in each hand, she studied them closely, noting the finely cut edges of the glistening metal that boasted a craftsmanship found only in the rarest of treasures.

"Ceana, the crosses from the blacksmith, they're here," Arabella called out. She left the front door and rushed to the makeshift bridal room. "I should say they're quite remarkable," she announced as she entered, lifting the necklaces for the others to see.

"They're perfect. Coric will be so happy!" Ceana took the necklaces and ran her fingers along their polished faces. "Mother, these are the gifts for Kenneth and Aiden—gifts for the groomsmen. The gold one is for Kenneth and the silver one is for Aiden."

"They are handsome gifts. The boys will be proud to have them," Sorcha replied.

The women each took turns admiring the two crosses, holding them to their necks as if wearing them for themselves. Ena was the last to examine the necklaces. She held the cross of gold into the air and then suddenly paused. The sound of approaching horses caught her ear. She quickly stepped to the window and gasped, "Nessa, here comes your father and the others!"

"We must finish here. They'll be calling on us soon," Sorcha said. She gazed at Ceana and smiled reassuringly.

"Nessa, fetch the bouquet. Arabella, draw some fresh water from the well. Quickly girls, quickly!" Ena gave the orders and the younger girls flitted about like swallows preparing for a storm.

Arabella grabbed a pail and left the women to fetch the water. The door slammed behind her as she hurried outside. She hustled past the storehouse and headed to the well.

At the well, Arabella found the well bucket tied to the

framing post. She tugged the rope to loosen it, but its knot only tightened. Setting down her pail, she leaned against the waist-high stone wall to unknot the rope.

The young man hiding behind the storehouse did not speak when she passed, he only watched. He watched her pass by. He watched her tug on the knotted rope. He watched her set down the pail and lean against the well to untie the knot.

Her slender figure was beautiful. Her white skin was beautiful. Her brown hair, cascading down her shoulders—it was all beautiful.

He remained silent in the shadow of the storehouse.

"Who did this!" Arabella muttered aloud as she fought the knot that bound the rope.

"Arabella?" Arabella heard Ena call from the house.

"I'll be right there," she called back.

"Ouch!" A sharp pain stung Arabella's finger. She glanced at her fingernail and its torn nail tip. Without a thought, she lifted her hand and removed the torn nail with her teeth. From the corner of her eye, she glimpsed a shadow inching up the wall of the well. Then, suddenly, two strong arms grabbed her waist and lifted her off the ground.

"Aaah!" she cried.

"Bella!"

Relief rushed over her.

Kenneth set her down and turned her in his arms.

"Kenneth, you scared me to death!"

He smiled at her. "Why were you scared? I wouldn't let anybody get you." Still clutching Arabella in his arms,

Kenneth stepped backward and pulled her with him. A grinned formed on his face when she resisted.

"I have to get the water. Your mother's going to fuss."

He pulled her closer. "My mother can wait. She'll get her water when—"

Kenneth suddenly tripped on the pail, stumbled backwards, and fell. Arabella fell with him and landed on top when the two hit the ground.

"Glad I could soften your fall," Kenneth said, unable to conceal his smile.

"Kenneth, I can't believe you! You're supposed to be with the others, getting ready for tonight!" Arabella stared at him and then giggled. "You have made a mess of me. What am I going to do?"

"You look like a princess ready for a coronation! You don't need to do anything … save fix your hair here … and there … and over here," Kenneth teased Arabella. "Truly … you're lovely—," he stopped and stared when his eyes caught hers.

Arabella stared back at Kenneth, following his eyes as he traced her face. She waited.

Her eyes were a deep green. Her lips were fashioned with supple lines that turned with the curve of her smile. Her cheeks were slender and well-crafted, making her lovely. *You are beautiful, truly beautiful.* The words in Kenneth's mind were so loud he was certain she heard him.

Arabella stared at him. And she waited.

Then Kenneth slowly lifted his head, closed his eyes, and kissed her.

The press of his lips against hers sent a shot through Arabella's heart like a magic spell cast upon her, forever binding the two as one. Her mind went blank, and she pressed her lips deep into his.

Her lips were tender and sweet, their very touch struck Kenneth like a jolt from heaven. All of his life came to this moment, and he could not stop kissing her. He lifted his hands to cup her face as their lips held one another's—

"Arabella," Nessa called. "Did you get the water ... Arabella?"

"Oh my, the water!" Arabella whispered, pulling away from his kiss. She lifted her head and yelled, "I'm over here Nessa. I am getting the water. I'll be right there." She couldn't keep from smiling at Kenneth. Then the two jumped to their feet, and Arabella dusted off her dress and straightened her hair.

"I'll get the rope untied. Get the pail ready." Kenneth pointed at the pail and then hurried to untie the knot. He worked the rope, but the knot was too tight. He dismissed the knot and let go of the rope, eyeing Arabella. He wanted to kiss her again.

She was waiting for him.

Kenneth smiled at her.

Arabella smiled back. And then she caught herself. "Will you hurry? I'm going to get in trouble!"

Luag's home made for a suitable spot for Coric to prepare for his wedding. As the groom, he would have to clean up properly and be well-shaven and handsomely presentable. Luag's wife had insisted that Coric use their home to allow the women their necessary privacy at Alpin's home.

Coric sat on a footstool alone in the room where Luag's family normally slept. His mind danced with a hundred thoughts as he rose and paced to the window. Outside, the rolling countryside lay peacefully beneath the afternoon sunshine and the early stalks of spring barley had sprouted. He paused and stared at the field and its polka-dots of gold.

Gazing out the open window brought forward a montage of childhood memories—the smells, the sounds, all that Renton offered a young boy. How many times had he raced his brothers and Ronan across the fields, each hoping that they had what it took to be the victor? How many trees had he climbed with Kenneth and Drostan? How many sprinting jumps had he made into the river, trying to splash his brothers?

He thought of the battles that he and Drostan and the others had pretended to fight, the forts they had built, and the wooden swords they had carved. All of that had passed. Those days were tucked away in another time and place. He missed them. He missed his brother.

Drostan would've been proud of Coric—standing ready for marriage, a man of 23 years, preparing to receive his bride. Drostan would have been 28 years old this year. He would have taken a wife and fathered children of his own by now. He would have already lived his wedding day. And had Drostan been present, he likely would have devised some clever test for Coric, some right-of-passage for him to prove himself. Coric would never know. What was done could never be undone.

What would Drostan say if he were here today? Coric wondered, picturing his brother's hands on his shoulders while speaking to him of battle, and manhood, and women, and God.

The wooden door of the room scraped the floor as it opened. "Coric. How are you?" Alpin asked, entering the room.

Coric returned from his distant world, "Father … I am well … I was just thinking about things."

"This is a big day for you, and for Ceana, and for our families."

"Yes, Father, yes … yes it is," Coric stumbled on his words.

"Is something the matter?"

"No, Father, no … all is well … I need to finish dressing," Coric replied.

"I won't keep you. But as your father, I wanted to take a moment to offer you some words that should prove helpful in the days ahead," Alpin said with a steady, purposed voice. "That is, should you choose to heed them." He smiled and waited for a response.

Coric struggled to return a smile.

"Coric, need I say how pleased your mother and I are with you. You are a fine man, a brave man, and you have much wisdom and courage. Ceana is a fortunate woman. You are my oldest living son. Drostan has rested. The family looks to you to rise up and carry the leadership of the family in the years ahead—"

"But Father," Coric interrupted, "I don't have that right. I have not earned it. It's Drostan's right … I shall not take that from him."

"Coric, you did not take it from him … your brother has given it to you. His sacrifice was for you and for me and for all of us. When he took up his sword at Ae, he understood the consequences. He was willing to pay the price expected of a warrior. He did it to protect the freedom of Dalriada, a cause he was willing to fight for, and even die for. His blood was not shed in vain."

Coric winced at his father's words.

Alpin stepped aside from Coric and looked about the room. Turning to face Coric, he spoke with measured intent, "Coric, Drostan gave what he gave, so you could have what you have. Drostan willingly, knowingly, did this. He fought for his family, for his brothers, for our homeland, and for the freedom to enjoy them in peace. Take what he has given you and live it with all your might."

Coric sat down on the edge of the bed. He thought of his brother and then gazed up at his father. "I understand. I know what Drostan has done. I will make him proud." Coric's words hung in the air. His cheeks tightened and he swallowed. "And Father, I will make you proud," he said.

Alpin nodded his head, affirming his son. "Coric, I'm already proud."

Dalriadans both young and old lined the path traversing the village of Renton. They stood shoulder to shoulder, awaiting the commencement of the marriage procession. Each wore their finest adornments, for this was Renton's first wedding in three years.

Shops and buildings of stone and wood formed the backdrop behind the villagers on either side of the path. The structures were an appropriate visage of Renton's humble heritage. As well, the buildings to the west served as a suitable shade from the warm, late-afternoon sun.

Conversational murmurs buzzed in the air as word spread that the procession was nearing. Then the loud sound of cheers and applause erupted when Donald, leading a stark white mare, turned the corner at the edge of town. Happy sounds of bagpipes and flutes, lofting above the noise of the crowd, complemented the exuberant cheers—the procession had arrived.

Coric and Ceana appeared after Donald. The two rounded the corner walking hand-in-hand. Ceana waved to the people to the left and right, while Coric stared ahead in stoic form, occasionally glancing at his bride. The two paced behind Donald as the procession migrated toward Renton's abbey.

The bridesmaids of the party, including Arabella, followed the wedding couple, while Kenneth and Aiden walked as escorts alongside the ladies. To complete the festivities, the young girls of the village, anxious to participate, tossed pink Autumn Joys into the street as the procession passed. Arabella vicariously absorbed it all, even slowing on occasion to collect the flowers that landed near her.

Weddings had always been festive in Renton, and this marriage came with heightened excitement, as Coric, son of Alpin, embarked upon a holy union. It was an important matter to the people of Renton, for Alpin, a respected leader, was regarded by many as the head of Dalriada, a title Alpin would not claim for himself. The union also held importance to more than Renton. In taking the hand of Ceana, daughter of Latharn of Milton, Coric would forge a bond between two of Dalriada's leading villages.

Upon reaching the abbey, the wedding members fanned out like wings on either side of the abbey's stone steps. The men took their place to the right, facing the entrance of the abbey, and the women stood opposite to the left. As custom dictated, the cleric would perform the wedding ceremony outside the abbey in the native language of Dalriada. This was to be followed by a second service inside the abbey. There, the service would be performed in Latin, the language spoken by the clergy in the house of God.

Gilchrist climbed the steps of the abbey, and a quiet hush fell over the people. The clergyman nodded and surveyed the eager faces before him, with each returning an anxious smile.

The ladies in the wedding party were the most excited, and the most lovely. Arabella and Nessa wore cream-colored gowns and both wore their hair tucked properly in a bun. The two stood side by side, giddy with the enthusiasm of young maidens. Ceana was no less giddy, and on this day, she was radiant, her hesitation gone like mist vanishing in the morning sun. Her hair hung neatly in thick braids, woven with flowers and white ribbons, while her long white gown reached the ground and hid her feet. She held a bouquet adorned with delicate yellow daffodils and white wild flowers that had been gathered by the young girls and given to the bride as a gift.

Kenneth and Aiden carried the appearance of statesmen, standing in orderly fashion beside their brother. The three appeared virile and strong. The boyish softness and charm of youth had melded into the sober ruggedness of manhood.

Kenneth wore his cross of gold and Aiden his cross of silver. In accordance with Dalriadan tradition, the groomsmen sported ceremonial weapons. Kenneth carried an axe, a tool for dropping trees and shaping wood to provide for one's family. The instrument also doubled as a weapon, symbolizing the preparedness of a man even amidst his daily tasks. Aiden donned a bow, a weapon designed to engage an opponent from a distance, demonstrating a readiness to defend oneself and one's family. The bow also served as a tool for gathering provisions, such as hunting game. Coric, the bridegroom, bore a sword. Custom assigned the sword to the groom, the man of honor. The instrument was one of focused purpose, designed purely to fight and defend. With the sword, Coric displayed to his bride, and all witnessing, that he was willing to fight for her, to defend her and her honor to the death.

The wedding members, both beautiful and strong, stood anxious at the abbey's stone steps. They faced Gilchrist, with Coric and the groomsmen to the right and Ceana and the bridesmaids to the left. Standing in such an arrangement allowed the groom to keep his right arm free in order to take up his sword, should he need to defend his bride during the ceremony.

As customary in times of peace, the groom was to hand his sword to his first man to begin the ceremony. The act represented his willingness to put down the sword and dispel his appetite for battle, a declaration that the groom was offering his whole heart to his bride. This was custom.

Coric broke from custom.

Gazing at Gilchrist, Coric lifted his blade. "I hold this sword today in remembrance of Drostan, my brother. He and others have given much, so that on this day, we could have much. May Drostan, and those brave men of Dalriada, be honored." Coric lowered his sword and held it at his side.

Gilchrist nodded, acknowledging Coric. Then the clergyman's eyes turned to the party gathered before him.

"Good people of Renton, we unite today to witness a most holy ceremony before God and man," Gilchrist addressed the crowd of Scots. They had come from as far north as Cashel and as far south as Milton.

"Coric and Ceana have joined together before us to seek a covenant and God's blessing of that covenant. In the eyes of God, a covenant is a sacred promise. Often, a man makes a promise. He gives his word and seeks to keep and honor that word. In time, a man often finds himself lacking, wanting, unable to secure the fidelity, diligence, and resolve to preserve the words of his spoken promise. As such, how can a man, a sinful man, a broken vessel of a man, find the fortitude to stand fast in his word and hold to the surety of his promise? I tell you he cannot. Such a man is utterly bereft of the strength required for such a glorious endeavor. That is, by himself he is powerless—powerless without the Hand of Almighty God, and His Christ, to provide the much needed strength. In such a predicament, a man must seek God, he must seek help from the Lord above. As so, on this day, Coric has sought the aid of his Father in Heaven to meet him in his humble time of need. Coric now stands here before you, and before me, before God in Heaven, to seek the blessings, the grace, and the power of Christ to secure his covenant with his beloved Ceana—a covenant that, in God's mercy, shall be a lasting covenant that rejoices in prosperity and endures in trials. What we witness today is a promise given in faith, in hope, and in love—and with God as their Guarantor, a promise that shall survive throughout this life unto death."

Gilchrist's voice continued with his message of hope, filling the cool evening air. At first, the cleric's words tickled Arabella's eager ears, but soon her fanciful thoughts carried her to a distant daydream. The swirling words of the clergyman faded to a hum and her attention wandered and settled on Ceana. The evening sunshine fell gently on the bride's shoulders and flowed onto the white wildflowers entwined neatly into the braids of her sandy-brown hair. Arabella determined that she would adorn herself the same on her wedding day, someday. She let her thoughts carry her farther away, where she no longer heard sounds but only saw images passing by in her mind's eye. She saw Kenneth holding her, peering into her eyes. His expression was strong, but tender. He pulled her close to him and he bent to press his lips against hers.

Her thoughts suddenly broke and scattered in her mind. Her past came forward to the very day she comforted Kenneth at the abbey seven years prior. That day was a cold, hard day. She let go of those thoughts and allowed her mind to focus on Kenneth and how he had surprised her at the well. She remembered how he grabbed her and stumbled and that wonderful feeling when he caught her and kissed her. She mused softly and giggled.

The giggle startled her.

She glanced to see if anyone had noticed. The others appeared intent on the cleric and his message. He was addressing Coric, speaking of bravery and honor and duty.

Arabella sighed in relief. She leaned forward ever so slightly to peek at Kenneth. He was staring back at her. The smile in his eyes embarrassed her, and she blushed and lowered her head. A moment passed, and then she peered up at Gilchrist and vowed that she would not let Kenneth, or thoughts of him, distract her again.

That evening, Renton held a feast under Dalriada's open sky. The fading sun illuminated the horizon with streaks of magenta and indigo emanating forth. The atmosphere was rich with a cheerfulness that had long been absent from Renton, especially Alpin's household. Venison and lamb cooked over two large, open fires, filling the air with an appetizing aroma. Children ran about, playing hide-and-seek, where every tree was a gameful hiding spot. The men and women sat and ate, trading stories of children and marriage and telling tales of their own husbands and wives. Often, the stories were embellished with charitable recollections designed to exaggerate their spousal plights.

As the plates grew empty and bellies grew full, Latharn pushed back his chair and rose before the crowded wedding table. Being the father of the bride, he called the party to attention. The jovial mutter of conversation dulled to a hush.

Latharn raised his wineglass and spoke, "To all of you good people, on behalf of my family and those of Milton, I wish to convey my deep gratitude for your kindness to us on this fine day. What we have witnessed today was a sacred pledge between two special people—a pledge to one another, to God, and to the villages of Renton and Milton. Their pledge symbolizes a bond between our people ... that together we shall remain happy, fertile, and strong."

Latharn paused and gazed at his daughter. "To my darling daughter, whom I have held with fondness since the day I first received you … you are a gift from above. It is as if God, Himself, gave to me one of His angels." He smiled at Ceana, the smile of an adoring father.

Latharn turned to Coric, "And to you, Coric, now my son, this is a happy day. We first met in sorrowful times, a time when we together mourned the loss of good men, courageous men. Your brother was among these men … he was a noble warrior. I am proud to have fought at his side. Dalriada honors his bravery and passion. And I see, too, that you are fashioned from that same rare mold, a man of courage and honor. I am happy for Ceana and proud to receive you as my son."

Latharn paused as claps of approval echoed from the gathered guests.

Latharn spoke above the clapping hands. "Please … please. Grant me but another moment." He turned to Alpin, "Alpin, as I have spoken of Coric's honor, I wish to also say, on behalf of my entire family and the people of Milton, that my toast extends to you as well. Your wisdom, your courage, and your leadership are recognized far and wide throughout Dalriada. Your father before you and his father before him are praised as men of noble character, serving the cause of our beloved land. The name of your family is to be commended, and therefore it is my high privilege to grant you my daughter, as you have granted me your son. May He who watches over the sun and the moon and the stars, watch over these two and this great land we share!" His words reached a crescendo and he lifted his glass high into the air.

The table guests raised their wineglasses to join the toast, tapping glasses together up and down the table and following the toast with whistles and cheers.

During the speech, Kenneth had been inspecting the handsome cross hanging from his neck. He quickly released the trinket and grabbed his glass to toast with Arabella, sitting across from him. As the cheers ended, he hurried to tap his glass to hers. The two vessels hit with a *clank*.

Kenneth laughed at his clumsiness, and he winked at Arabella. Her lips pursed, she frowned, and then she returned her attention to Latharn. Kenneth had hoped for a different response, maybe an affectionate kiss lofted into the air and blown in his direction. He rested his wineglass on the table and stared at Arabella. He'd lost her attention completely. His brow furrowed as he studied her.

As Latharn sat, Alpin rose. He smiled and addressed the attendants, "Kind people of Milton, friends of Renton, and countrymen of Dalriada. I am grateful for your presence this evening, joining my family as we begin a new dawn in our lives. I speak for Ena and my children, as well as myself, when I offer you our gratitude and affection. Please receive our warmest thanksgivings. We have been granted a lovely daughter, gifted with all grace and beauty, one who has been given a sharp mind and a caring heart of equal distinction." Alpin nodded at Ceana as he finished his words.

Ceana blushed and turned her head to the side to deflect the attention.

Alpin's gaze fell to his son Coric, who sat erect and attentive in the chair beside him. "Coric, my son, I see in your countenance that you have found the one who completes you. This is a blessing, Son. From the day you first took a step, you were a fighter, and this is evident even today in your earnest pursuit of life. A warrior's heart is in your blood, as if it were destined in the heavens from eternity past. You have not deviated from this path in your pursuit in becoming a man. Your heart bears the strength of the lion and your sword the cunning of the fox ... together the two are a formidable match for any man, young or old. I charge you now, before both God and man, to hold firm the vows you have spoken, the covenant that you and Ceana have made with your lips and have sealed in your hearts. Be of noble character. Help those in need. Be generous in all things. Give and do not take. You have been granted much. Use your strength for the good of others, to the glory of your Lord. Someday you will pursue a cause far greater than yourself ... much will be asked of you. I encourage you my son, be willing to give what is asked."

Alpin's words fell upon his sons like a mantle of great weight. For Coric, the pride of his father and the expectation of courage lit his heart as though a torch had been passed to him and pressed firm against his chest. He was not alone. Kenneth had abandoned Arabella's rejection and had locked his attention on the man standing before him—his father's words had fallen upon his ears with a searing, sobering conviction. Aiden, too, was struck by his father's exhortation. His mind retreated back to that cool autumn morning in the barley field when he was a boy. It was the last day he and his brothers stood with Drostan. Drostan had taken up the mantle and lived the very words their father had spoken.

Aiden felt a constriction in his throat. He labored to swallow as his chest heaved in and out. Admiration for his brothers overwhelmed him. Drostan and Coric had come so far, proving themselves men. He wondered if he could ever attain such heights.

By this time the sun was setting behind the western hills,

and only the moon on the far horizon and the amber light of the fires remained. The flames illuminated Alpin's face as he continued to speak, "Latharn, men of Milton and men of Cashel and Renton, to all Dalriadans who have joined us, we are Scots. We are a people of a long and cherished heritage. Our forefathers have toiled much for this beautiful land we call Dalriada. I am grateful for the bonds we have forged this day. I am grateful for each family here tonight. Friends who have traveled from distant villages across our lands, I thank you all."

Alpin paused for a moment. He stared blankly into the distance, distracted. With a calm demeanor, he returned his focus to his audience and lifted his glass, then his eyes turned to Coric and Ceana, seemingly babes. He offered a toast, "May your days be bright, prosperous, and filled with happiness. May your affections bind your spirits as one and grant your hearts peace." He turned to the others, "I beg of you ... continue your merriment on this, the finest of nights!"

The Dalriadans resumed, clinking their glasses and consuming their wine.

Alpin placed his wineglass on the table and removed himself from his dinner guests, troubled by the distraction in the distance. Striding past the fires, he stepped into the darkness of the barley field.

The light of the moon shined down on a moving silhouette, advancing quickly through the trees.

The silhouette broke from the woods, and a man on a horse materialized. He rode with purpose, his destination was evident—the wedding feast.

Instinctively, Alpin released a sharp whistle. The rider's

head swiveled and then the horse turned. An eerie feeling crept over Alpin. His hand moved to his waist to find his knife, but it wasn't there. He planted his feet and prepared for the horse and rider.

When the man arrived, he tugged the reigns of his horse and stopped the beast ten feet from Alpin. The man glanced at the fires and then peered down at Alpin, the moonlight exposing a maze of painted images on the man's arms and neck.

Alpin's fears were confirmed.

"Pict," Alpin said. "What is it you seek?"

Constantine took notice of Alpin's absence. He approached Luag and Latharn as the two lingered beside a nearby fire, conversing over wine. "Have you seen Alpin?" Constantine asked, "I can't find him."

Luag turned toward the tables and then glanced at the other fire. "No, I haven't seen him since he spoke. Is something wrong?"

"No. I was going to ask him—"

"Is that him in the field?" Latharn interrupted.

Constantine turned in the direction Latharn was pointing. "It may be," Constantine muttered. He squinted to improve his sight and then started toward the figure.

"Cousin, why do I find you alone in the dark?" Constantine called out as he approached Alpin.

Alpin turned to Constantine but said nothing.

"Are you growing soft? Can you not handle these tender moments?" Constantine said with a grin.

Luag, following behind with Latharn, chuckled at Constantine's remark.

"I wish it were only that," Alpin replied.

"What's troubling you?" Luag asked.

"I assume you didn't see the rider."

"Rider?"

"Yes, a Pict."

"A Pict," Luag replied, "What was a Pict doing here in Renton?"

"He came with news from the north. Viking ships have reached our lands and they have brought war to the isles along our northwestern shores. The Picts in the northeast fear they may be coming east."

"How can we be certain they're Vikings? Picts can't be trusted," Luag muttered.

"The Picts have seen their ships. You men know of our fathers' stories. Their ships are distinct. From the description, they are Vikings," Alpin said. He eyed his three companions. "Be sure of this, any Viking is a threat to our land and our people—they are killers, merciless killers. Should they venture south into Dalriada ... God help us."

Alpin turned and glimpsed the rider departing beneath the moonlight. Then the shadowy form all together disappeared into the distant trees.

CHAPTER 7

THICK SMOKE FILLED THE AIR ABOVE A SMALL northern Dalriadan village. The smoke carried an acrid, charred stench. Halfdan sat on his horse, watching the flames engulf the iron shop at the edge of the village. The inferno's heat burned against his skin. He smirked as the black clouds rose into the sky. It was a suitable announcement of his arrival.

The billowing orange flames steadily swallowed the helpless iron shop. Its owner could do nothing. The unfortunate blacksmith lay in the doorway of the shop with an axe protruding from his back. The wooden building struggled against the flames and finally collapsed, crumpling into a heap of burning char and burying the blacksmith beneath its members.

Halfdan mused at the sight. Then he coaxed his horse and trotted through the burning village. Flames poured from the wooden structures while bits of ash and soot floated lifelessly into the air.

The calamity fell upon the town not long prior, when the Vikings suddenly appeared from the west and descended violently upon the unsuspecting village. Like a tornado, the monsters overtook the shops and decimated the people. No warning. No mercy.

Their ships had landed on the northwestern Dalriadan shores only days prior, bringing with them the necessary instruments of war: horses, swords, axes, bows, and men—many men.

As with past conquests to the Isle of Britannia, the Norsemen, or Vikings, as they were often called, were consumed with enslaving their victims—or killing them. The captured men were useful for amassing lumber and building camps. The captured women were for other purposes. Some would become slaves or concubines in the Viking camps, while others would be carried away by ship back to Norway, never to be seen again.

Halfdan the Black was their leader, the son of the notorious Norse King, Gudrod the Hunter. Like his father, Halfdan the Black was a vicious man who found pleasure in dominance. His conquest had begun with the destruction of the small villages of the Orkney Islands, north of the Isle of Britannia. He and his marauding Vikings had waylaid villages and destroyed families, enslaving the souls of those who had the grave misfortune of encountering him. For Halfdan, the morning onslaught was not a raid, but a mission. He wanted the land, and he wanted it all.

Halfdan continued forward on his horse, parading through the small village adorned with its burning buildings. Corpses, either burned to death or run through, lay strewn throughout the village. He dismissed the bodies. They were not his concern, but rather pawns, casualties of conquest.

Another round of screams echoed from the far end of the village. Halfdan's men had found more prey.

The sky above grew gray with smoke, shielding the sun's light. The spring air, once fresh and crisp, now reeked with a burnt, dead odor.

Halfdan lingered in the street. His interest soon faded to apathy. He was not a patient man. He scanned ahead, peering at his men. A dozen were standing at the far end of the village, gathered outside a single building, arguing with one another.

"Are we not finished here?" Halfdan shouted from his horse in his native Norse tongue.

The bickering ceased and the men turned toward Halfdan with a blank stare. Their large axes and swords hung idle in their hands after failing to penetrate the building.

Halfdan glared at the men. "What are you waiting for! Burn it to hell, we're done here!"

Jorund, a large Viking wearing a rugged horned helmet, called back, "We saw women and children run inside and we—"

"Burn it!" Halfdan yelled.

"But I think you'll want to see the women—"

"I don't give a damn who's inside—burn it before I burn it myself!"

Jorund cursed under his breath. He grabbed a burning piece of wood from a nearby heap of rubble and threw it onto the roof of the building. The dry straw began to steadily feed the hungry flames. Jorund eyed the door, waiting as the flames grew and quickly spread. The screams of the children inside hardly pricked his ears.

Jorund bent to grab a second torch. As he lifted, the man beside him suddenly stiffened and fell to the ground. The man's limp body hit with a thud—an arrow extended from his forehead. A second arrow flew from the flames and a second Viking fell.

Halfdan watched from his horse, boiling with anger. He glanced over his shoulder and then to either side. Then he cupped his hands to his mouth and roared, "Kodran!"

The Vikings nearest the building scrambled to find cover from the arrows. Jorund signaled his men for more torches and motioned for them to spread the flames along the sides of the building. The men exhumed pieces of burning wood from the nearby fires and hurled the makeshift torches at the small structure.

Within moments, the entire roof was aflame. Four Vikings gathered at the front of the building beside Jorund and they waited for the Scots to flee. Another arrow flew from the jarred shutters and a third Viking fell. Then a loud cracking sound erupted from the building. Its walls labored to stand. Instantly, the front door burst open and a wave of smoke flooded from the doorway. Two figures appeared, enveloped in smoke. The silhouettes cut frantically through the air with swinging swords, slicing their blades left and right in search of the enemy.

The Vikings leapt to avoid the flying steel, but the attack was too swift. Another Viking fell, sliced through the gut by a swirling sword. Metal clanged against metal as more Vikings joined the fight.

Behind the fighting men, the flames slowly swallowed the building. A portion of the roof collapsed and the screams of the children echoed from within. Two more Scots exited the smoky doorway. One held a bow. The other, the elder of the two, held a sword. They guarded the doorway as women and children fled the flames. A moment passed and a large woman emerged in the doorframe. The woman lifted two small children in her arms and disappeared around the corner of the building.

Smoke continued to pour from the building's windows and doors, and then a young woman with hair as red as fire appeared from the flames, coughing violently and shouting a man's name each time her throat cleared. She hesitated a moment longer before navigating through the smoky haze. Struggling forward, she reached the edge of the building and rounded the corner. Suddenly, a Viking grabbed her arm and pulled her to him.

The young woman screamed.

The Viking dragged her to the center of the street.

She plowed her heels into the ground and dug her nails into the man's arm.

The Viking dropped his sword, tightened his arms around her waist, and lifted her off her feet.

As the young woman hovered above the ground, she cocked her leg and delivered an upward thrusting knee, ramming her boney joint square into her captor's groin.

The man released her instantly and groaned in pain. When the woman's feet touched down, she attempted to run but the Viking lurched forward and grabbed a fistful of her long red hair.

The woman's head spun and she tried to fight. It was then that a large Scot emerged amidst the smoke and flames. He had come from the eastern forest. He was a hulk of a man and he carried an axe that matched his size. The massive axeman's arm lifted in a blur and the weapon flew from his hand and buried itself deep into the chest of the Viking brute. The impact was fatal. The Viking's arms fell limp and he collapsed where he stood. The woman freed herself and stumbled back on her heels, disoriented. Regaining her balance, she brushed her hair from her eyes and stared mesmerized at the large Scot.

"Run, Rhiannon!" the large Scot said.

"Dorrell!" she exclaimed.

"Run!"

Rhiannon ran past the burning building toward the forest.

Dorrell turned to face his enemy. He quickly surveyed the battle and saw that only two Scots still remained in the fight. Dorrell drew his knife, spun the weapon in his hand, and clasped the blade in his palm. He reared back his arm, aiming at Jorund, but he never released. A blow from behind hammered down on his skull, and his world went black.

Halfdan sat on his horse, waiting. "Kodran!" he shouted a second time.

The older Scot stood in the middle of six Vikings. He clutched his sword with both hands, half bent and gasping for air. Blood seeped from his shoulder. The Scot who'd first exited the doorway stood next to him. The young man glanced at his elder and then jumped in front to defend him.

Jorund and his men circled the two Scots, waving their weapons at the younger Scot, taunting him and daring him to swing.

The young man lifted his sword aloft and charged the Vikings. Without warning, the butt of a sword materialized and thumped hard against his exposed ribs. Kodran, the Viking warrior, had appeared from nowhere, as though he'd dropped from the sky above. It was Kodran who had delivered the blow. The young Scot doubled over and heaved for breath, reeling from the strike to his torso.

Kodran stepped past the younger Scot and slowly walked toward the elder. Kodran twirled his sword in the air, forming a swiftly moving circle of steel. He moved closer, pivoted, and brought his blade down hard against the older Scot's sword.

The weapon flew from the elder Scot's hands and tumbled to the ground.

The young Scot yelled and jabbed his tired blade at Kodran.

Kodran sidled and kicked the young man's sword, quickly disarming the boy. Finished with his entrance, Kodran rested his sword and turned to Halfdan, "Should I kill them now?"

"Kill them," Halfdan replied.

Kodran strode behind the older Scot. The man was bent in two, heaving for breath with his hands on his knees. Kodran stared at the man's sweaty neck and he lifted his sword above the man's head.

"Father!" the boy shouted.

"Father? Wait, Kodran," Halfdan uttered, now speaking in the Scot tongue. "Kodran, lower your sword. We must take a moment of care." Halfdan dismounted his horse and walked toward the company of men.

Kodran settled his sword and kicked the older man in the back of his legs. The Scot dropped to his knees and sunk in doom.

The young Scot turned to face Halfdan as he neared, "You can't do this."

"I can't do what?" Halfdan replied. He stopped a foot from the young Scot and glared into his eyes. "I do as I please, boy!"

Without a thought he slapped the boy, and the boy stumbled sideways. Then he stepped past the boy and approached the father. "Do you know what I hate more than a Scot?" he yelled at the man. "Do you?"

The doomed man shook his head.

"I hate the son of a Scot. The son of a Scot is an irritating pest that seems to reappear with some noble regard for a father long gone, crying pathetic words of retribution ... as if the fool could do something about his pitiful plight. That is why I kill the son first, then the father."

"No, I beg of you. We mean no harm. We only—"

"Silence! You are a waste of my breath." With the speed of a cobra, Halfdan ripped a jewel-handled knife from his belt and sunk the blade into the boy's chest.

"Father ...," the boy gasped. He tried to lift his arms, but his limbs drooped and his eyes closed.

Halfdan removed the bloody blade and the boy's body sunk to the ground.

"No!" the father shouted.

Halfdan turned his back and walked to his horse.

"No ... no," the father sobbed.

"Kill him," Halfdan muttered.

A second hadn't passed before the father felt a cold sting run through his heart. He stared down to see the red tip of Kodran's blade piercing his shirt, then the blade suddenly disappeared. The Scot's body slowly slumped over and fell to the earth.

Halfdan mounted his horse and turned to leave. As he rode off, he yelled back to his men, "We eat, we sleep, we find another village."

Kodran gazed down at the bloody corpse lying at his feet. He smirked. Then he bent, grabbed the dead Scot's shirt, and cleaned his blade.

Jorund stood idle, watching Kodran finish his work. Jorund shrugged and promptly slid his battle-axe through his wide leather back-strap and walked to the motionless body of the Scot called Dorrell. "He's still breathing. Good. He's big, he'll do well at cutting trees. We'll keep him." He peered at his men. "Carry him to the carts. I'm going after the girl."

Jorund walked past the burning building, turned the corner, and disappeared to hunt his prey.

CHAPTER 8

"I SAID, GIVE ME ANOTHER!" SEARC BARKED AT the tavern owner standing behind the waist-high bar.

"The day is young. Go find some fresh air," the tavern owner replied.

"I don't need air. I need another drink. Or do I have to pour it myself?" Searc said, emboldened by the alcohol coursing through his veins.

The tavern owner, and most of Renton, had grown tired of Searc's common outbursts. His foul moods occurred frequently, coming like an unwanted visitor. Over the past several months, Searc's visits to the tavern had devolved into a habit—with the ale promising friendship and vowing goodwill, but never fulfilling either.

"You're not going to find what you're looking for here, Searc."

The voice in the background hit Searc with a sudden shot of sobriety.

"Every time you do this, you wake up in a field wondering if it was worth it. It is not going to bring your father back," Aiden said.

"Aiden, my dearest friend, join me. We should sit and

talk and consider the crimes against us." Searc leaned against the bar and gave Aiden a curt smile. Then he tilted his head back, raised his empty mug above his mouth, and waited for the single lonely drop of ale to drip onto his tongue. The drop plunged to his chin, and he looked at Aiden and grinned.

"We should kill them Briton devils, Aiden," Searc said. "You and me … we should do it … we should kill'em!"

"Searc."

"We should, Aiden. It's the only right thing to do." Searc paused and scanned his empty mug once again. "Have a drink, Aiden … my friend here was about to pour me another."

Aiden leaned against the bar and stared into Searc's glazed eyes. "Searc, I didn't come here to drink, I came to get you out of here … to do something to clear your mind."

"Do something! What do you want to do! If you want to go south with me and find some Britons and kill'em, then sure let's do something!" Searc pushed away from the bar in an overly dramatic manner.

"Searc, let's sit. The Britons can wait. We can stay here and talk." Aiden pointed to a table in the corner of the tavern. He glanced at the man behind the bar. "I'll take a pint," he said and he turned to Searc. "See, we can sit. All is well."

"Yes, all is well," Searc mimicked.

The sun remained high in the summer sky while cotton clouds sailed below, only occasionally shading the sun's light as they passed. Alpin moved from the searing sunshine and stepped onto the wooden planks of the walkway leading to the blacksmith shop. The shop's thatched awning provided the shade he was looking for.

Kenneth followed behind his father.

Feragus, the blacksmith, poked his head up when the two stopped at the shop front, filling the shop's doublewide doorframe.

"I need those shoes in three days, Feragus," Alpin called out to the blacksmith. "I don't want my horses running free without them."

"Yes, of course. You'll have them," Feragus said, stopping his work to address his customer.

"Three days, right?" Alpin reminded.

"Yes. You know you'll have them. How many times have I brought you shoes, nails, pots—whatever you ask? I'll deliver them in three days, as we agreed." The short, heavyset, older man was busy with his words. He was a fastidious and nervous man.

Alpin snickered at the blacksmith's grumpy retort. "I'll tell my mare not to fret, that the noble Feragus is hastily preparing her shoes."

"Well, that would be kind of you. You can be certain they will fit her well," Feragus said as he wiped his brow with a dirty rag, smearing a black smudge across his temple. He shoved the rag into the front pocket of his shirt and peered at Kenneth. "Is he as pushy at home, lad?" the blacksmith asked, wearing a wild-eyed look on his face.

"Well, at home he—"

"That's a fine necklace you have there, son," Feragus interrupted, pointing to the cross hanging from Kenneth's neck.

"Thank you, sir. It was a gift given to me ... from my brother."

"I know," the man said with a twinkle in his eye. "I made it. Did you notice the fine edges—I fashioned them just so. The gold has to be just right, not too hot before the cut."

"Yes sir, I noticed how—"

"You must be the favored brother," the blacksmith interrupted a second time.

"The favored brother?"

"Well, yes," Feragus said with an eager smile. "You were given the cross of gold."

"Oh ... well ... my brother, he—"

"Take care of that ... it's a gem."

"These horseshoes," Alpin interjected, "three days, right?"

"Yes, yes, three days. You'll have them in three days," Feragus groused. He shuffled around a scarred iron anvil mounted on top of a three-foot-wide stump and glanced back to the rear of his shop. "My fire!" he exclaimed and hurried to the fireplace to tend its dying flames.

Alpin chuckled to himself, gazing on as the bustling blacksmith nurtured his oven back to life. Suddenly, he was startled by a tap on his shoulder.

"Father, who's that?" Kenneth asked, pointing east toward the edge of Renton.

Alpin peered out the doorway.

In the distance, three men were approaching on horseback. They rode abreast and carried a banner of colors.

Alpin reached down and felt the handle of his sword. "Get Aiden," he muttered.

Kenneth shoved open the tavern door and stormed inside. Aiden was sitting at the corner table, sipping a pint with Searc. "Aiden, Father wants you."

Aiden lowered his mug, his face holding a puzzled expression.

"Come on," Kenneth said.

"What is it?" Aiden asked.

"Riders, coming from the east. I don't know who they are, but Father wants you."

"Can't you see we're having a drink, Lord Kenneth? I am sure your father can handle this. He's a mighty man," Searc said carelessly.

"Shut up, Searc. You can sit here and drink for all I care."

"Lord Kenneth, I hath offended thee," Searc said, slurring his words.

"Aiden, I have neither the time nor patience for this. Let's go!" Kenneth demanded, and he turned and vanished through the doorway.

The three riders reached the edge of Renton. Alpin remained under the awning of the blacksmith shop, watching as they approached. Feragus stood behind him.

The shops and merchant carts no longer had their visitors. The women and children had disappeared. The men of Renton aligned along the shop fronts and waited as the riders neared.

The riders slowed to a trot as they entered Renton. They glanced about, surveying the men gathered on the street. The rider in the center called out, "We are seeking Alpin of Renton."

Alpin stepped into the street. His hand never left his sword. He moved toward the middle of the street and then walked toward the foreigners, keeping the sun to his back.

"I'm Alpin. What is your need, Pict?"

Their painted arms affirmed their origin. The black inked sketches on their skin were detailed and distinct, forming intricate shapes and lines.

"I am Deort, Captain of the Pict Guard," the rider in the center stated. "Oengus, Lord of the Picts, approaches. He desires a word with you, a word you should take heed to hear and consider." The rider's intonation was even, his tone terse.

"Oengus! Where is he?" Alpin replied and glanced to his right.

Kenneth had returned and was now standing at Alpin's side. He caught his father's glance and peered back at the tavern, hoping to sight Aiden approaching.

Deort sat up in his saddle. "Lord Oengus comes. We are his forbearers," he said. He paused and then spoke smugly, "It is a wise man who sees what lies ahead. Lord Oengus esteems the eyes of his forbearers."

As the Pict spoke, Alpin noticed an entourage cresting the hill in the distance. "Our High Lord Oengus graces us with his presence," Alpin muttered.

Kenneth stole a second glance back toward the tavern in search of Aiden. *Where is he?*

The Pict entourage stopped at the edge of Renton. Oengus left the assembly and rode his muscular white steed toward his forbearers. When he reached them, he coaxed his horse to the front. He scanned the men of Renton and then locked on Alpin. "It has been some time since we last saw one another face to face, Alpin. The years have been generous to you."

"Oengus, you are still the same … your love of grandeur hasn't left you," Alpin retorted. "What brings you to Dalriada? Surely you have amassed enough power and wealth to find all that might appease you in Pictland."

"Alpin, the matters at hand extend well beyond power or wealth. You've heard the reports of the enemy to the north, I presume? They are vicious and merciless, and they attack our lands as we speak!"

"We have already heard the reports and confirmed them for ourselves, Oengus. We know of the attacks."

"Then you know they are Vikings?" Oengus said and peered at the men along the street. "Do you know this?" he asked the men, his voice now growing louder. "They are led by a vicious man, Halfdan the Black. They seek to take your people, and my people, as slaves. Some say they are using the men to build camps in the northwest … and they ship the women to their homeland across the sea. They are animals! They have overrun towns in northern Dalriada and have recently made movements toward Pictland."

"We Scots have fought the Vikings before … they bleed just as all men bleed," Alpin said. "We will see to the protection of our land. It is not your worry."

"Don't be a fool, Alpin! These men are murderers. They will push farther south into Dalriada and take every soul they find—with sword or chains. They have no conscience, no mercy. Your men stand here as if this is yet another fine day, with no worries in their minds. They will consume you in your sleep!"

"You have come here for a reason, surely it wasn't simply to insult us," Alpin replied.

"I have come to make peace," Oengus said. "Our people have had differences in the past, but now we face an enemy greater than either of us. Join us and we can defeat them. Alone, I fear neither has a chance."

"You fight to defend your land, and we will fight to defend ours," Alpin said. "That should suffice. We have no interest in aligning with the Picts."

Oengus sat agitated. He turned in his saddle to address the bystanders, "It is more than simply fighting to protect your land ... our land. This is an opportunity to come together and unite to form a people of greater strength. Together, we will show the Vikings, the Britons, and all men that they cannot stand against us!"

His words lingered in the air and no one spoke.

Kenneth heard the sound of shuffling steps behind him. He turned to see Aiden and Searc heading in his direction. Searc struggled to walk a straight line while Aiden kept him upright.

Oengus continued his proposition, "To be strong, we must unite against this enemy. I am here today to provide an offer of unity to you and to your families." Oengus' horse slowly veered to one side, yet he held his gaze, scanning the men as he spoke. "I seek your loyalty and offer you my protection and surety. I ask you to pledge your sword to me, and in turn, I will see that you and your families have your necessary provisions and every measure of protection. This will keep our lands strong and free."

The Scots murmured among themselves, for the Pict lord's request for loyalty bore the same signs of subjugation that the

Dalriadans had earlier escaped when fleeing Ireland—men who ask for loyalty, yet demand far more in return.

Alpin eyed the men of Renton standing along the street. Each was staring back at him, anxiously waiting for him to speak.

Alpin's eyes shut. He rubbed his jaw with several strokes of his palm, fighting to quell his anger. He peered at Oengus. "Your words of unity and peace are illusions, Oengus. You ask us to fight as one with the Picts as though we held an alliance, but your pledge of loyalty is properly a pledge of fealty. The men of Dalriada are free, why would we surrender our most sacred possession? You would have us work our land and serve you, so that *you* could provide for *us*. That is what you are promising? Dalriadans have never cared for such schemes!" Alpin squeezed the grip of his sword. "Do not take us for fools, Oengus. It would be best that you leave."

"Don't leave!" a voice blurted out.

A surge of anger pulsed down Alpin's spine as the words entered his ears. Alpin peered over his shoulder to see Searc standing behind him.

Searc pressed his hands on his hips, laboring to stand erect. "We should hear more from the fine lord," Searc said. "It's time we stop doing nothing, we've done nothing too long. Maybe we should consider what the good Pict says. Together, we could put an end to our enemies—we could put an end to them wretched Britons!"

Alpin glared at Searc. He clenched his teeth, causing the muscles in his cheeks to ripple as they tightened. "You have spoken beyond your understanding, boy. We are done here!" Alpin directed Aiden with his eyes, giving a silent, irritated command.

Aiden grabbed Searc's forearm and tugged him backwards.

"No!" Searc said, ripping his arm free. He stepped away from Aiden and turned to the men in the street. "We've had enough of our people doing nothing," Searc's words spilled out in a drunken mixture of beggary and anger. "We should have killed the Britons long ago, but we've done nothing! My father's blood lies on some far away field, and what do we do? Nothing!"

"That's enough!" Alpin exclaimed.

Kenneth claimed Searc's arm and twisted and pinned it behind his back. Searc lurched forward and tried in vain to break free. Then the two brothers spun him around and marched him back toward the tavern. He resisted every step.

"We should listen to the Pict—"

Searc's drunken words ended abruptly when Kenneth's fist struck his ribs.

Oengus watched as Searc and his escorts departed. He peered down from his perch atop his tall white horse and grinned at Alpin. "I believe the boy hears the wisdom of my offer … you'd be wise to hear it, too." He paused and then finished, "I make my offer to you today. I will not offer it again."

Alpin resisted the urge to pull his sword and charge the man. He resisted the urge to cut him down where he stood.

"You parade into Renton as a mandated king, and you proffer some lofty notion of loyalty," Alpin said. "We do not fear the Vikings! We will not give up our lands to them, nor will we come crawling to an old Pict who charades as a friend, yet whose heart intends to rob us of land and freedom. You speak of unity, while your desire is to chain us to your whims and have us do your bidding! It won't happen, Oengus!"

"You should weigh your decisions more carefully, Alpin … I fear that in your stubbornness, you will give up far more than you hope to keep."

"We've given the blood of our fathers and our sons for this land. I have watched the blood of my own son spill for Dalriada … our land will never be yours, not as I live. We will watch over our people, you watch over yours. Now leave our village."

Oengus spat on the ground at Alpin's feet. He jerked his head and signaled his entourage. Then he spun his horse and scowled at the men of Renton before fixing his gaze on Alpin. "You will look back on this day with regret, Scot! With deep regret!" He turned his horse sharply without looking back and rode away with his men.

Alpin stood motionless, watching as the last of the entourage crested the hill and disappeared. "Pompous fool," he muttered to himself.

Kenneth returned without Aiden or Searc and stood by his father's side. "Father, if the report of the Vikings is true, then should we prepare to fight?"

Alpin stared off into the distance. "We are preparing. Luag rides now to Dumbarton and Melton. I've also sent men to Cashel to gather Constantine and his men. The clans of Dalriada will gather in Renton within days. We will meet these Vikings and we will fight them. They will not take our land!"

"Why wouldn't we have the Picts fight with us?" Kenneth asked. "Would we not be stronger?"

"Long have I known Oengus. He is a man thirsty for power and hungry for prominence. His tongue is cunning and deceitful. His plea for our loyalty, in return for provision and protection, is but a veiled attempt to have us do his fighting ... in return, we become his subjects, like peasants to a king."

Alpin placed his hands on Kenneth's shoulders and He stared intently into his son's eyes. "Kenneth, you serve no master. You serve no king. You pay respect only to the Creator above. Few men have known such fortune. Our people, in generations past, have had men—men of their own blood—proclaim themselves leaders, but even these men grew corrupt in time. For over fifty years now, the people of Dalriada have pursued a life free from the oppression of such men. In times of war, we unite under a leader, but when trouble has passed, we return to our lives as free men. No one above us, no one below us. Was life not meant to be lived as such?"

"Father, I hear your words. And yes, it is good to be free. But, if the Vikings are strong in number, wouldn't we do well to have even the Picts fight at our side, and after the fighting we go our own way?"

"Kenneth, Oengus was asking for a vow of loyalty. But he means for us to submit ourselves to him, that we would serve him. In the end, when the fighting is over, having given our pledge of loyalty—a pledge of fealty—he would rule over us and demand from us as he pleases. Unity may be strength in battle, but in times of peace, it grows like a plague into bondage. I will not have that for you, or for any man. Do you see, Son? As a gift from God, you and I were born as free men. And we shall live, and die, as free men."

CHAPTER 9

TWENTY-THREE DALRIADAN MEN SAT WITH anticipation in Renton's meeting hall, sealed behind the closed shutters of the old stone structure. Mounted candles hung from the walls, and two square lanterns sat at either end of the large oval table centered in the room. Only the stray strands of silver sunlight, cutting through the western-facing shutters, added to the dim illumination of the musty hall.

The men had come from Dumbarton, Melton, Cashel, and other small villages across Dalriada. They were husbands and fathers, shepherds and farmers. Among them were Latharn, Guaire, Constantine, and Luag.

The younger men filled the benches lining the walls of the hall. Taran claimed a seat at the center table before his father dismissed him to a bench along the wall, opposite the wall where Coric, Kenneth, and Ronan sat. Searc came late and sat next to Aiden. The older men, leaders of a dozen Dalriadan clans, occupied the seats encircling the hall's large wooden table.

Alpin stood and spoke first. "Men of Dalriada, your presence here in Renton is appreciated. As you know, an enemy has arrived in the north and has attacked and destroyed several villages. These evil men are Vikings. Sailing their ships along the north shores of Britannia, they have crossed the sea and have brought both weapons and destruction with them. It has been reported that they are encamped at the Isle of Skye. They have pushed inland to the northern regions of Dalriada, burning our villages and slaughtering our people as they move."

"Alpin, are the Picts behind the attacks?" Latharn asked. "They have long sought to overtake our villages in the north and claim the land as their own."

"No, this is not their doing," Alpin responded. "As some of you know, Oengus, leader of the Picts, came to Renton with two dozen men. He came to ask for our swords, as he claimed. What he wanted was not simply our swords, but our servitude." Alpin paced the floor, then stopped and stared at the men at the table. "I was not inclined to submit our people to him, that we should be his subjects."

The men shifted in their seats and murmured back and forth.

"Oengus is not the reason we are here," Alpin stated. "His request assures us that he is not behind the attacks. He was clearly troubled at the reports of the Vikings … Oengus is not our concern. Our concern is the Vikings. We must stop them from taking and murdering our people. This enemy is here for conquest, and the Picts are only another pawn in their path."

"From what we've heard, the Vikings have many men, some say a thousand," a man from a western village said. "They are skilled fighters. Defeating them will not come without much bloodshed."

"Alpin, I agree. Our force must be sizeable to defeat them," Guaire added.

"Men of Dalriada," Coric said, standing up from his seat along the wall. "How many capable men are each of you able to gather, men who are strong with the sword and bow?"

"Coric, it will require many more than the men of our villages. If the Vikings have a thousand men, then we will need all of Dalriada to defeat them," Constantine replied.

"Gathering all of Dalriada is a considerable task. Every man will have to realize that his own land, his own family— even his own life—is at stake. Otherwise, I fear many will remain home, believing they are protecting their farms and flocks," the man from the west said.

"And those far off won't simply appear with a sword in hand. They'll need to be called and rallied by a leader ... dare I say, by a king," Guaire proposed, gazing about the room.

The hall quieted. Those at the table shared glances and stares as memories of days long gone returned and brought no pleasing comfort.

"We have let our kings pass, Guaire," Alpin replied, breaking the silence. "Recall from our forefathers, some sixty years ago, when the Vikings first raided our lands. Even then, the Vikings were savage men. This is not the first time our people have faced these animals. Our people pushed them from Dalriada ... and yes, for a season, the wars left our people broken. The death of our king left factions, our own people fought one another, claiming their rights on Dalriada ... and the Stone of Destiny was lost in the midst of that civil war." Alpin paused, catching glimpses of the men as they stirred at the recounting of the legendary Stone. He lingered and then proceeded, "A piece of our heritage was lost, not to be recovered. Our people, our lands, they were shattered. And for what? Power? Wealth? Strong leaders become even stronger kings. Our land has seen what this can do to a people, men with strong wills and selfish ambitions, forcing their way upon others. We've seen it! We know it! Such authority inevitably ends in tyranny!"

Every eye, every ear, lay fixed upon Alpin. He entranced the hall as he paced and opined.

"I do not wish to be subject to a Viking, nor a Pict … nor a Scot," Alpin insisted. "Nor will I subject others to a misery that I myself would not endure. I will fight to keep Dalriada free of such oppression!"

Most of the hall nodded in approval—but a furtive few sat stoic.

Constantine lifted from his seat. He walked behind the table of men. Then he stopped. He glanced at Alpin before turning his gaze to the others. "Men of Dalriada, I understand my cousin's concerns. His passion for freedom is great—this same passion burns in my gut, as it burns in his, and yours. But make no mistake, we are at war. We must assemble a large army, a strong army … one that can match the strength of the Vikings. We must unite our towns and villages. To do this, we will need a leader, a man of courage—a man who knows the hellish woes of battle, yet is unafraid to face them head on. We cannot win this battle divided. To stop the Vikings, we must be of one mind, of one heart."

Constantine paused a moment. "Well, is there a man among us who disagrees?"

The men encircling the table whispered back and forth,

exchanging words and glances, yet none offered a voice of opposition.

Taran rose from the bench where he'd sat silently, biding his time. He moved toward the older men sitting at the table. Glancing first at Alpin and then at Constantine, he found no resistance. Inferring approval, he eased toward an opening among the men and pushed his red hair behind his ears. Then he placed his hands on the oaken oval and leaned his frame forward.

His bright mane glowed like flames as he lowered into the light of the lantern. He spoke in a clear, steady voice, "Good men of Dalriada. I agree with Constantine. We need a strong man, a noble man, one who is able to lead our people to fight and defend our land. We need a leader."

Taran's eyes darted from man to man, eager to find their attention. "But we don't simply need a leader. We need a man who will inspire our hearts! We need a man who will unite us as one!" Taran pushed away from the table and stood erect, "We need a king!"

The fiery redhead's arm shot upward and his hand tightened to a fist. Then, pumping his fist in the air, he exclaimed, "We need a king who will gather our warriors and lead them into the throes of battle and carry Dalriada to victory!"

A smile decorated Taran's lips as he watched the men nodding, some with earnest, chewing his words and swallowing them. He pushed back from the table and began to circle the room. "Good men of Dalriada, I do not take this lightly. I see the gravity of what is before us. We must find a man willing to lead, dare I say, wanting to lead … a man whose heart will not stop until Dalriada sees her salvation."

He paused for a split second and then asked, "Do you see this?"

"Aye," approvals echoed from several in the room.

For the moment, Alpin bit his lip and allowed Taran to proceed.

"Then, with your blessings, I propose that there is no man better suited for this than my father—Guaire of Dumbarton! He is the man to lead us!"

The hall erupted. Taran's words had fallen like a lead mallet upon the ears of those from the north. The large wooden table vibrated with pounding fists as the northern clans demanded to be heard. Opposite the fist-pounders, two Dumbarton men rose behind Guaire, applauding in approval. The man to Guaire's left nudged his shoulder and encouraged him to stand.

Guaire's eyes found Alpin, and the Dumbarton leader chose to remain seated.

"Men, men, rest your tongues ... rest ... REST!" Luag bellowed, his guttural voice reverberating in the still air of the warm room.

Gradually, the men settled and found their seats.

Luag sat forward in his chair to address the room. "Men, it is unity that will bind the hearts of our people. On this matter, we agree. Discord will only steal away the very trust we long to keep. Guaire is a capable man," Luag glanced at Guaire, "yet he himself would admit that decisions of the past can linger ... even though time has moved on."

Guaire offered Luag a half-hearted nod, conceding the point.

"This proposal, from those of Dumbarton, has not united the hearts of this small assembly. How will it win the hearts of all Dalriada?" Luag paused and a sober silence entered the room. Luag slowly rose and stepped to the front of the table. "Allow me to be clear. There is no perfect man among us. There is not one who sits here today who would make a perfect king. Yet, I contend we do have a leader who has shown himself worthy."

Luag turned to his right and stared at Alpin, the only man he dared to follow. Returning to the others, he measured his words and spoke, "Alpin of Renton, son of Eochaid, is a man who has proven his courage and his sword on a dozen battlefields. He has fought for freedom and peace in our land. We are a free people today because of men like him and his father before him. Alpin lost his father in battle, and he witnessed the sword that stole away the life of his son, Drostan—a man, a young man, who gave his very blood for our land."

Luag faced Alpin and the two locked eyes, standing ten feet apart. "My brother, you have given much for your people. I know that. I am asking you … reconsider your stance. We are in need, and the hour is before us. I am asking you, will you lead us?"

No clamoring erupted. No disruption broke out. The men at the table sat quiet, awaiting Alpin's response. Alpin's sons watched with the same eagerness from their benches along the wall, excited for their father to speak.

Coric and Kenneth had remained transfixed since their father had begun the meeting. Aiden, too, had sat with anticipation on his bench near the door. The three were anxious to hear their father address Luag's proposition, though it would be wrong to say their minds were of one accord. Coric and Aiden waited in hopes that their father would draw his sword, loft his blade into the air, and declare that he would receive the crown of Dalriada. That he would show he was the one warrior who could unite the Scots against the Vikings. Kenneth, sitting beside Coric, waited for something much different. He held to the earlier words of his father that still whispered in his ears—the words that esteemed the great goodness of freedom. He believed his father, that freedom from tyranny included freedom from kings and crowns and men. To Kenneth, freedom was too high a price to purchase a king.

The young and old men alike sat in expectation. Moments passed as they waited for Alpin to speak.

Alpin stared long at Luag. Then he turned to the others, meeting the eyes of each man, gauging them, weighing them. He drew a deep breath, then spoke calmly, deliberately, "How often do we know the outcome of the things we wish for? We would fail to act at all if we were to know the future and what it holds. We believe we need so much, yet we don't fully grasp the very things we seek … often ending up with something much different than what we first desired."

The words fell from his lips like pieces of a puzzle.

Alpin continued, "I have heard your offering. Your sentiment is far too generous. I have spoken of my fears of the vaunted notions of leaders and kings … and where such lofty ideas can carry a people. I ask, 'Do not people, in vying to be free, unwittingly seal their fate by placing their most precious gift into the hands of fallen men—hands hoped to be trusted and presumed to be good?' It is a dangerous step that a people would take, when they seek to secure the very thing they are giving away."

Conflicted, Alpin continued to address the men of

Dalriada. "My fellow Scots, I have heard neither jeering nor rebuffs from Luag's request. As such, I will presume that this request of his is something you wish for me to seriously consider."

The men remained fixed in their silence.

"I likewise know that our people must unite and fight the Vikings in the north. As in times past, we are facing a day where we must secure our land so that our people may know freedom and peace again."

Alpin hesitated. He gazed at Guaire and then at Constantine.

Tension hung in the angst-filled hall.

Alpin's chin dipped slightly. "Men of Dalriada, I recognize the threat before us. I, too, recognize the great need of our people to come together as one. I shall take this solemn charge to lead our noble people, and I vow to you this day, with all earnestness, that together we shall rally the hearts of Dalriada and thrust our sword deep into the soul of the Viking beast!

"I grant that I will lead the Dalriadans in battle, but I will wear no crown upon my head, nor respond to the calling of king from your lips. It shall be together that we put an end to this Viking invasion. And when we see the matter to its rightful end, with God as my witness, I will be released of this charge … freeing the men of Dalriada, and freeing my own conscience, from the plague of tyranny."

The room erupted in cheers, and the men rose from their seats, nodding and applauding. Constantine, Luag, and Latharn stood among them, clapping with approval.

Coric lifted to his feet and joined the men. He glanced at

Aiden, standing in the back of the hall, and nodded. Aiden's chin dipped in return as he clapped.

Alpin's assent was what many in the hall had come to hear. The Dalriadans had their leader. They had their swords and their bows. They had a united spirit. And they were prepared to fight.

No one noticed when the door of the large hall opened. Taran was the first to leave. And Searc was next.

Coric and Ronan moved through the room and joined Luag. The three grinned and embraced one another.

The remainder of the men in Renton's hall took turns congratulating Alpin.

Kenneth sat, clasping his hands, alone on his wooden bench. One by one, the men approached his father and offered their praise. Kenneth watched as his father received their words and conversed with them cordially.

As the last of the men stepped away, Alpin peered across the hall. His eyes fell upon Kenneth.

Kenneth did not move from his father's gaze. He only nodded his head and offered a smile of congratulations.

CHAPTER 10

MUTTON STEW SIMMERED OVER THE STONE oven's hot flames. Ena supervised a dozen women as they busily finished preparations for the evening meal. The aroma of hot stew and the smell of baking bread filled the cooking area and seeped into Renton's adjoining hall.

"Let the men know we will be serving supper shortly," Ena said to Ceana and Arabella as the two hovered beside the serving table, cutting their fresh baked loaves.

Ceana set down her knife and stepped to the door leading to the meeting hall. "Arabella, come with me," she said.

"Let me finish here," Arabella replied. Then she cut her last slice and followed Ceana.

Ceana tapped lightly on the door and waited for a response.

She tapped again, but still no response came.

"Let me see if I can get my father," Arabella said and she stepped in front of Ceana. She cracked the door and peeked inside the hall. Her father was standing in the center of the room, speaking with Alpin and Latharn. She opened the door wider and waved. Constantine, oblivious to his daughter's gestures, continued to engage his audience of two.

"He doesn't see me," Arabella said. "Let's go in and get him. He'll tell the men the meal is ready."

Arabella took Ceana's hand and pulled her through the door. The girls ambled into the hall of men and moved toward Constantine, trying not to draw attention to themselves.

"Taran, where have you been?" Guaire asked.

"I had to get some air, Father. I couldn't stomach it any longer … these fools and their bloody wisdom," Taran said, shaking his head. He peered about the room then eyed his father. "Father, would you come outside? I need to speak with you—privately."

"Son, I should not leave. Let it wait until later—"

"Father, Alpin cannot lead these men. He is a double-minded man!" Taran whispered tersely, agitated to the point of anger.

"Not now, Taran!"

Taran's jaw tightened. He spun and moved toward the door—but stopped suddenly when he glimpsed Arabella. She was coming toward him. He turned slightly and paused as if contemplating a thought. As Arabella passed, he stepped back and bumped her.

"Excuse me, my lady," Taran said.

"Oh, my lord, I am sorry. Do forgive my clumsiness," Arabella pleaded.

Taran smiled at Arabella and then glanced at Ceana, dismissively. "There is no need to forgive such an innocent brush, especially from one so lovely. You seem to be on a quest," Taran noted. "I'm sure I can assist you."

"Oh my lord, you are quite generous, I am trying to get to my father, Constantine. I must tell him the evening meal is ready."

"Ah, Constantine of Cashel. You are Constantine's daughter." Taran fixed his gaze on Arabella's lovely green eyes. "I am Taran, son of Guaire of Dumbarton. I must confess, I am embarrassed. We've met before, I do believe. It was here, at Renton's summer festival, some ten years ago. As I recall, Constantine's daughter was quite a young lassie. And now, the same young lady stands before me as the rarest of beauties. Come with me, I am certain I can steer a path through the men and take you to your father."

Arabella peeked at Ceana. Ceana frowned, as she was all too familiar with Taran. With Melton and Dumbarton in close proximity, she and Taran had met on prior occasions, none of which had she found particularly memorable.

Arabella turned to Taran, "My lord, Taran, you are generous with your offer … and please do forgive my clumsiness. But the two of us must relay a message to my father before the ladies in the kitchen grow impatient with our dawdling."

"Very well, Lady Arabella, I shall allow you to pass. But the night is young. Surely we'll have the mutual pleasure of visiting again." The words had hardly left Taran's mouth before he grabbed her hand and kissed it. When finished, he raised his head and smiled at Arabella. He slowly lifted his arm in the direction of Constantine, and in a theatrical gesture, he extended his palm outward and freed the ladies to pass.

Arabella grabbed Ceana's arm and the two shuffled past Taran through the crowd of men toward Constantine.

Taran gazed at Arabella as the two departed. He raised his hand and slowly rubbed his mouth. Then he smiled to himself, relishing the lingering scent of Arabella's touch.

The aroma of the stew settled in the rustic hall while the twin lanterns on the oval table illuminated the evening meal. With supper nearly finished, the men found their previously empty bellies now warmed with mutton and ale, and the mood in the hall had an ease that had not been present in the earlier deliberations.

Alpin pushed his empty soup bowl toward the middle of the table and then wiped away a dribble of stew that perched on the stubble of his beard. He turned to Constantine, waiting for him to finish his last bite. "Constantine, we'll need all the men we can assemble. We'll need them from every village and town in Dalriada."

Constantine swallowed his mouthful of bread and rested his spoon in his wooden bowl. "I will gather the men from Cashel. I figure I'll have forty or fifty, plus others from the north." Constantine gazed to his left at Latharn. "What about Melton, and those in the south? How many can you bring?"

Latharn tossed his napkin beside his finished meal and pushed back from the table. "I would say I could gather about eighty men once I return to Melton and send the word out. When they hear of the Vikings and our plan to unite against them, you'll have an army of angry Scots looking for a fight."

"That's good, we'll need them," Alpin replied. "I want to make it clear to the men that we must gather every capable man in Dalriada to fight the Vikings. We need to attack first. We need the element of surprise. That's our best chance." Alpin's eyes circled the hall. The men were finishing and preparing to leave. "Excuse me, gentlemen," Alpin said to his two companions as he rose from his seat.

"Men," Alpin addressed the assembly, "I hope that you have enjoyed your meal. The women worked hard preparing it for us. I thank them." He paused and collected his thoughts. "Many of you will leave in the morning to return to your towns and villages. You know that we must gather every capable man to fight the Vikings. By the reports we've received, we believe the Vikings could reach us within a matter of weeks at the pace they're moving through the land. But we are not waiting to be attacked—we must bring the attack to them. As you carry the news of our plans, I ask that you carry this message as well, 'The Scots of Dalriada have united as one, to fight for the land we hold sacred. As our fathers have fought before us, so too will we stand and fight. Our time to stand is now!' So I charge you, gather your men, your horses, and your swords. In ten days, we shall meet here in Renton and march north to meet the enemy. We must secure our land as a free land for our families and for the families of our children to come." Finishing his speech, Alpin lifted his mug from the table and raised it in the air, "For Dalriada!"

"For Dalriada!" The men's words echoed back, filling the hall.

The evening grew late, and most of the men had drifted from the meeting hall. Some found rest in tents while others built campfires not far from the hall. Smoke from the fresh wood lofted into the cloudless night, and the fires brought a warm comfort to the cool evening air.

Kenneth left the hall after his father finished his parting

message to the men. He wanted to be alone. He wanted to think. He found a spot away from the commotion and he sat in the grass under the stars. He gazed up at the spring moon, full and round. Then he filled his eyes with the twinkling lights that dotted the darkness. The night sky was vast and beautiful. It had always been beautiful. He lost himself for but a moment before his thoughts migrated back to Renton's hall. His father's acceptance of the men's call gnawed at him. It was not that he felt his father wasn't the right man to lead. In his heart, he knew he was. The nagging feeling stemmed more from seeing that it had become a reality. Maybe if his father had declined, it would have shown the Viking attack was of small concern, or even someone else's concern. Yet his father's acceptance of the call to lead only proved that the threat was real. And alas, joining the men and leaving Renton was just as real.

Kenneth tired of stewing in thought. He picked up a nearby rock and threw it at a tree. The rock struck the trunk and fell to the ground. "Enough of this," he muttered to himself and he rose to his feet and strode back to the hall.

"Where is she?" Kenneth asked Nessa. His sister was carrying the last of the bowls from the large oval table and was heading to the adjoining kitchen.

"Where is who?" Nessa replied.

"Arabella."

"She's cleaning up your mess, that's where she is." Nessa gestured with her head toward the kitchen. Reaching the door, she pressed her back into it and pushed it open.

Kenneth peeked through the open doorway and glimpsed Arabella leaning over a tub of water, scrubbing the evening cookware. He held his finger to his mouth to signal Nessa to keep quiet. Then he followed her through the doorway and crept behind Arabella.

"Nessa, do you think this water is still good, or should I—AHH!" Arabella jumped a foot off the ground when the two pairs of fingers jabbed her ribs.

"Got you!" Kenneth teased.

Arabella spun and hurled a bowl at Kenneth. The dish missed as he ducked.

Kenneth laughed and clapped in delight.

"Kenneth, don't ever do that again. That's mean! A girl could die from such a scare!"

Kenneth stepped toward Arabella and attempted to catch her flailing arms as she scolded him. "Arabella, I only wanted to take you away from the awful drudgery of these chores. The night is beautiful. Won't you come with me and leave these dishes behind? Come on, you have to see the moon tonight."

"And let the bowls wash themselves?" Arabella replied.

"Kenneth, why don't you help finish the dishes," Nessa proposed. "Then you can have your romantic evening under the moonlight."

Kenneth scanned the pile of dirty bowls. "Alright, how about this, you two finish the dishes and I'll do my part by getting the horses ready? It's a great plan, I'll bring them to the front of the hall." He grinned and stepped toward Arabella. "I'll meet you in front, and we can ride the east path for a mile or two. You'll enjoy the air. What do you say?"

He stared into her eyes and coaxed her with raised eyebrows.

Arabella gazed at him, unable to resist. She smiled. "I'll

be done in a moment and I'll meet you in front … don't keep me waiting," she fussed.

Kenneth nodded. "See you there." He turned and grinned at his sister, then hurried out the door.

"What is it with you two … he seems to glow every time he looks at you? Did you put him under a spell?" Nessa asked.

"I have to confess, I adore him," Arabella said, chuckling to herself. "But I hate it when he scares me like that. Somehow though, he makes me laugh … even when I want to be mad at him."

Arabella stooped over the gray dishwater and grabbed another bowl. She mused at the thought of Kenneth surprising her. Then she scrubbed the bowl and dunked it in the water.

Arabella finished the bowls and wheeled the tub of gray water to the rear door. "Nessa, can you give me a hand for a moment?"

Nessa set her rag down and helped Arabella muscle the wheeled cart over the threshold.

"Thanks, Ness. I can get it from here." Arabella let the door close behind her, and she pushed the cart through the grass, far enough away to dump the water.

A few men loitered by a nearby fire, warming themselves. Arabella moved past in the shadows and found a suitable spot to empty the tub. She straightened and flexed her stiffening back before taking a moment to rest. Then she lifted the side of the tub and tipped it, letting the water rush across the grass.

At first, the hand on her shoulder startled her. Then

she smiled and giggled. She started to speak as she turned, "Darling, when will you—ohh!"

"My, I do enjoy an affectionate greeting. I didn't realize we had grown so close ... and so quickly," Taran said, smiling, his ego enlarged from the dinner ale.

Arabella stood dumbfounded.

Taran stepped closer and grabbed Arabella by the arm. He smirked, "You know, you needn't call me 'darling.'" His eyes moved across her face and then down to her breasts. "But go ahead, if you must," he said with a snicker.

A crazed flicker danced in his eyes. Arabella could smell the alcohol on his breath. She was afraid. "Lord Taran, please remove your hand from my arm," she politely insisted.

"My lady, I certainly wish you no harm. I simply wish to visit with you on this fine night," he said, and then his grip tightened.

Kenneth waited with the horses at the front of the hall. *Where is she?* he thought to himself. He tied the horses to a nearby rail and went inside the meeting hall. When he opened the door to the kitchen, he found Nessa sweeping the floor.

"Where is Arabella?" he asked.

"She went out to empty the water," Nessa said and pointed to the rear door. "She may have walked around to the front. Did you see her outside?"

"No, I didn't see her. That's why I'm here," Kenneth said, irritated, and then stepped out the back door. He stood under the night sky and scanned the area for Arabella. He noticed two men warming themselves beside a nearby fire, but couldn't find Arabella. Frustrated, he marched from the hall. After several paces, he spotted two more figures standing in the dark next to what appeared to be a washtub cart.

"Arabella?" Kenneth called and he moved toward the figures. Something wasn't right. He quickened his pace. Then he heard the cry—"Kenneth!"

Taran pushed Arabella away when he heard Kenneth approaching.

Losing her balance, Arabella stumbled, bumped the corner of the cart, and tumbled backwards.

Kenneth leapt and reached for her as she fell, but Taran caught him by the torso and spun him around. In the blink of an eye, Taran cocked his arm and delivered a thundering blow to Kenneth's face. The punch landed square and knocked Kenneth to the ground.

Kenneth rose to one knee. He shook his head and peered at Taran. Without a second thought, he lunged forward and tackled Taran around the waist. He drove his legs over and over, pushing Taran backwards until the two fell and landed in the wet grass.

"Stop it ... stop!" Arabella yelled.

Kenneth ignored the shouts as he mounted Taran and began punching him repeatedly in the head and jaw. Taran raised his arms and twisted under Kenneth, anything to block the blows and shield his face.

Two pairs of hands suddenly grabbed Kenneth's shoulders and yanked him from Taran.

Taran jumped to his feet.

"Need some help?" one of the two men asked Taran. The

two who had hovered by the fire were Dumbarton men, and they were now holding Kenneth firmly in their grip.

Taran nodded at the men as he wiped his mouth. Then he moved forward and stepped face to face with Kenneth. "You shouldn't have done that, son!" From nowhere, a blow slammed Kenneth's gut, followed by a second to his jaw.

Kenneth bent in half, gulping for air. The two henchmen clutching him held tight as Kenneth stooped and spat blood from his mouth.

"Stop!" Arabella screamed again. But the passion of adrenaline and ale had already pushed the men too far.

Kenneth stood erect and lifted his head. Taran glared into his eyes. "Boy, be sure you know who you're dealing with before you decide to interfere in another man's affairs." Taran raised his fist to strike again.

The punch never landed.

Coric's shoulder rammed Taran like a lightning bolt, lifting him off his feet and back onto the soggy ground.

Kenneth wrestled against the hands that bound him and managed to break his right arm loose. But it was Ronan's punch to the jaw of the bigger man that ultimately set Kenneth free.

The bigger man stumbled and Ronan continued to pound him.

Aiden shoved the second man holding Kenneth. The man spun and threw a punch, catching Aiden in the ear. When his opponent recoiled, Aiden returned a blow to the man's chin and followed with a punch to his chest.

Gasping for air, the man reached for Aiden. He had forgotten about Kenneth. But Kenneth hadn't forgotten about him, and Kenneth felt compelled to thank the man for letting him go—then he did so with a hard kick to the stomach. The man fell and rolled on the ground, grabbing his midsection and groaning in pain.

"Knock it off, boys. Knock it off!" Luag's voice boomed in the darkness, startling the young men.

Those on the ground jumped to their feet. Those on their feet turned in attention, each cutting glances at one another and sheepishly rubbing their fresh wounds. No one said a word.

Luag stepped closer. "I don't care who started this and I don't care why it started. Drop it, and drop it now! Our fight is not here and it's not with each other. Save your fighting for the devils in the north! You are Scots, you are brothers. Now act like it!" He glared at the boys in disgust. "I don't want to see this kind of foolishness again." Saying no more, he turned and tromped away.

Taran and the two from Dumbarton brushed themselves off and departed on a path opposite of Luag into the darkness. The three never looked back.

"What the hell happened?" Coric said. He stepped to Kenneth and inspected his brother's eye where a large knot crowned his cheekbone. Kenneth fidgeted with his sore hands and stared at Coric while his eye was being examined.

As Coric tended Kenneth, Aiden approached Arabella to see if she was hurt. She was shaking, and her blouse was partially torn. "Did Taran do this?" he asked, noticing that her shuttering frame made her appear helpless and vulnerable. "Are you alright, Arabella?"

Arabella gazed listlessly at Aiden. Tears streamed down her cheeks. "Yes … I'm alright," she said, clasping the torn folds of her blouse and cupping the fabric to her chest. Then she lowered her head in humiliation.

Kenneth brushed the grass from his shoulders after Coric finished his examination. "I saw Taran grabbing Arabella," Kenneth muttered to his brother. "I couldn't control myself. I felt like killing him."

"It sounds like he had it coming," Coric said.

Kenneth shook his head, still caught in disbelief. Then he stepped past Coric and went to Arabella.

Aiden moved aside as Kenneth approached.

Kenneth took Arabella's hands in his. He glanced back at his brothers and Ronan. "Thanks for the help ... I could've used it sooner," he said, then gave a brotherly smirk.

"Holler if you need us to save you again," Coric replied, grinning back at Kenneth. The three turned and walked past the abandoned fire before disappearing into the night's darkness.

Kenneth returned his focus to Arabella and held her close. He brushed her hair off her forehead and tucked it behind her ears. "Are you alright?" he asked, staring over her pitiful frown and spying a moist trail of tears on her cheek that glistened in the moonlight.

Arabella was silent. She lifted her hand and gently touched Kenneth's swollen eye. A moment passed and she laid her head on his chest. Then she held him close and she cried.

Kenneth tightened his arms around her. Her body was soft and warm. He loved her. He rested his chin on her head and gazed up at the moon.

Arabella remained speechless. She didn't want to speak. She wanted to hold Kenneth. She wanted to hold him forever.

As she clutched him, she thought of her first parents and how she lost them. The terror of that day repeated in her mind. She thought of Constantine and Senga, how they had rescued her and gave her a renewed chance at life. Another wave of pain struck as she recalled losing Senga. Her losses seemed inescapable. Her feelings for Kenneth, in some ways, made her wounds more raw and more painful. The man she loved stood before her, holding her, yet in a matter of days he would leave her. She wondered, even feared, that he may become like the others she'd loved.

She felt the urge to run, to run and hide. She wanted to leave. She wanted to leave with him. If they left, they could make a life together, while staying meant that war would soon find them. She knew she couldn't ask Kenneth to run away with her, but that didn't stop her from wanting his heart, his whole heart. She knew he'd have to leave while she stayed behind, waiting for his return, praying for his return. His heart would be forever torn if she stole him away, ripping him from his father and brothers, who in a matter of days would march to fight.

No, she would not force him to choose. She would not hurt him. She would not leave him. She would wait for him.

She stood clutched in his arms under the moon's soft glow. She didn't speak. Her heart was too sore to speak. She simply stood and let him hold her.

CHAPTER 11

THE MOON FLOATED IN THE SKY OVER RENTON, casting its midnight glow down upon an insignificant cluster of willows standing on the outskirts of the small village. A steady breeze blew through the trees, swaying their long lanky arms back and forth, though no one noticed. Chirps of bush crickets and the repetitious hoot of a long-eared owl echoed in the night air.

The swaying willows hid the moon above and produced a swath of dancing shadows in the darkness below. The darkness offered a suitable spot for men to meet in secrecy. It was there that Taran and Searc first conspired.

"We could do so much for our people if we had a man of passion as king," Taran said. "Those fools think Alpin can lead Dalriada. The man has deceived himself as well as the others. He's not able to lead our men to victory over the Vikings. He doesn't have the heart for it. He's been a weakened man ever since he lost his son."

"Why can't the men see that?" Searc replied. "He's afraid to fight, even against the Britons. Why do they think he'll have the heart to fight the Vikings? They are far worse than the Britons."

"He's a coward. His call for freedom will fall on deaf ears when the men realize he lacks the courage to be king. We can't let this happen to our people. We need a man with the heart to call himself king!" Taran said, sowing his seeds. "We need the others to see this."

"Oengus, the Pict, is willing to help," Searc said. "He came to Renton several days back, but Alpin refused to listen—his stubbornness will get us all killed."

"Yes, if Oengus were to return to Renton to seek a truce, then the Scots and Picts could align. Together we could stop the Vikings," Taran said, manipulating his words with care. "Once we defeat the Vikings, we could turn south, and our armies could bring an end to the Britons."

"Yes, we could do it. We could crush the Vikings and the Britons!" Searc exclaimed, excited by the possibility of revenge.

"Shhh," Taran warned.

Searc lowered his voice, "But Alpin will never concede to Oengus."

Taran grinned as his patsy took the bait. "You're right. You're exactly right," Taran said, feigning as if he'd never considered the thought prior to that moment. "I know a few men who would be willing to listen to Oengus, men able to lead the Scots when we unite. The men I am thinking of, they will be in Renton in ten days when we assemble to battle the Vikings." Taran strained to look into Searc's eyes, hardly able to see him in the darkness. "Searc, you must do something for me. Something that will help us all."

Searc nodded.

Taran leaned close and whispered in Searc's ear.

๑

Three riders, bearing painted flesh, rode across an open green meadow in northern Dalriada. The sun was high in the noon sky, yet it remained veiled behind an endless expanse of thick gray clouds. The riders moved forward, lofting a long wooden staff with a single white cloth attached to its tip. The riders purposed to show confidence, but in truth, they were unsure if the man they were seeking would respect the white cloth's declaration of peace.

The three riders slowed as they crossed the field toward the distant army. There, a countless number of men and horses fanned out across the earth, surrounding a single brown tent. Beside the tent, a blazing red fire burned. Its smoke billowed high into the air.

Kodran trotted his horse around the northern perimeter of the army of men and beasts. A second Viking trailed behind him. Kodran had nearly finished his patrol when he spotted the three riders crossing the field. Kodran shouted to his cohort, and the two turned their horses and headed to the center of the camp.

"Halfdan," Kodran called from outside his leader's tent. "Three riders are approaching from the east. It looks as if others are not far behind," he said with a heavy breath.

Halfdan emerged from the large brown tent. He slid his sword into its sheath. "Get my horse!" he commanded the guard beside the tent, and the man vanished behind the brown tarp.

Halfdan, Kodran, Jorund, and a dozen others mounted

and rode to meet the three riders. When they neared the riders, both parties slowed, measuring one another in silence. Halfdan peered at the white flag and mused dismissively as it fluttered in the wind.

One of the men with painted arms spoke first. "I am Deort. We are Picts, servants of Lord Oengus. We come in peace," he said, uncertain if the Vikings understood.

Halfdan released a wad of spit into the air. It landed on the ground beside the Picts. "I care not of your lord nor your peace. You'd be wise to return along the path you came and warn your lord of the wrath of Halfdan the Black!"

"You speak our language," Deort replied, surprised. "Then I trust you know our offer of peace is sincere?"

"A language is easy to master when you surround yourself with servants and slaves who speak such," Halfdan replied. "This is not our first conquest of your land. As for your peace, we don't need it. We find and take as we desire, and peace is not among our pursuits."

Deort tried again, "Please consider my words and weigh them carefully. Our warriors, too, are strong. The people to the south, the Dalriadans, they as well are capable of assembling a sizable army, and they are tenacious fighters when their land and lives are at stake. We have seen and heard of the destruction brought by your Vikings. We know of your strength. My Lord Oengus respects your strength. Though you are capable of much, if you pursue an untimely battle with the Picts and Dalriadans, your losses may be more severe than you're willing to bear. I simply ask that you consider a peace offering with Lord Oengus. We believe we have much to offer. You will see as much if you take heed and speak with my lord."

Halfdan was a man of few interests beyond fighting. But at this moment, the cunning of his mind trumped the hot-temper of his heart. Gaining more knowledge of the Picts and Dalriadans could prove useful. With little to lose and much to gain, he spoke, "Where is this 'Oengus' you speak of? Is he too cowardly to meet face to face? Or does he hide behind his men and fight from the rear!" Halfdan's horde laughed at the insult.

"Lord Oengus is not short on courage, rather he is long in wisdom and patience," Deort replied. "He is well aware of your savagery and your quick hand with the sword. My lord has loyal men who ensure his intentions are met. We have been sent to seek your presence. If you are agreeable, then we have accomplished our purpose."

"Your purpose is to stay alive and hope that my men do not press a blade through your chest!" Halfdan growled. "Enough talk. Bring this 'Oengus' to me."

Deort nodded to the Pict with the white flag. The man turned his horse and trotted back several paces. Then he lofted the flag above his head and waved it side-to-side.

In the distance, a large band of Pict riders slowly crested the hill and advanced.

Oengus sat tall on his white steed. "I am Oengus, Lord of the Picts," he announced, flanked on either side by a dozen painted men decorated with intricate patterns extending up their arms to their neck and cheeks. The opposing assemblies stood twenty feet apart, glaring at one another—the Picts with their maze of body ink and the Vikings with their ominous horned helmets. The Picts stirred and sized their unfamiliar foe, assessing the Vikings like a badger to a boar. The tension was palpable.

After a moment of silence, Halfdan spoke, "You are Oengus. The one who believes a small white flag and a few painted men will stop my warriors from taking as we please. I question your wisdom!"

"I am well aware of your zeal to take as you please, but I am here to offer you the very things you desire … yet at a price not so costly," Oengus replied.

Halfdan chuckled. "Go on," he permitted.

"As a leader of men, I assume you have a purpose for the things you pursue. We are alike in many ways. As such, I ask that you come with me, that we may have a word together." Oengus drew his horse to the side and gestured for Halfdan to follow.

With a quick nod of the head, Halfdan signaled Kodran and then tugged his reigns and trotted beside Oengus. Kodran and Jorund followed.

Deort eyed the Viking henchmen and coaxed his horse to keep pace, watching the two closely as they moved.

When the five riders had separated a dozen paces from the others, Oengus stopped his horse. He peered across the field and then turned to face Halfdan. "This land has much to offer, but you will encounter resistance with every step you take. Resistance can be costly. I can help you achieve what you desire … while ensuring your losses are few."

"Your interest in protecting my losses is intriguing. You have something to gain, I presume?" Halfdan replied.

"Indeed, we both have much to gain, me as well as you. We seek peace and you seek conquest. To secure our mutual pursuits, I ask that you cease any intrusion against the Picts, and in return, I will show you a land to the south, a land abounding in resources and beauty," Oengus said, and his mouth arched into a grin.

Alone, Kenneth stood on the bank of the stream, watching the twisting waters pass. The stream flowed by that morning as it had every morning. Kenneth had come to the same bank many times before. He had always found an ease in gazing upon the stream, watching its water freely flow, endless and unhindered. Though now, as he watched the water pass, he was struck by the realization that whether he stood at the banks or whether he turned and walked away, the stream would continue to flow—with or without him.

On this morning, he struggled. Arabella filled his thoughts. The terrified look on her face when he found her in Taran's grasp had left its imprint on his mind. He despised Taran for what he'd done, and adding to that, Kenneth hated the thought of Arabella living in despair— despair that would come if he were to die in battle. Kenneth treasured her. Standing alone on the bank of the stream, he determined he would keep her from such sorrow.

Kenneth lifted his hand and touched his bruised eye, as if to verify the encounter had happened the previous night. He winced. The pain assured him it had. He bent and picked up a stone from the bank. The cold wet form sat lifeless in his hand. He tossed it in the air and caught it as gravity brought it back to him. Then he gazed at the stone for a long moment before hurling it into the stream. It plunged into the water with a plopping sound and sank out of sight. He remained fixed, watching the ripples on the water emanate like growing circles from where the stone had disappeared. The ripples quickly faded as the water carried the distorted rings downstream.

Kenneth knew he must go. He had to go. He would take his sword and gear and head north with his father, brothers, and the other men coming to Renton—all within a matter of days. They would pursue their enemy and fight to defeat them. He would miss Arabella. He would miss her dearly.

Memories of Drostan returning home crept into his thoughts, memories of that awful wooden cart and his lifeless body. *Is that how Arabella will find me?* he wondered. He recalled the day he and Coric stood on the far side of the barley field that cold autumn morning, seven years back. How the two had desperately wanted to be men—he and Coric both. A smile leveled across his lips as he remembered Aiden's wild charge, and how the three of them had wrestled on the rocky path before their father and the men had surprised them. He realized how the men must have seen them as mere children, sparring as if lost in make-believe.

Kenneth didn't stop the tear that inched down his cheek. Dear Drostan. It was the last day he and his brother spoke, the last time he saw him smile. Drostan seemed so old then, yet now he seemed so young. He gave so much.

Kenneth remembered his father's and mother's agony and the years it took to recover from the loss. It had been such a bitter Providence. *Why were life's lessons so hard? What was to be gained, or learned, from such a deep loss?* He found no answers to his questions.

Kenneth tried to dispel his thoughts and empty his mind of Arabella and the despair that could one day come to her.

His duty was to fight. Honor demanded that he stand with his brothers and defend Dalriada. *Yet in these noble actions, what would become of Arabella if she were to suffer loss yet again?* He shook his head and tried not to think of it.

He bent down and grabbed another rock.

He looked at the stream. Its water flowed by, pushing downstream between the edges of the banks, seeking something to pour itself into, something larger than itself.

"Aiden said I'd find you here!" Arabella called out from high on the bank behind Kenneth.

Kenneth spun to face her, "How long have you been here?"

"Only a moment."

Kenneth peered at the stream and tossed his rock into the passing water. "Can't a man find peace and quiet?"

"I wasn't trying to disturb your peace," Arabella replied and began to descend the bank. "I was just trying to find you. I was hoping to talk to you."

"Some would say that's disturbing one's peace," he said. He tried to act as if he was teasing and wondered if she knew he wasn't.

"Kenneth, I am not trying to bother you. I only wanted to see you."

"Well, I came here to think a little," he said. His eyes left the peaceful waters, and he turned and gazed at Arabella, who now stood before him.

"Thinking about last night?" she asked.

"Yes, last night … I could kill that fool, Taran. Who does he think he is?"

"Kenneth, let it go. He'd been drinking … it was stupid."

"He even tried to enthrone his father as the leader of

Dalriada, as if to be some sort of king … and he wasn't drunk for that!" Kenneth ran his fingers through his matted hair. "Dammit, why is this happening?"

"What Kenneth?"

"My father, the Vikings, that snake Taran—all of it!" He paused, staring at Arabella. "You know I'm going to fight. You know we're leaving in nine days."

Tears moistened her eyes. She shook her head without speaking, resenting him.

"Say something!" Kenneth exclaimed.

Arabella said nothing, she simply gazed at him in disbelief.

"It's not right," Kenneth said. "I will not love you and then break your heart!"

His words hit her ears and plunged her into a wave of confusion. "What are you saying, Kenneth? What do you mean, 'you will not break my heart?'" She stared at him, scanning his eyes, his face, wanting him to speak.

Kenneth struggled inside, and Arabella reached for his hand, but he pulled away.

"Kenneth, I will not stop loving you because of some war!"

Kenneth said nothing. He turned from her and faced the stream in silence, afraid of how he would hurt her.

Arabella refused to let him fade from her. She would fight. She brazened and spoke, "I think your father is wrong. I think he should make a truce with the Picts. Maybe then the Vikings will see who is stronger and will leave Dalriada. I know you may think that is selfish, I see that."

"You think it is strong to submit to the Picts? That makes

no sense. Why can't you support me, why can't you support my father? The men have made their decision."

"I am saying that I hope they made the right decision. Kenneth, there is so much at stake. And yes, I do support you … and your father … if they believe this is the only way. And if it is the only way, then do not think that your time away from me will cause my heart to grow cold. I'm not going to lose you, Kenneth. I know the Lord will bring you back to me."

"Arabella, do you realize the heartbreak that many will suffer before this war is over? War brings death, just as it did to my family when Drostan died. Do you not see that this same grief will return? You yourself have lived this … more times than one should bear. I will not bring this agony upon you again!"

"I don't understand you, Kenneth. What are you saying?" Arabella wiped her eyes before her tears could spill.

Kenneth shook his head and then stepped away and walked to the edge of the stream. He gazed down at the still pool beside the bank. The pool's glass-like water displayed an eerie reflection—one that revealed the lost countenance of a young man. *Who are you?* he asked himself. He hovered over the pool in silence as Arabella stood in watch behind him.

The two remained wordless as the stream's water passed. Neither ready to speak. Neither ready to listen. All they could offer the other was silence, while the sound of the trickling creek crept into their ears, entrancing them both.

"Kenneth?" Arabella said with a quiet, questioning voice.

Kenneth turned and gazed at her. His face held no

expression. "You should go," he said. "You should go back to Cashel."

"Kenneth, why are you talking like this?"

"Arabella. Your father will be gathering his men in Cashel. Go to him. He will need your help to prepare things." Kenneth's words were terse and hollow. "I must go now. My father will need me here in Renton." He turned and walked up the bank, leaving Arabella behind.

Arabella remained alone beside the stream. She stood in solitude as Kenneth slowly disappeared from sight. Turning toward the creek, she watched helplessly as the cold waters passed quietly by.

Bang!

The slam of the wooden door startled Ceana. "Coric, are you alright?" she called out from the bedroom where she sat stitching a buckle to a boot.

No one answered.

She tensed.

"Coric?" she called again. As she rose from her chair, Arabella materialized before her. "Arabella, why are you back so soon? I thought you were with Kenneth."

"I was with him. And now I am not with him!" Arabella said as she stormed past Ceana. She hurried about the room and began to gather her things, clumsily shoving the items into a woven bag.

"What's troubling you? Why are you packing?" Ceana asked, bewildered. "You are welcome to stay with us until the men return to Renton."

"No, I don't believe I am!" Arabella snapped. She skirted across the room and stubbed her toe on the bedpost in her haste. The blow was painful. She grunted and hobbled before inadvertently dropping her bag and dumping its contents on the floor. Without stopping, she snatched her fallen items and crammed them back into the bag. "Kenneth insists that I return to Cashel to help my father prepare his men. If that is where I'm needed, then that is where I shall be."

"Arabella, you can't leave like this," Ceana insisted, wanting her to slow down, wanting her to reconsider. "You must have misunderstood him. Arabella, you're just upset."

Arabella ignored her, only pausing to scan the room for the last of her items. Then she pushed back her hair and grabbed an overlooked blouse and shoved it into the bag.

"Are you afraid he won't come back?" Ceana asked. "Is that it?"

Arabella stopped. Her lips pursed and she met eyes with Ceana. "Maybe it would be better if he didn't come back!" she shouted and ran past Ceana towards the door.

Ceana reached for her, but she was too quick.

Opening the front door, Arabella glanced back at Ceana. She didn't say a word, she only shook her head and rushed away, slamming the door behind her.

The house went silent. Ceana drew a deep breath and stared down at the floor. She walked to the door and stepped outside to find Arabella.

Not far away, Arabella sat alone beside an old elm tree, crying. Ceana went to her.

"Tell me what happened," Ceana said quietly. She sat down and placed her arm around Arabella.

Arabella didn't fight her tears, she fought her

sadness—and a past that frightened her. She wanted to be with Kenneth. *Why did he leave me, why did he let go?* She hated herself for letting him walk away. She hated herself for getting too close. She hated to admit that she loved him as much as she did.

The two remained together under the branches of the old tree, staring off into the distance. For a long time Arabella sat without saying a word. Her heart was broken, and silence was her only comfort.

CHAPTER 12

SEARC ARRIVED IN PERTH, THE LAND OF THE
Picts—the land of Oengus. Two days had passed since he
and Taran had met in the shadows of Renton's moonlight.

Searc quietly rode through the darkness to a copse of
spruce trees and dismounted. The pungent scent of the
hearty evergreens saturated the air. He tied his horse to a
waist-high branch and made his way through the trees to a
clearing. Still tucked in the veil of the evergreens, he knelt
and pushed aside two bristly limbs and peeked out at the
giant stone monster towering in the distance.

There, across the clearing, loomed the Pict castle. The
enormous structure stood arrayed with flaming torches that
sat like sentries mounted atop its massive rock walls. The
flames lit the darkness above the castle, causing the hovering
night sky to glow with an ominous ambience. The sight was
unlike anything Searc had ever seen. It was an icon of Pict
strength—Searc had come to the heart of Pictland.

Time passed and Searc remained cloaked in the
thickness of the trees. He sat in the darkness, mulling over
Taran's words and rehearsing their plan in his mind. He
pictured himself speaking to Oengus, and a sudden feeling

of dread rushed over him as he thought of entering Oengus' den and facing the Pict lord alone. *What if Oengus refuses to hear me? What if he looks at me as his enemy?*

No, Oengus will listen. Searc wrestled with his doubt. *He wants a truce. He wants the Scots to join him.*

An owl hooted in a nearby tree and spooked Searc. He took a deep breath to settle his nerves. He began to perspire. The night was still young, and he wondered if he should wait until dawn before approaching the castle. But he knew he could wait no longer.

He returned to his horse and rode forward, leaving the protection of the spruce grove behind him.

"Halt, there below!" the tower guard shouted from his parapet as a lone rider approached. The rider slowed to a stop in front of the massive doors of the castle entry. "State your business."

The light of the castle torches flickered across Searc's face as he eyed the parapet and spotted the guard. "I am Searc, son of Gormal of Renton. I wish to speak with Lord Oengus." Searc's words echoed against the castle wall, making him feel even smaller than he already felt, if that were possible.

"Lord Oengus is resting. What is it you seek at this hour of night?"

"My message is urgent. Lord Oengus must hear me. It is a matter of grave importance. I beg of you, allow me to speak to your lord."

The tower guard turned and disappeared from sight. A moment passed and Searc heard the exchange of voices above. He shifted on his horse and glanced over his shoulder into the darkness. The anticipation made him antsy.

"Wait there … you will be escorted by our men," the guard shouted and then sunk into the shadows of the parapet.

Searc's heart raced as he sat in the silence of the night. *This is the right thing to do. We need the Picts.* Searc tried to convince himself the plan would work. *The men of Dalriada, the people of Dalriada, need to hear Oengus. Alpin was a fool for refusing him. He had his chance.*

Searc's grip tightened on his reigns, and he tried to steady his breathing.

Suddenly, a steely thud sounded in his ears, and the large castle doors jarred against one another and began to move. The dark opening between the wooden giants grew wider, and two men on horseback emerged from the shadows. They approached and stopped on either side of Searc.

"Dalriadan," one of the men said, "dismount and follow me."

Searc stood in a dimly lit chamber within the musty bowels of the castle. The walls were stone, the floors were stone, and the entire chamber was altogether unwelcoming. Searc's heart beat loudly within his chest. The idea of speaking to Oengus grew more unsettling, and doubt began to gradually quash what little of his courage remained. It was then that thoughts of Aiden crept into Searc's mind. He wondered if Aiden would consider him a traitor—standing there in the Pict castle, pleading for a moment with the Pict lord, scheming to unseat Aiden's father.

Aiden was Searc's only friend. He'd always been good to Searc. Where others cared little of Searc, it was Aiden who'd been faithful to stand beside him. Surely, in time, Aiden would see that this was the right decision. Searc labored to push the thoughts from his head and clear his troubled mind.

A moment later, the far door of the chamber slowly opened, and a man in a long robe entered. "Dalriadan, what brings you to my home at this late hour?" The voice was severe and unfriendly.

Searc stood as still as a stone, gazing at the man. He recognized Oengus from his visit to Renton, but he appeared older in the dim glow of the chamber. The candlelight deepened the wrinkled skin surrounding his eyes and mouth, aging him notably. "Lord Oengus ... my lord, I am indebted that you would grant me a moment of your time. I am Searc of Renton, son of Gormal. I hope you find my message pleasing. I believe we share a common goal ... one of great importance."

Oengus peered at Searc, studying his face. "I know you," Oengus said, resisting a grin. "You are the one who tried to bring reason to the men of Renton when I called on your people to join me, yes?" Oengus stopped and folded his arms. "I am not sure I'll find much pleasing at this hour, the moon is high and my mind begs of rest. What is it you so urgently desire to share?"

"Lord Oengus, when you visited Renton, not many days ago, you spoke of the Viking attacks in the north. We too know of these attacks. We agree, they must be stopped—"

"Your wise Alpin does not share this sentiment," Oengus interrupted. "Have you come to tell me he has changed his mind?"

"Alpin is blind in his pride ... he doesn't see what others around him so clearly see. Many in Dalriada do not agree with him. They see wisdom in joining the Picts against the Vikings."

"So the others in Dalriada have sent you to inform me that Alpin has been supplanted, and the others wish to pledge their loyalty to me?"

"Well, you see …," Searc stumbled for words, "there are others that—"

"Come out with it!"

Searc trembled. "There are others in Dalriada who see things differently than Alpin, yes. It would be good for you to return to Renton to offer again your call for unity, that the others assembling in Renton may give ear to your message."

"Assembling in Renton?" Oengus said. "Assembling in Renton to consider uniting with the Picts?"

"No, not for that purpose … but if—"

"Then for what purpose! My patience is wearing thin, boy!"

"The Dalriadans are assembling in Renton to prepare for war against the Vikings."

Oengus turned from Searc, hiding the smile that crept across his face. He gazed up at a grand painting hanging on the wall. The picture displayed an older woman in a long, purple gown sitting in a red chair. The woman was adorned in jewels, with a white sash covering her shoulders and draping over her breasts. Oengus remained fixed on the painting, admiring its maternal subject.

Oengus snapped from his trance and spun to face Searc. "So the men of Dalriada are gathering in Renton to war against the savages in the north. I suppose this was Alpin's idea—how clever to fight the Vikings from a position of weakness, how clever to fight them alone." Oengus' ire grew as he spoke. His pasty white skin reddened as blood pulsed through his veins. "The man is a fool! Many will die in this noble war of his. Many who could have been spared, had he the sense to join me." Oengus took a breath and evened his tone, "Only, his pride would not allow it."

"Lord Oengus, it's not too late. If you'll reconsider your offer of alliance and speak to the men of Dalriada when they assemble, then they will listen to you. They will join you. Guaire of Dumbarton is a strong and wise man. His son, Taran, is a strong man as well. These men will listen to you. They will convince the others that aligning with you is our best hope to stop the Vikings. Alpin will have no choice but to concede."

Oengus allowed himself a moment, and a plan unfolded in his mind. "And when the Vikings are defeated by our alliance, your Dalriadans will honor their pledge of loyalty, of fealty, to me, yes? I will ensure their security, their prosperity, and their peace, and they in turn will pledge to me their land, their swords, and their loyalty, yes?" Oengus rubbed his chin as he mused at the thought.

"My Lord Oengus, I do believe our men will see the wisdom of such an alliance. We can rid our lands of this evil. With your leadership, we can crush the Vikings and others in Britannia. After the Vikings are defeated, I beg of you to finish the task and destroy the Britons as well. I pray that no heart in Dalriada, or Pictland, is settled until both Vikings and Britons are destroyed!"

"You seem quite anxious to cleanse our lands, young Scot … tell me, where is it that you grow this hatred for both Viking and Briton?"

"Just as you despise the Vikings, I despise the Britons.

The devils killed my father at Ae, and Alpin did nothing to stop them!"

Oengus' eyes settled on Searc. His mind schemed. A thought formed and pleased him. "Searc of Renton, you have shown much courage in coming a good distance to bring this important message. Clearly, you treasure Dalriada, or shall I say, you treasure Britannia. I share your passion in ridding our lands of the heathens in the north ... and the south. With an alliance between our people, we can achieve such things." Oengus gave a fatherly smile before finishing, "When will the Dalriadans meet in Renton?"

"Eight days from now, men across Dalriada will assemble in Renton. You should come and speak to them at that time. I'm certain they'll receive you."

"In eight days ... very good." Oengus placed his hand on Searc's shoulder. "You must go now. Tell no one of our visit. I do not want Alpin to devise a plan to shipwreck what promises to be a day to remember ... a day that will not long be forgotten."

CHAPTER 13

A LONE RIDER CAME FROM THE EAST. THE PAINTED Pict approached the Viking camp, a camp transforming into a veritable fort.

The Pict was met by a dozen Vikings.

The men escorted the Pict through the front opening of the half-built fort and traversed the grounds to the fort's north wall, where Halfdan stood outside his chamber.

The Pict spoke and provided a message to Halfdan.

The message was brief.

Halfdan nodded his head without saying a word.

The message was delivered.

The Pict was escorted from the fort and disappeared as quickly as he came.

Halfdan looked to the south—and his mouth arched into a crooked smile.

CHAPTER 14

ALPIN WRESTLED WITHIN HIS SOUL. THE DECISION in Renton's hall three nights prior provided no escape from his doubts. Standing high on the ridgeline and looking over his homeland only seemed to make the decision more difficult to live out. Taking the Scots to battle would be hell.

Alpin had ridden up the steep rocky ridge alone, a single man on a single horse. Here he had hoped the seclusion and silence of solitude would clear his mind of concern and worry—worry for his family and the people of Renton and Dalriada. The sunlight, at times able to revive the sullen heart, was locked behind the lowering clouds. Without its warm rejuvenation, Alpin was left alone under the gray sky to fight the troubles that vexed his soul.

From below, the quiet solitude of the ridge had promised relief, a place to sit and consider. But now, as he stood high on the ridge overlooking the vista, the thatched rooftops dotting the hills below seemed to cry out to him. The small homes of Renton sat like fragile hearts begging for peace and protection, hearts that cried for an escape from a coming darkness, hearts that hoped for a great good to arise and keep them from evil.

But he was no savior, no hero. How could it be, that his people would place their hope in him—that he would now be the protector of their Promised Land? Years ago, with the passion and strength of youth, he would have taken hold of such a mantle and charged forward to slay the enemy. He would have delighted in the justice of burying his sword into the hearts of the hateful ones, knowing such deeds were noble. Yet now, he was a different man. Though his spirit despised injustice and his passion burned to live amid a people free from tyranny, his soul carried a hole, an emptiness that would never be refilled. How could he, a man who was unable to protect the life of his own son, protect the lives of a thousand sons?

Life's madness twisted inside him. And all the while, the frail dwellings below pleaded to him, haunting him, fueling guilt and doubt in his heart. Alpin knew he had things to fight for, precious things. He hoped that someday, in a better time and place, he could face himself again and be proud of the deeds he'd done, proud of what he'd given.

In a week's time, the men of Dalriada would gather. Renton would be overflowing with zealous men, anxious to defend their homeland. They would look to a leader to carry them forward, a leader who could take the hearts of a myriad of men and make them one. Yet Alpin doubted himself. Thoughts of losing Drostan at Ae ate at him. The loss had cracked and scarred the once sturdy man.

For the sake of his son, and those willing to give as Drostan gave, Alpin realized he must dispel the doubt that whispered to him and find the courage to lead as the men needed him to lead.

The people needed a leader, and maybe needed a king.

A king could unite them. A king could speak into the hearts of the uncertain and unsure and open their eyes to a greater cause beyond themselves, a transcendent cause that was not bound to the mundane, the simple, or the insignificant. A king could lift their spirits and meld them as one. A king could take the passion and zeal of a multitude of men and harness them, focusing them with a single spirit that fought for the good of the many.

Alpin knew the merit of giving the men a king, but it was not a mantle he was willing to embrace. He was born a free man, he would die a free man, and he would not subject any man to the bondage of fealty or the debt of servitude. Yet could he banish fear and instill courage in the Scots without being their king?

Alpin sat down on a large jagged rock anchored in the earth. He gazed at the small thatched roofs below. He did not fear living and dying, rather it was other fears that plagued his heart. He feared that he again may lose those things dear to him in the days to come, that he would lose men and boys. And he feared the awful fear—the fear of losing another son. The horror tormented him. Foolishly, he gave his fears a foothold to take root.

Alpin was a fool for ruminating on his fears, for fear does not fight alone. Fear invites its two mistresses—Guilt and Doubt—when it stalks its prey. Together, these two fuel the misery of a man's soul. They are perverse in their ways. Guilt haunts a man with failures of the past, taunting him in shame. Doubt, on the other hand, assures a man he is doomed to fail again in times ahead, testing every thought and questioning every motive, obliging a man to defend himself or perish. They are the bewitching enemies of every man.

These pernicious foes toyed with Alpin's heart. He could do little to resist as his eyes closed and he was carried away into a dream. In the dream, Alpin sat beside a well, holding a small stone in his hand. The stone was like a pearl—white, smooth, and round. As he sat, two shadowy figures came to him and lifted him to his feet. Standing at his side, one figure beckoned him to peer into the well. The circular stone well led down to a deep, dark blackness that seemed to stir as he gazed inside.

As Alpin stared down into the darkness, the second figure stole his stone and cast it into the well, laughing as he released the gem. Alpin lunged forward, grasping for his jewel, yet it passed out of reach and dropped into the black water below.

Alpin gaped into the blackness of the well, hoping to glimpse the white stone beneath the rippling water. He saw only his reflection, a reflection of himself as a younger man. Alpin grew mesmerized. As the waters settled, the face gazing back at him was the face of Drostan. He was staring up at his father through the water. Alpin's soul crumpled. Nausea wrenched his stomach and sorrow gripped his heart. Memories of Drostan flooded over him—the touch of his skin, the sound of his voice, the smell of his hair—all torn from him.

A tear dripped from Alpin's eye and fell into the well, rippling the water below and chasing away the sweet, sad reflection. "I'm sorry, Son," he whispered.

Alpin woke from his dream. The laughing voices of the shadowy figures echoed in his ears. A fury inside of him burst out in rage. He yelled and hurled his fists into the air like a blind madman groping for his foes. Yet the figures had vanished, along with the water and the well.

Only the memory of Drostan remained.

Alpin struggled to regain his senses. He rose to his feet. The moist breeze felt real upon his skin. He was alive and clarity struck him, pushing aside his vexation and pumping new life into his heart. He stepped to the edge of the ridge and looked down over the small village below. He thought of his family. He thought of his people. He would fight for them.

"Father," a voice from behind him spoke. "Mother thought you'd be here."

The voice was familiar. Alpin rubbed his whiskery face and turned toward his son. "Coric."

"Father, are you well?" Coric asked, holding the lead of his horse and studying his father, puzzled.

"Yes. I'm alright."

The two stood silent, gazing at one another.

"Is something the matter, Father?"

Alpin peered at the ground and then up at Coric. He stared intently at his son and saw strength in the young man. "Son, I suppose every man has his demons. Far too long, I have tended to mine … but no longer," he said, finally realizing what he was fighting for—something beyond himself, something bigger than himself.

Coric gazed at him and nodded. After pausing a moment, he spoke, "Father, is this where you came before Ae?"

"It is," Alpin acknowledged. "Every man needs a place

to sit and measure himself, to weigh matters ... to clear the mind."

Coric released the lead of his horse and stepped to the edge of the ridge. He looked out over the small homes dotting the countryside of Renton. "You can see so much from here."

"And still, there's much you can't see," Alpin replied.

"Things you can't see?" Coric asked, perplexed.

"Those things that lie ahead ... the unexpected trials of life. But know this, it's not the trials that define a man, rather it's how a man faces his trials." Alpin gazed at his son, studying him. "Coric, the days ahead will surely bring many trials, possibly the greatest you'll ever face. No matter what happens to me, or to your brothers, never forget who you are."

"I will always be your son, Father ... in life or death. I learned that from you. I learned it from Drostan."

"Indeed, you are my son, as is Drostan. And you are a fine son, and a good husband, and one day you will be a great father. In all these things, you are a son of Dalriada, always remember that. And as such, you must always remember that you are a free man. It is your birthright, it is every man's birthright—let no man speak otherwise nor take it from you. Cherish this, Coric ... guard and treasure it."

Coric stared at his father, listening to his words. Slowly, his gaze turned, and he gaped over the open expanse and spoke to himself, as much as to his father, "You've always said freedom comes at a price ... I suppose all things worth treasuring do." A gentle wind blew against Coric's cheeks while his gaze remained on Renton.

"In a matter of days, we will leave for battle," Alpin said. "Hold tight to all that is worth treasuring in this life and the next, and when you fight, fight with all the fury of heaven and hell—for in many ways these are the very things at stake."

Coric turned to face his father, "Yes, Father ... I will," he promised.

CHAPTER 15

"I DON'T UNDERSTAND THE BOY," ALPIN SAID AS he took a seat at the table, staring at his wife. He reached with his hand and picked at the wick of a half-spent candle sitting in the table's center.

Ena dunked a dirty plate in the washtub, "And which boy is that?" she asked without lifting her eyes from the dishes.

"Donald. He's been acting odd. And when I speak with him, he closes up and says nothing."

Ena released her plate into the tub and dried her hands. She peered at Alpin, "How do you expect him to behave when his father is leaving to fight a war?"

"I don't expect him to crawl into a shell and play as if the world doesn't exist."

"Alpin, he's ten years old. His father is going away to fight, and the last time you left ...," Ena paused, her eyes moistened. She wiped her eyes and took a deep breath. She started again, "We are all scared, Alpin. He's afraid he'll never see you again ... or his brothers. He wants to be with you. That's how young boys are, they want to be with their father."

"Ena, I understand, but what do you want me to do ...

the men will be here in six days. There is much to prepare. The barley, the sheep, the goats, these need tending. And Donald has been helping me."

Ena walked to the table and sat next to her husband. "He needs more from his father than an opportunity to do chores. You know him … he wants to be like the older boys. I should ask, have you seen him with his bow? He tells me he's been practicing and asks if you've noticed." Ena said. She paused, reading her husband's face, awaiting a response. "You told Coric the men would need more food for the days ahead. You could take Donald hunting and get the meat you need. Let him go with you. Alpin, he needs his father."

Alpin stood and stepped to the window. He peered outside. "Do you see him now? There he is, as if he heard you. He's shooting arrows at the tree … and using your scarf as a target."

Ena rose and stood beside Alpin. "See, that's all he does, every day. But I'll take a willow switch to him for using my scarf," Ena said and smirked. "This is what I mean. He needs you."

Alpin put his arm around Ena. The sight of the small boy shooting at his mother's scarf seemed to lighten the tension of the day.

"You're right. He's been asking if I'd take him hunting before we leave. And he's even been sleeping with that bow of his the past several nights," Alpin said, allowing himself to chuckle.

"Nessa and I will take care of things here. We'll tend to the animals and the barley. Maybe one of the boys could stay back to help, and we'll have some of the other men, too, if we need them. Go, hunt with your son. He needs you."

Alpin knew she was right. He left the window and turned to the door. He glanced back at Ena. "Donald has been given a kind mother." He pushed the door open. "I guess that makes up for having such a whelp of a father," he said with a smile and then walked out the door into Renton's sunshine.

"Get a big buck! I expect a feast when you return," Kenneth said to Donald, who sat high on his horse. The young boy beamed with excitement as he prepared to leave with the men to hunt.

"Bring one home that's sweet to the tongue. Leave the bitter ones for the Picts," Aiden said. He and Kenneth laughed as they jeered their little bother.

"You can eat what you want, but the antlers will be mine," Donald said, dreaming of his prize. "Father says that he'll show me how to clean a buck," he finished, his eyes aglow and his smile infectious.

"Come now ... you'll have to silence your feet and steady your shot before you can boast of such a trophy," Coric replied, mounted on his horse beside Donald.

Together the two turned and trotted their horses toward the front of their home. Ena, Nessa, and Ceana stood outside, waiting to send them off with a satchel of apples and dry meat.

Coric bent down from atop his horse and kissed Ceana. She kissed him back and then whispered in his ear.

Ena and Nessa took turns hugging Donald's waist. "Do well and listen to your father," Ena said.

"Yes, Mother. I will," Donald replied.

Kenneth and Aiden watched as their brothers said good-bye to the women. Alpin stopped his horse beside the two. "You'll need to help your mother and keep an eye on things. As we discussed, we will be gone a night or two. The other men coming to Renton won't show up for another three or four days from now. Tend to the barley and the animals. When we get back, Coric and I and the others will help get the final things ready to head north. The grain bags are nearly full and the meat in the salt house should be ready to take."

"What do we do if the others show up early?" Kenneth asked.

"Bunk them where you can—the house, the barn, the meeting hall. Put them where you need. Constantine will likely be the first to come with his men. We won't be long on the hunt."

"We'll watch things here … hope Donald gets his prize," Aiden replied.

"See you soon, Father," Kenneth added.

"Good-bye, boys." Alpin tapped the side of his horse with his heels and moved ahead to Coric and Donald. He called back, "Be good."

After the hunting party departed, Kenneth and Aiden walked into the barley field with tools in hand. For Kenneth, the chore of cutting barley didn't help much in taking his mind off Arabella. He missed her. He recalled how Coric and Ceana had said their good-byes, and he scolded himself for how he'd treated Arabella. The more he worked, the more he thought of her. He didn't speak to Aiden much. Instead, he walked through the field and cut the barley, swinging his sickle one swing at a time.

He swung the tool in a rhythmic fashion, carrying out the rehearsed motion over and over again, while images of Arabella drifted through his mind. He guessed she was helping her father—and probably scared for the days ahead.

As the sun grew high in the sky, Kenneth and Aiden stopped to rest. The heat of the late spring day was warmer than usual. The two found shelter in the shade. Aiden claimed the large shade of the barn, and Kenneth sprawled beneath the willow tree next to it. They sat facing each other with little to say. Then the silence broke.

"What are you doing?" Aiden said as he wiped the sweat from his brow.

"What do you mean, 'What am I doing?' I'm taking a break. What are you doing?" Kenneth replied.

"I'm asking, what are you doing here when Arabella is waiting for you in Cashel? Why did you send her off before we had to leave? Wisen up, Kenneth, she loves you and there's a chance you'll never see her again."

Kenneth had no desire to discuss Arabella with his brother. He was bothered enough with himself, and this was a time to rest from work, not add to it. "Don't you think I know this? What does it matter to you anyway?"

"Well, if she was my girl, I wouldn't have sent her away … and I wouldn't be hanging around here," Aiden said.

"I'm not hanging around. I'm getting work done."

"If she was in love with me, I wouldn't be letting the barley stop me from seeing her."

"What do you know about love, Aiden? You wouldn't

understand," Kenneth said, wishing his brother would shut his mouth.

"I understand enough to know that I'd be with her before I left to fight a war."

"I can't be with her now. There is too much to do here in Renton. Mother needs us, and we have to get things ready for Father."

Aiden shook his head, "You're crazy, Kenneth. Arabella is rare ... beautiful, smart, funny ... she thinks the world of you, and here you sit cutting barley, getting ready for what ... to go out and get yourself killed?"

"Don't you see it, Aiden? Can't you see it? How many times has she had someone taken from her? How many times has her heart been broken? We are going off to war, and we might not come back."

"I still don't get you, Kenneth. Is your plan to spare her the pain of a broken heart by breaking her heart now? I'm sure she's thankful for that."

"What do you want me to do? Father is going to lead an army of Scots to fight a battle against those Viking animals, and I'm supposed to leave my brothers and the others and run away with her? I'm not a coward, Aiden!" Kenneth stood and grabbed his sickle.

Aiden rose and met his brother. "Kenneth, I'm not saying to run from the fight. I'm saying that it's been clear to me since you stepped into that field that you've had one thing on your mind, or should I say, one person. Clearly, your heart is somewhere else." Aiden paused and studied his brother. "We don't know what's going to happen with you, or me, or Father, or anyone, when we step into battle. But that doesn't mean you push away the girl that has gripped your heart since you were a boy, a girl that stares at you every time you enter a room … I'm going to ask again, what are you doing here when you may have only a measure of days ahead? Why aren't you with her?"

Aiden stared at Kenneth. Then he lifted his arm and mopped his sleeve across his forehead before speaking again. "Kenneth, she's a marvel, with a heart of gold. I envy you for how she treats you, how she—"

"I hear you, Aiden!" Kenneth's anger swelled. "I want to be with her … but when I look at her, it kills me to think of breaking her heart simply because I'm letting her get too close."

"You can't control everything, Kenneth. Let it go … let it go and *live*." Aiden held his gaze, glaring into his brother's eyes. He waited for Kenneth to say something, anything.

Kenneth gave no reply.

Aiden shook his head and turned away. He grabbed his sickle and walked back into the barley field, alone.

Arabella finished her bath and robed herself in a tired cream-colored dress suitable for chores. She looked at herself in the mirror and ran a comb through her hair. Her eyes were sad. Her thoughts wanted to wander, but she wouldn't let them. She refused to think about the things she couldn't change.

Water dripped from her hair as she pulled the wooden comb through her long locks, dampening the shoulders of her dress. She placed the comb on the dresser, wiped her eyes, and sighed. Then she walked away from the mirror.

As she passed by the window in her room, she paused at

the sound of muffled voices. She stepped to the window and peered out, but the voices had come from the front of the house and she could see no one from her side view.

Arabella grabbed the wooden stool from the corner of her room and placed it below the window. As she stepped up, the stool tipped and she stumbled. After catching herself, she clumsily righted the stool and cautiously stepped up again. Slowly, she eased her head out the window, hoping to better hear the voices.

"I'm wondering if you're the cause or the cure. She's been trying to look helpful the last few days, but her smile is gone," Arabella heard her father say. "She belongs in Renton. Being with Ena and the other girls would be the best thing for her, but she insists she doesn't want to be there. My guess is this has something to do with you."

"I didn't mean to bring her to this. I thought I could protect her by keeping my distance. I don't know what's ahead, and I didn't want to hurt her any more than she's already been hurt," she heard a second voice say.

It was Kenneth. She was certain it was *his* voice.

She withdrew from the window and went to the mirror. Her dress sat crooked on her shoulders and she straightened it, then she pushed back her wet hair. Her hands trembled and an antsy feeling rushed over her.

She smiled for a moment, but then a wave of sadness hit. She fought back, refusing her fears. She wanted Kenneth to hold her again and tell her that he loved her. She wanted to feel the warmth of his chest, the steady sound of his breath, and the tight grip of his arms around her. Whether he held her or pushed her away, her heart would forever break if she lost him. *Why not hold him for a moment and take the risk, rather than never hold him again?*

She wiped her eyes and promised herself she wouldn't cry. Hurrying back to the stool, she leaned out the window a second time.

"Kenneth, you know, as well as I, the pain of loss." Arabella listened as her father spoke. "I won't come between you two. This is something beyond me, something the two of you need to work through. But Kenneth, it won't be easy ... love and war are hard enough by themselves, and they certainly don't get easier when they're mixed."

"I understand, Constantine ... but I have to try. May I speak with her?"

Arabella gasped and leapt from the stool. She checked her reflection in the mirror and tried to press down the swelling below her eyes. Then she quickly ran the comb through her hair and rushed to the door.

Kenneth stood at the door. He lifted his hand and formed a fist to knock.

The door suddenly opened and Arabella emerged. She smiled. Her nose was red.

Their eyes met. His heart sank. He knew she'd been crying. He'd never meant to hurt her. He reached for her hand. "I'm sorry," he whispered.

Arabella stepped forward, and she wrapped her arms around his waist and clutched him.

Kenneth gazed down at her. "Will you forgive me?"

She stared up at him. "Yes, Kenneth, I forgive you."

He smiled. "Then will you come with me?"

She looked confused.

"Come with me," he said. "There's something I want to show you." His request was like a small boy asking a small girl to come and see a hidden treasure.

Her brow lifted and her expression turned to curiosity. It made Kenneth blush.

"You and me," Kenneth said. "We'll take my horse … come, you have to see something. We'll be back before nightfall." He grabbed her hand and coaxed her.

She took his dare and the two hurried to his horse.

Arabella allowed her heart to hope. She allowed herself to be thrilled by the crazy boy who wanted desperately to show her his secret surprise.

They passed Constantine as they ran. "Father, may I go with Kenneth … we'll be home by evening?"

Constantine smiled. "Go, enjoy yourself. I'll see you soon," he called back.

Kenneth mounted his horse and then reached down, grabbed Arabella's arm, and lifted her up behind him.

Arabella looked back at her father and called to him, "I love you, Pa-pa."

"I love you too, darling. See you soon."

Arabella found something soothing in the steady cadence of the steed. She held fast to Kenneth and gazed at the passing landscape as the two rode along the southern rim of Loch Lomond. The loch's surface lay placid, appearing as crystal under the radiance of the setting sun. Dalriada was rich in beauty. Arabella lost herself in its adornments—its rolling hills, timid lochs, and green forests of pines, willows, and oaks.

Arabella leaned her body into Kenneth's. "Where are you taking me?"

"You'll have to wait and see ... but we have to hurry," Kenneth replied and shook the reigns of his horse to spur the animal forward.

Arabella enjoyed the moments holding Kenneth as he steered the horse across the sloping terrain.

In time, they arrived at the foot of a tall, steep hill. Looking up, it seemed like a small mountain. The hill was south of Cashel and west of Renton. Arabella had seen the hill from a distance many times in the past but never up close, much less had she climbed it. The hillside was draped with thick, lush grass, dotted here and there with rocks and boulders.

Kenneth dismounted his horse and surveyed the hillside. He craned his neck and scanned the sky. Dusk drew near, but the sun was still up—only it sat out of sight on the far side of the hill. Kenneth helped Arabella down, and then he tied his horse to a tree. Together, they began the ascent on foot.

"When do I get to see the surprise?" Arabella asked between gasps of breath as they climbed.

"You'll see soon enough," Kenneth said. He reached out his hand and grabbed her palm, helping her past a patch of loose rocks.

When the two were halfway up, they stopped beside a boulder jutting out from the sloping hillside. The boulder sat adjacent to two smaller rocks, forming a cave-like depression below their granite underbellies. Using the two smaller rocks as steps, Kenneth climbed to the top of the large rock. He turned and bent to help Arabella. "Give me your hand," he said, and he lifted her up next to him. The two sat on the large rock and rested with their feet dangling over its edge.

Kenneth pointed to the northeast and said, "That's the way we came, we should be able to see Cashel from the top, if the skies are clear enough." Kenneth looked east at the hills in the distance. "And see those two hills over there that almost come together?" He pointed again with his finger. "Renton is just beyond those hills."

Arabella looked at Kenneth and smiled. She liked how he talked to her. "Yes, I see them," she said. "It's beautiful up here."

"Okay, enough rest. We have to get going if we plan to make it to the top in time." Kenneth hopped to his feet and peered at the sky. A swath of dull gray clouds crept along the northern horizon, and thunder echoed in the distance.

Kenneth glanced at Arabella, still sitting on the rock. She seemed unsure. "The thunder sounds far away, we'll be fine," he reassured her. Then he helped Arabella to her feet, and the two continued the climb.

As they neared the summit, Kenneth paused to catch his breath. Arabella trailed just behind him. "Let's hurry," he said.

Arabella quickened her pace. On her third step, her foot clipped a buried rock, and she lost her footing. "Ahh!" she cried.

Kenneth reached for her and grabbed her waist to keep her from falling. "I can't have you getting hurt. We haven't made it to the top yet," he said. He stepped in front of Arabella with his back to her and bent down. He pointed over his shoulder to his back, "Up you go."

"You can't carry me, it's too steep."

"Hush and get on," Kenneth replied.

Holding Kenneth's shoulders, Arabella lifted herself onto his strong frame and folded her arms across his chest. Kenneth held her legs to his sides and began to climb the final stretch to the top. Taking long strides and letting his knees bend low as he stepped, he playfully bounced her on his back as he moved up the hill. Arabella laughed out loud, half thrilled and half terrified. She realized Kenneth had a way of making her feel that way.

The two reached the top. The hill had been steep and daunting, yet its plateau was level and welcoming. It flourished with thick green grass and dense patches of clover. Kenneth set Arabella on her feet, and the two sat down on the soft ground.

Arabella gazed out across the panoramic vista. It was filled with large mountains to the north and west and smaller foothills to the south and east. Together, they formed a circular valley that surrounded the hill like a castle moat.

As Arabella surveyed the view, Kenneth settled his eyes on her angelic visage. The setting sun illuminated the smooth skin of her cheeks. Her long brown hair blew in the breeze and rested on her shoulders, dancing now and again with each gust. Her shirt rippled as the wind blew, flapping and pressing against her figure. She sat peacefully, clasping her hands together around her knees while staring off into the distance. Kenneth watched her. And he treasured her.

Arabella slowly turned, ready to ask Kenneth of his

surprise. It was then that she caught him—caught him staring at her with a boyish fascination. Her lips curved into the coy smile of a young girl, and Kenneth knew he'd been caught. He lay back in the grass and laughed aloud. Arabella leaned forward and swatted his leg. "What are you looking at?" she asked, already knowing the answer.

Kenneth sat up. "I'm enjoying the view. Is there something wrong with enjoying the view?" he responded.

"No ... nothing wrong with that," she said, and her smiled widened. "The view up here is worth enjoying," she replied, noticing Kenneth's unshaven face and the dimple in his chin.

"I brought you here to see something special," he said, working to change the subject. He glanced west into the distance. "The timing has to be just right. It'll last for only a moment. I'm glad to say our time wasn't wasted ... look over there, look at that." He lifted his hand and pointed toward the shrinking sun resting on the horizon.

Arabella gazed at the sunset. The gentle beams of the western sun reflected off the bellies of the gathering clouds. The scene was like a painter's palette, strewn with fiery oranges and deep purples melded together in a sublime sight of glory. The magnificent tones burst forth and folded over the sleepy mountains of Dalriada. "It's beautiful," Arabella whispered.

Kenneth took her hand, "Arabella, that's you. You are my sunset. When you are with me, I can't stop looking at you, and when you are away, I can't stop thinking of you. You ... you captivate me."

He held her eyes in his and refused to look away. "Since the day I first saw you, you dazzled my heart. Your smile, your laugh, the silly things you say—you captivated me from the start. If I were given a single wish, I would wish that every day, for the rest of my life, I would wake to see you next to me and end each day the same. My one desire is to spend my life with you, to grow old with you."

Arabella's eyes moistened. Kenneth extended his hand and touched her cheek. "Arabella, only the Lord knows how many days we have in life … I want to give all of mine to you." Kenneth drew a deep breath and then he asked, "Would you be willing to take them? Arabella, I am asking you, will you take me … will you marry me?" His pulse raced as the words left his lips.

Arabella's heart erupted in her chest, "Kenneth … yes, I will marry you! Yes, yes, I will marry you—and I will give you every day that is mine to give."

A smile rose in Kenneth's eyes, and he slowly dipped his head and removed his gold cross necklace. Then he leaned toward Arabella, "I want you to have this … as my promise to always love and keep you." He finished his words as he placed the cross around Arabella's neck.

Arabella lunged forward and hugged him, and the two fell back into the soft clover. Wrapping his arms around her frame, Kenneth pulled her tight against his body. Arabella lifted her head and the cross of gold dangled from her neck just above Kenneth's chin. She gazed into his eyes.

Kenneth grinned. "I was sure you were going to say, 'no.'" His grin widened.

She giggled and smiled back at him.

"Arabella, I love you with my whole heart—it will always be yours."

He kissed her.

She kissed him back and held him, letting her heart sing and never wanting to let him go.

The sun set with only a remnant of light still hovering above the hills. Then a sudden crack of thunder bellowed in the darkening sky, closer than before.

"Goodness," Arabella said. "My father, he'll be looking for me. We must get back!"

"I don't want him angry at his future son-in-law," Kenneth teased. "Let's go." He stood and lifted Arabella from the grass.

They headed down the hillside, retracing their steps with what little light remained. The breeze intensified into a stiff wind and blew briskly against their backsides.

Kenneth led and Arabella, keeping hold of his hand, followed close behind. The two continued down the hill, passing the large stone where they had earlier rested. A deep roar of thunder boomed overhead, and suddenly heaven released its waterfall.

"This came from nowhere," Kenneth shouted, lifting his palms as if catching the rain. "If it continues, we'll never make it to the horse and back to Cashel in time. I think our only choice is to head back up a little and take cover under the large rock."

"Can't we make it home, if we try?"

"It's too risky to keep heading down the hill ... and we'd never make it riding the horse in the rain, not with night upon us."

Arabella nodded and the two hurried back up the hill.

They returned to the oversized rock and ducked beneath its shelter. The nook was dry and would protect them from the deluge. Though there was little room for two, it was a preferable alternative to the drenching storm.

Once settled in the nook, Arabella gave up on making it back to Cashel. They talked for a while about happy things before Arabella eventually laid her head in Kenneth's lap and closed her eyes.

Kenneth sat with his back against the rear of the rocky shelter. He covered Arabella with his arms as she quietly fell asleep to the steady pitter patter of the falling rain.

Kenneth sat in the dampness of the dark night. He could faintly see the silhouette of his bride-to-be. Each time the lightning flashed, he caught another glimpse of the beautiful young woman who had promised to be his.

How is she mine? he thought.

He felt as though he was the most fortunate man in the world. There were no thoughts in his heart at the moment, save the thought of being with her.

He ran his hand gently over her hair as she slept. He was intoxicated by her love for him—that she desired him as hers. And he marveled that she was his. His soul was the soul of a man finally content. He slowly nodded off to sleep.

And the rain fell through the night.

CHAPTER 16

MORNING CAME TO THE HILLSIDE. THE RAIN HAD turned to drizzle. The sky had begun to brighten, but the sun had yet to crest the eastern horizon.

Arabella woke first.

She opened her eyes. Kenneth's lowered face hung above her. His eyes were closed. His lips were slightly open, just enough for his steady, rhythmic breath to pass in, then out. Thoughts of how he'd come for her in Cashel slowly stirred in her mind, and how he simply had to show her the hilltop sunset. She remembered their argument days earlier, and how her heart ached when he had pushed her away. She was glad to be with him now, and she didn't mind the rain.

She lifted her head and eased up.

Kenneth stirred as she rose.

"Are you alright?" Arabella asked.

"Oh, my neck feels like it was struck by a dagger." He sat up straight, and he grimaced as he rubbed his neck and stretched. "I'm too young to ache like this," he said and chuckled. "Did you survive the night?"

"Yes, a few aches here and there, but I'll recover," she replied.

Kenneth looked out at the drizzle and then upward at the reddish-brown fungus growing on the underside of the rock that sheltered them. "Glad I didn't know that was above me all night," he said and smiled at Arabella.

She laughed at him.

"You know we've got to get you back to Cashel. Your father is probably out looking for us, worried to death about you."

Arabella scooted next to him and placed her hand on top of his. "Kenneth, last night …," Arabella said, staring at him. "I am happy to become your wife. I can't believe this is truly happening to me … to us. I want you to know how much you mean to me. You mean everything." She stared at him for a long moment and then spoke again, "I know you want to take me home, but we don't have to go back, Kenneth."

A surprised expression fell upon Kenneth's face, "Arabella … we shouldn't do this."

"All I am saying is to think of the life we have in front of us. I have dreamt of this day since I was a young girl. And now that it's here, it could all be taken away."

"Don't say that, you don't know that."

"I know that men die in battle. I know the Vikings are killers. I know that they murdered my mother and father." Arabella's eyes welled with a certain sadness. "And had Constantine not found me, I likely would have been left for dead."

"You're not making this easy."

"It's not easy, Kenneth. It's real."

"Do you think I want to leave? You know I want to be with you, Arabella. We've been through this."

"But it doesn't make sense. If you must fight, why don't

we get help? The Vikings are attacking us and they'll attack others too. Why won't your father get help from the Picts?"

"Help us? They want to own us," Kenneth said.

"They are people too, just like us. They have families—"

"They're not like us!" Kenneth exclaimed.

Arabella spun her head and folded her arms across her chest. She peered at the sprinkling rain and refused to speak.

"Hey, don't do that … I didn't mean it like that," Kenneth said.

She glared over her shoulder, staring him in the eyes. "Then how did you mean it? My mother and father were Picts, and I am a Pict … am I not like you? Am I some hideous creature?"

"That's not fair. I'm only saying that Oengus is not like us. He wants to take our people and call them his. He wants to lord over his people and ours. He doesn't care about you or me, or any Dalriadan. He wants to rule."

Arabella wiped her cheeks and gazed at Kenneth, face flushed and eyes red. She shook her head slowly back and forth, disbelieving that he couldn't understand.

"Arabella, I heard him with my own ears. He wants us to pledge our lives to him, as though he was some sort of king." Kenneth crawled from the shelter and stood, uncaring of the falling drizzle that wet his frame. He turned and gazed at Arabella, still sitting under the overhang, "I have to agree with my father. He's not going to live under a king, especially a Pict king. Men should live their lives as free men and not have to serve other men, not even a king."

"Maybe if there was a king, the Vikings would not have attacked us. But we'll never know because we won't let ourselves stop to consider such an awful thing as having a

king, all the while the Vikings come and kill us one by one."
Arabella's brow furrowed in frustration. "Kenneth ... don't
you see ... I don't want to lose you."

Kenneth rubbed his head, irritated, plowing his hands
through his damp hair. His eyes narrowed and he spoke,
"There is a problem with kings, Arabella ... they are all men.
And in the end, all men of power abuse their power. They
steal freedom from their own people, the very people they
promise to protect."

Arabella moved from beneath the rock. She stood and
walked away from Kenneth.

"Where are you going?"

"I can't breathe in there. I need some air," she replied.

"Stop, Arabella."

Arabella turned. "You're not listening. You sound like
your father. You don't always have the right answers ... have
you considered that maybe you're wrong?"

"What does that mean? Is it wrong to want to be free?"

"I'm not saying to let go of freedom. I'm saying the Picts
could help stop the Vikings without everyone getting killed."
Arabella stopped, trying to calm herself. "Maybe we could
have freedom—and remain alive to live it."

Kenneth said nothing.

She stepped toward him. "Kenneth, I heard the men in
the hall. Some considered joining the Picts. They spoke as if
that is our only chance to stop the Vikings."

"You're siding with Taran! The one who wanted to have
his way with you!"

"How dare you!" Arabella exclaimed, her face flush with
anger. "It's your father who wants his precious freedom, even
if it costs him the lives of his sons!" Arabella slowly faded to

her knees like a falling leaf. Her heart ached for Kenneth, as though she'd already lost him.

Kenneth stared at her withered frame, feeling the burn of her words—and his own.

Arabella's chin lowered to her chest, the drizzling rain hiding her tears.

Kenneth approached and hovered beside her. Then he gently took her hands and lifted her to her feet. He put his arms around her. "I'm sorry … I shouldn't have said that." He placed his hand on Arabella's chin and lifted her head. "Arabella, the things before us are what they are. Some things we cannot change. Some things we simply have to face … I love you. I will do everything under heaven to make it back to you. I promise you, Arabella … I promise."

Arabella peered deep into his eyes, desperately wanting to believe his promise.

The two held each other on the side of the hill. The drizzle retreated, but the empty clouds remained, hiding the sun from view.

Time passed before Arabella spoke. "I love you Kenneth, son of Alpin. Though my heart is large enough to have you, my hands are not strong enough to hold you. Go, and do what you must do. And may God above keep you and bring you back to me."

Kenneth nodded. "He will bring me back. I will come back to you," he vowed, and he lowered his head and kissed her.

He released his lips from hers. Then he turned and motioned for her to follow. They stepped to the large rock, and together they climbed up and faced the top of the hill.

"It was only last night that you promised to be my bride," Kenneth said.

Arabella gazed at him and tried to smile.

"Are you ready to tell your father the news?" Kenneth asked. He took a long breath. "We have to go."

"I know," Arabella said softly. "And, yes, I want to tell my father." As she spoke, her eyes moved beyond Kenneth and then grew distinctly wider. "Kenneth, what is that?" she said with a haunting sound filling her voice. She pointed over Kenneth's shoulder into the distance.

Kenneth spun on his heels. To the east, beyond the distant hills, large pillars of smoke rose into the sky. Kenneth stood motionless, staring at the billowing black clouds.

"Renton!" he yelled. He jumped from the rock and rushed down the hill. He paused and turned back, "Come, let's go! We must get to Renton!"

The two descended the hill and ran to Kenneth's horse, still tied to the tree. Kenneth reached the animal first and untied the lead. Together, the two mounted the stallion and rode for Renton.

CHAPTER 17

THE STALLION SNORTED FOR AIR AS IT GALLOPED east across the hills. The beast's muscles pulsed, its long slender legs flexing and surging with each stride. Kenneth pulled the reigns to his right, steering the animal to a shortcut through the flat terrain of the woodlands. The horse darted through the forest, cutting left and right as it weaved between the trees.

At the edge of the woods, a dead pine tree lay fallen across the path. "Hold on!" Kenneth shouted. Arabella's grip tightened as the horse leapt over the dead log and burst into the open meadow. On the far side of the meadow, a single hill stood between Kenneth and his home.

When the two reached the crest of the hill, Kenneth tugged the reigns and stopped the horse. He couldn't help but shudder at what stood before his eyes.

Orange flames snapped and popped as fire devoured the thatch-roofed house he called home. Everything was in flames—the house, the barn, the storehouse—they appeared like three giant torches, heaving their black smoke into the sky.

Kenneth shook the reigns and jabbed his heels into the

sides of his horse. Arabella squeezed herself against him as the horse leapt forward and sprinted down the hill. The smoke thickened as they drew closer, and a pungent smell of burning wood, thatch, and barley filled the air.

At the bottom of the hill, there was no sign of life except two crazed hens running wild and squawking in terror.

The stallion neared the house and Kenneth pulled the reigns and jumped to the ground. "Mother ... Aiden ... Nessa ... where are you? Aiden ... where are you?" He ran to the front of the house. A burning shutter fell and Kenneth jumped back as it toppled down in front of him.

Kenneth waved his hands to clear the smoke from his face as he stared at his home. Every inch was engulfed in flames—only the front wall was still recognizable. Fighting the fire would be futile. Nothing was left to save.

Kenneth moved forward and called out, "Mother ... Aiden—" His foot hung on something mid-stride, and he suddenly found himself falling, then his body smacked the ground. Gazing back through the haze, he spied a prostrate figure. He crawled toward it and glimpsed the charred remains of a man. The grotesque stench of the burning flesh made his stomach convulse and a surge of warm vomit filled his mouth. He heaved and spat it out.

No! he prayed.

He stood and wiped the vomit from his lips. Then he grabbed the leg of the corpse. Tugging with both hands, he pulled the charred body from the smoke.

A wave of relief came. The man's face was badly burned, but Kenneth was certain he'd never seen the man before. The blackened pants and the dark leather boots were not typical of Scots.

Kenneth bent and studied the man, wondering who the hell he was and why he was there. Then the wind shifted to his backside and the swirling smoke lifted. There on the ground, ten feet from his home, were two more bodies lying dead. They were of similar dress, and though they were not burned like the first man, they were covered in blood. One had a cut running from his chest to his waist. The other had a large wet circle of red staining his shirt directly in the center of his belly.

Kenneth stood over the men, surveying their corpses. He released a horrific roar, "AAAGGGHHH!" Then he kicked the body nearest him and shouted at the man, "What do you want!"

Arabella ran to the front of the house. Seeing Kenneth standing over the dead men, she froze and felt as though she were trapped in a nightmare.

Kenneth turned from the house and sprinted to the barn. He circled the burning building, not sure of what he was looking for. As he approached the backside of the barn, he noticed a wadded garment lying beside the well. Kenneth slowly stepped toward the garment, grabbed it, and held it chest-high. He recognized it immediately—Nessa's shawl.

Kenneth inspected the garment and found multiple splotches of blood, but no holes or cuts. He tried to envision what must have happened, wondering why the shawl was sitting there, yet not certain he wanted an answer. He prayed his sister wasn't hurt.

As Kenneth lowered the shawl, his eyes fell to the well and a chill ran down his spine. He hesitated, wanting to turn and walk away, to run away, but he resisted the impulse and stepped forward. Slowly, he peered over the wall of the well and down into its dark, eerie shaft. There, he found only a black placid pool of still water. He exhaled and pushed away. Then he dropped the shawl and let it fall to the ground at his feet.

His family had to be somewhere. He glanced at the burning barn and then scanned the field. From the corner of his eye, he noticed something in the grass twenty feet from where he stood. He hustled toward the object and stopped in his tracks, surprised at what he found—Aiden's sword.

He picked up the weapon. Its blade was dirty and dripped red, as if the sword had been bathed in blood.

Kenneth seethed in anger.

He breathed hard, in and out, trying to think. *Aiden and Nessa must have been outside when the fight began. But where are they now? Mother … where was she when the men struck? Would she have been in the house when the fire was set?* He tried to dismiss the awful thought.

His mind twisted with images of others—his father, and Coric, and the men. *Had they seen the smoke? Could they even see it from where they were?*

Arabella rushed to Kenneth as he stood in his stupor holding Aiden's sword. "Kenneth, I've found no one! Do you know where they are, did they go somewhere?"

"No, they were here when I left. I've seen no sign of my mother … Aiden and Nessa must have struggled with these men. I don't know if they escaped, or were taken, or worse. I have to find them!"

"Who were the men on the ground?"

"I don't know. They don't appear to be Picts. No paint. I can only guess they're Vikings."

"Oh, God, what's happening!"

"I don't know, Arabella. I don't know what's happening!"
Kenneth cursed in rage and drove his brother's sword into
the ground. He stared at his hands, they were covered in
blood. He wiped his palms on his sleeves, pleading with his
conscience that the blood was not Aiden's.

Kenneth turned toward Renton. Smoke continued to fill
the sky above the village. Then he jerked his head and peered
across the field at the small home tucked behind a grove of
cedar trees. It was the home Coric had built for him and
Ceana. No smoke—a promising sign.

Kenneth grabbed Arabella's hand, "I'm taking the horse
and going to Renton. My guess is Aiden went there to help.
Go to Ceana's and check on her, I'll return when—"

"I'm not leaving you, Kenneth," Arabella protested.

"You have to check on Ceana, and I have to see if Aiden
needs me! Renton is burning. I don't have time!"

"Kenneth, I'm going with you!"

He shook his head in frustration. "Then we must leave
now." He mounted his horse and pulled Arabella up behind
him. As they departed, he steered the animal in the direction
of Aiden's sword. Nearing the weapon, he reached low and
grabbed it by the handle without breaking stride. "We may
need this."

Kenneth spurred the horse north toward Renton. His
heart thumped in his chest as guilt and anger tore at his
insides. "I have a bad feeling if Aiden left his sword," he
muttered to himself.

"When we get to Renton, I don't know what we'll find,"
Kenneth said, not turning his eyes from the path they rode.
"I want you to stay on the horse until I know the others

are alright." He turned in his saddle to check on Arabella and saw tears streaming down her cheeks. She nodded and tightened her arms around his waist as the horse galloped forward.

The small town came into sight—the image was surreal. Tall tongues of fire ascended upward like an over-stoked furnace. Several of Renton's buildings were ablaze and quickly fading, while others had already submitted to the inferno and now stood like charred wooden tombs. The meeting hall, the tavern, and the blacksmith shop choked out chimneys of thick black smoke from their windows and doorways. The thirsty flames lapped up the thatch roofs, leaving the air rife with a thick odor of burning wood.

As they drew closer, Kenneth's eyes caught the movement of figures ambling in disarray through the smoky street ahead. Kenneth snapped his reigns and urged his horse toward the pitiful, blazing village.

They entered Renton from the south. Buildings lay crumbled on either side of the path as fire sucked the life from their wooden forms.

Renton was a nightmarish chaos. Several older women stood weeping as if entranced in some terror-induced spell. Others were running about, tending the wounded and sobbing over the dead. An older man, Renton's tanner, sat on the side of the path holding one arm and rocking back and forth. He looked up at Kenneth in a listless daze, wearing a long smudge of soot smeared across his forehead and a once white beard now black and red. The lifeless bodies lying among the rubble numbered young and old. They were the people of Renton, Kenneth's people.

The struggle was fresh and raw. Within a single day, Kenneth had left a town of life and had returned to an aftermath of death. The battle had found Renton—the enemy had found Renton.

Kenneth leapt from his horse and drew the sword that Aiden had lost. "Arabella, don't get off," he demanded, this time unwilling to take 'no' for an answer. Gripping the sword tightly in both hands, he stepped forward, swiveling his head and straining to see through the smoke, uncertain of whom he'd find. His movements were deliberate and cautious as he advanced in front of the steed carrying Arabella.

Upon reaching the body of a fallen Scot, Kenneth paused and then stepped over it, but not before glancing down at the figure and grimacing at the carnage. He swallowed and pushed ahead. He had to move forward, he had to be ready to fight. He had trained for this a thousand times with his father and brothers, and he remembered his father's words, "If you ever pick up a sword to fight, be prepared to use it—prepared not just to swing, but to kill."

Kenneth moved through the village, advancing toward the blacksmith shop as it popped with fire. His sword stirred in his hands. Suddenly, a figure moved ahead, stumbling into the street near a fallen stack of wooden barrels. The man lifted his head and stared at Kenneth with a bewildered expression on his face.

"Feragus," Kenneth uttered and he ran to the blacksmith. "What happened here? Feragus, what happened!"

The blacksmith sat in shock and said nothing.

Kenneth lowered his sword and shook the blacksmith, "Feragus!"

Feragus snapped from his fog. "Kenneth, my God ... they were everywhere ... all at once," he said, his voice faint and dry. His eyes wobbled, and his head bobbed back and forth as if the muscles in his neck had been severed. Then his eyes blinked rapidly and closed.

"Feragus," Kenneth shouted.

Feragus moaned.

Kenneth called to Arabella, "He needs help!"

Arabella sat on the horse staring back at Kenneth, lost in a trance. Cacophony reigned—fires crackled, women shouted. Panic seized Arabella. *What's happening?* She instantly broke from her trance, pointed, and screamed, "Kenneth!"

Kenneth turned to see a large man emerging from the supply house, one of the few buildings still standing. The man carried an overstuffed sack on his shoulder and was moving awkwardly, limping toward a horse not far away. The man's clothes were similar to those of the men lying dead at Kenneth's home, but this man also boasted a heavy metal helmet that extended over the top half of his face, leaving only his mouth and beard exposed. Formed into the metal lid were two thin slits for the eyes, while a pair of sharpened horns protruded from the top of the helmet. Trampling through the smoke and flames, the man appeared as the Devil himself, stalking the burning streets of Renton.

When the invader heard Arabella scream, he lifted his head and surveyed the street. His movement stopped when he spotted Kenneth. Instantly, the man hurled his load to the ground and drew a long black sword from a sheath tied to his back. Then he released a deep guttural cry and rushed toward Kenneth, his limp evidently cured by a quick dose of adrenaline.

Kenneth tensed, drew a deep breath, and shifted his weight. For a moment Kenneth paused, then his fingers tightened around his sword and he leapt forward to meet the man.

The Viking closed the gap in a blink and swung his black blade upward before slicing it down swiftly upon Kenneth.

Clank! Metal struck metal, and the clashing swords resonated in a cold, steely echo.

The vibration of the colliding blades stung Kenneth's hands. Kenneth twisted his wrist to avoid the blow and pushed hard, forcing the man's sword to the side. Then Kenneth leaned and shifted left to regain his footing.

The Viking didn't hesitate. He recoiled, spun, and swung his sword a second time, reaching to strike Kenneth's midsection.

Kenneth jumped and dodged the blade. The man repeated his onslaught, swinging his weapon back and forth, hungry for flesh.

Kenneth retreated backwards with each attacking swing until his backside struck the wooden post of a shop awning. He was pinned, wedged between the post and his enemy.

There, the man lingered a moment and reassessed his prey. He peered through the slits of his helmet, moving his head ever so slightly from side to side. Then he stared straight at Kenneth. Kenneth could feel his heart race as he caught the man's gaze through the thin slits—two round orbs, glowing like the eyes of a wolf on a dark summer night. The man swung his sword. The sharp edge came fast toward

Kenneth's neck. Kenneth ducked and the blade sunk deep into the soft pine post. The bitter wood held tight, gripping the angry steel.

Kenneth sprung upward. He lifted his foot and shoved it into the man's kneecap. The joint snapped and buckled. The man dropped to one knee, and his broken leg folded lame to one side. As the man lifted his head, Kenneth struck his bearded chin with the butt of his sword. The Viking's jaw cracked, and his head snapped back. The man groaned and struggled to right himself. It was then that Kenneth buried his blade into the man's chest.

The Viking shuttered and tumbled backwards to the ground. Kenneth removed his sword and stepped forward, looming over his adversary. He stared down at the man, at his fallen body, at his cruel metal helmet. Blood slowly pooled on the man's lips, and then a stream trickled from the side of his mouth down into the thick hair covering his cheek.

Kenneth nudged the Viking with his foot. The man's lifeless body gave no response. He was dead. Kenneth had never killed a man before. His father had told him that such a day would likely come. That day had arrived, but it wasn't as glorious as Kenneth had once thought. Rage had been his fire. Defense had been his cause. *God forgive me*, the words echoed in Kenneth's mind.

"No! Stop!"

The shrilling screams rattled Kenneth's ears. He spun. It was Arabella. Two Vikings had found her and were circling her horse like a pair of crazed hounds. One was grabbing her leg and trying to dislodge her from her horse. The man was short and stocky, built like a stump with tree limb arms. The second man, taller than the first and brandishing a crossbow, left his partner and fronted the horse and grabbed its reigns. As he wrapped the straps around his hand, Arabella kicked the animal and the beast thrashed wildly. The tall Viking threw his crossbow to the ground and grasped the reigns with both hands while his partner moved to close on Arabella.

Kenneth stood motionless, staring at the invaders. The call to defend, the call to protect, was now upon him. The fight had come. Blood and death had come. There was no other choice. Kenneth settled in his heart that he would fight. It would end in life or in death, but he had to fight—and on this day, he would give all he had to give.

Kenneth tightened his grip on his sword and took a step forward. An angry scream erupted from his throat, "Aaaahhh!" His slow steps suddenly turned into a madman's rush, and he stormed forward with reckless abandon.

The shorter man pivoted and squared himself.

Kenneth lifted his sword aloft and swirled it down and around, making his cut from the side rather than striking the enemy's helmeted head from above.

The Viking lunged to evade the blow.

Kenneth twisted, cutting nothing but air. He righted himself and faced his opponent, taking a moment to resize the man.

A raspy metal sound shrieked through the air as the Viking drew a long, wide dagger with sharp jagged teeth lining its back edge. The tool was capable of tearing flesh and grinding bone. The man flicked the weapon back and forth in his hand, taunting Kenneth.

Kenneth broke and swung his sword, and the Viking

lifted his dagger against Kenneth's oncoming blade. Kenneth delivered a bruising blow, yet the Viking blocked the blade and held firm. Again, Kenneth swung and rammed his sword against the Viking's dagger, this time knocking the weapon from the man's hands.

Empty-handed, the man leapt at Kenneth. He planted his shoulder into Kenneth's waist and drove him backward. The two stumbled several steps before tangling their legs and falling. Kenneth's sword flung from his grip as he hit the ground. Then his lungs emptied when the Viking landed on top of him. The blow was devastating. The man's helmet had thumped against Kenneth's brow when the two collided to the earth, leaving a deep splinter of pain shooting through Kenneth's skull and a one-inch gash above his left eyebrow. Kenneth shook his head to subdue the pain, but the melee resumed. The two wrestled back and forth before Kenneth found his bearings and spun the Viking. Then Kenneth positioned himself on the man's backside and he wrapped his arm around the man's neck and tightened on his throat. It felt to Kenneth as if he were squeezing the trunk of a willow tree. Kenneth drew his grip tighter and pressed his fingers deeper into the man's neck while peddling with his legs to right himself and lift from the ground.

Once upright and sitting on the man, Kenneth released his chokehold, spun the stocky man beneath him, and threw three swift punches to the man's face. His last punch struck the man square in the nose, and a sickly, wet popping sound confirmed the Viking's bludgeoned nose was broken.

Suddenly, from nowhere, Kenneth's legs were being pulled. The second Viking was dragging him, stopping Kenneth before he could finish his kill. Kenneth bucked and kicked to free himself. The stocky Viking remained sprawled on the ground, coughing and gasping for breath, with blood spewing from the two holes that were once the base of his nostrils. The wounded Viking wheezed a few deep breaths and lightly touched his swelling nose to assess the break.

After the tall Viking had dragged Kenneth a dozen paces, the man lifted Kenneth's legs into the air and pushed him sideways, spinning Kenneth on the ground. Immediately, the man began kicking Kenneth, targeting his ribs. Kenneth rolled with each kick, struggling to avoid the blows. After several kicks, Kenneth grabbed the Viking's foot and twisted it sharply, attempting to break the man's ankle. The man yelped in pain and he lost his balance and stumbled sideways, ankle intact.

Kenneth jumped to his feet. The tall Viking spun to face him and Kenneth landed an uppercut to the man's jaw. He followed with two more jabs to the abdomen. The man doubled over and held his belly, laboring to recover. Kenneth glanced about, hunting for his sword. He spotted the stocky Viking's dagger lying in the path and dashed toward the weapon.

When Kenneth reached the dagger, he scooped it up and clutched its thick rugged handle in his palm. Instantly, the tall man appeared from behind and wrapped his arms around Kenneth's torso. The man's muscular limbs steadily tightened like a noose, binding Kenneth and crushing him as though he were wedged in a vice.

Kenneth, struggling to breathe, realized he had to break free—quickly break free. Or else it would be over. But it couldn't be over. Not here. Not now. A fury surfaced from deep within. Enraged with determination, Kenneth dipped his chin to his chest and thrust his head backward violently with every shred of force he could muster. The impact nearly cracked both their skulls. When his head connected with the Viking's chin, he heard the sound of the man's teeth shatter.

Lights flashed in bright explosions before Kenneth's eyes. He convulsed in pain.

The big man released his hold and his hands flailed upward to his ruined mouth. Kenneth gripped his newfound dagger with both palms and thrust the large blade backward, catching the oversized Viking in the midsection. Lowering his wrist, Kenneth gave the blade a second shove and plunged it farther into the cavity of the man's chest. Finished, he yanked the handle and ripped the steel from the Viking's body. The man stooped over and fell to the ground, the fog of death misting in his eyes.

Kenneth stumbled away, dizzy, his head throbbing in pain. He touched his scalp and felt a sharp edge on the back of his skull where he had struck the Viking. He dug with his fingers and removed a small object and held it in his palm. He then realized he was holding the broken tooth of the tall man.

A commotion stirred behind Kenneth—the rustling of a horse. Still in a daze, Kenneth could hardly perceive his surroundings. He turned and peered toward the north path out of Renton. Feragus was standing hunched in the middle of the path with buildings burning on either side of him, and he was waving a piece of wood with a large red flame. And then Kenneth saw the horse—and its two riders. "Arabella," her name crept from his lips.

The stocky Viking riding the horse cursed the blacksmith as he slowed the animal. He tightened his grip around his female captive and combed the area for another route of escape. As the Viking rider formed a new plan, the frightened horse below pranced in anxiety, troubled by the crazed blacksmith and his oscillating torch. The Viking yelled and slapped the spooked animal. Then the man pulled Arabella against his chest and yanked the reigns and turned the horse east.

Kenneth watched as the horse moved forward. Horror seized him—the Viking was leaving Renton with the woman he loved.

BOOM!

Kenneth leapt forward as a building crashed down behind him. Embers from the fallen structure brushed his backside. The blacksmith shop had given way to the fire's hot flames, spewing cinders and ash high into the air as the building crumpled. Within moments, the toppled building settled and lay dead, and a black billow of smoke emerged to broadcast its demise.

Kenneth regained his wits and looked up to find the fleeing horse. Yet now, the animal was heading straight for him. The Viking's intent was singular—he would trample Kenneth and end the fight.

No time remained.

Kenneth jumped to the side to evade the massive beast. He landed on his side with a thud and yelped when he hit the ground, nearly impaling himself on a pointed object that jabbed his backside.

The Viking never looked back after missing his prey, but kept the horse moving headlong on the path out of Renton.

Kenneth reached behind him and grasped the rigid object he had landed on—the tall Viking's crossbow. He gripped the handle and lifted the weapon. Pulling back the draw, he found his enemy's backside in the crossbow's sights.

He pressed the trigger and the arrow flew.

The slender shaft soared toward its mark and lodged into the stocky Viking's spine. The man froze, slumped, and slowly slid off the horse into a motionless heap on the path, leaving Arabella on the beast, upright and now alone.

Kenneth lowered the bow and took a deep breath. Then he lifted to his feet and rubbed a mixture of grime and blood from the side of his face.

In the distance, Arabella slowed the horse and turned the animal.

Exhausted, Kenneth stood at the edge of Renton staring at Arabella as the horse approached. Then he peered over his shoulder at the town of his youth, its burning structures slowly relinquishing their last gasps of life. The soulless bodies of those he had called friends lay strewn across the dirty streets. He glimpsed his brother's bloody sword lying in the middle of the path, the path that crossed through the broken heart of Renton.

Kenneth turned back to Arabella, his head and heart wrestling over the woman he loved. The crash of another burning building echoed behind him. Arabella's horse paused. Kenneth gazed at Arabella in a stupor. He stood motionless as though he were a statue covered in flesh. She was close enough that he could see her crying, yet far enough that she was safe.

He shook his head slowly, telling her *no*—he would not let the woman he treasured come any closer. "Go ... you must go! Tell your father of the slaughter of Renton!"

"Kenneth, if I go, then come with me!"

"No Arabella, I cannot … I must find Aiden and the others," he called back to her.

"Kenneth, I will stay with you. We can wait for your father and the others to return." Her horse danced below her as she spoke, terrified by the inferno raging in the distance.

"Arabella, you can't stay, you must go. You must go now!" Kenneth pulled a piece of burning wood from the nearby rubble. He held it low in his hand. His brow furrowed in sorrow. His jaw tightened in anguish. "I love you, Arabella. My heart will always be yours! I will fight until the Lord carries me home to you!"

Kenneth drew back his arm and hurled the burning wood at the horse, yelling at the beast, "Yahh!"

The horse turned and jerked to separate himself from the miserable man. Yet Arabella's eyes held to Kenneth, not allowing him to leave her sight.

Kenneth shouted again, "Go! Go to Cashel and wait for me … I will come for you!" Then he turned and ran into Renton's flames.

Arabella watched as Kenneth's silhouette disappeared into the dark gray smoke, "Kenneth!"

The sun that had radiated so richly upon her and her betrothed at last dusk now stood high overhead, crowning the destruction of Renton. Yet with all its brilliance, it could not break through the smoky haze that hid the man she loved.

CHAPTER 18

A DEEP MOAN STRUCK KENNETH'S EARS AS HE pressed through the thick smoke engulfing Renton. The sound curdled his blood, not because the sound was loud, but because it was awful. He could hardly see beyond his own steps, yet could hear well enough to know that someone was in agony. Kenneth stepped forward.

The path was familiar to him. It was Renton's path to the abbey. He had walked it before, for weddings and burials. As Kenneth moved ahead, the juxtaposition of the joy of Coric's wedding and the sorrow of Drostan's burial now held an eerie irony. His feelings were no longer of joy or sorrow, but anger—raw, palpable anger.

Another groan sounded.

Kenneth headed straight along the path to the abbey. To his right lay the burning remains of the tanner's shop. To his left stood the supply shop, one of the few buildings still standing. Renton's abbey was not far away. Kenneth eased forward, watching and listening, wondering if at any moment a Viking would burst from the smoke in ambush.

Kenneth righted himself and drew a deep breath. He gazed at the ruins of the town, and then his eyes eased downward to the ground. And there it was. Lying at his feet sat a gold cross, his gold cross. The same cross he'd placed around Arabella's neck as a promise of marriage. As he bent and lifted the necklace, he felt his anger growing like a monster inside him. He was angry—angry at himself for letting the Viking animals destroy his home and village, and for letting them manhandle his beloved Arabella. "I should have never let this happen … I should have never let them touch you, Arabella," he whispered to himself. He tied the cross around his neck and realized how much he already missed her. It was then he vowed that he would return to her and place it upon her neck once again.

Another groan woke him from his mesmerized trance. He paced forward and then stopped. Through the haze he surveyed the path in front of him, and his eyes found the gloomy visage of the abbey. The haze slowly cleared, and there in the grass, not ten paces from the humble structure, lay a man sprawled on his back. He hurried forward. It was Gilchrist.

A long gash, likely from the blade of a sword, had opened the cleric's belly. Kenneth scanned the cleric's frame, looking for other wounds. Seeing none, he knelt in the stained red grass beside Gilchrist.

Gilchrist released another agonizing groan. The laceration in his belly was deep enough to expose his entrails. His head tossed side to side, then his eyes clenched shut. Barring a miracle, his breaths were numbered.

Kenneth grabbed the cleric by the shoulders and shook him, "Gilchrist, it's me, Kenneth."

Gilchrist's eyes opened, his breathing intensified. Spittle flew from his lips as he exhaled several breaths in rapid rhythm. He stared into the sky, gazing past Kenneth as if he was invisible.

"Gilchrist, can you hear me?" Kenneth shook him again. "Say something!"

The cleric gave no response.

"Gilchrist!" Kenneth patted his cheek firmly.

Gilchrist snapped from his stupor. His eyes focused on Kenneth, his pupils combing over his face. His stare held an ominous gaze, like thick dark clouds hovering and stirring, yet his lips released no words, no sounds, not even a whisper. It was though he lay trapped in his body with no ability to speak.

Kenneth lifted Gilchrist's head and pushed away the cleric's sweat-soaked bangs from his brow.

Then a moan spilled from the clergyman's throat. His breaths came in an erratic, panicked pattern. He glanced down at his open belly and then back at Kenneth. A moment passed, and Gilchrist repeated the motion again with his eyes, looking down and then back at Kenneth.

"What are you trying to say? I don't understand!"

Kenneth eyed Gilchrist's stomach and glimpsed the cleric's hand, twitching above his waist and pointing with a crumpled finger. Turning sideways, Kenneth peered over his shoulder in the direction the cleric was pointing.

"The path north?"

Gilchrist's eyes widened. He panted, struggling in pain and wheezing as he breathed.

"Are you saying north? Did the men who did this head north?" Kenneth asked in a loud voice as if the cleric were deaf. "Did they take anyone with them, Gilchrist?"

A small curl formed on the edge of the cleric's mouth.

"Yes, north, they went north. Did they take Aiden, Nessa, or Mother?"

Gilchrist's mouth opened and he tried to speak, "Nes—"

His breathing slowed and his lips fell straight.

"Gilchrist!" Kenneth shook the cleric. "Gilchrist!"

Gilchrist blinked slowly, and his gaze settled on the gold cross hanging from Kenneth's neck. Then his ice blue eyes widened and froze in place like molten glass dipped in water. A frigid chill rushed down Kenneth's backside.

Alas, the cleric's breathing relaxed. His eyes slowly shut, and he let go.

Kenneth's horse blistered across the wet earth. The beast carried the angry Scot down the muddy trail tracing the northwest bank of Loch Lomond, a trail littered with hoofprints and wheel tracks.

From the prints, Kenneth estimated the Vikings numbered well above a hundred. He wondered if he could catch them—and what he'd do if he did. With every hill he crested, his heart pounded and his stomach turned, wanting—and not wanting—to see the Vikings ahead of him.

If he was fortunate, they would stop to rest or camp. Maybe he would see smoke from their fires. Yet with the sun just reaching noon, he figured the Viking raiders would not be camping soon. He pushed the horse forward, thankful he'd found the animal abandoned behind the abbey.

As Kenneth rode, he couldn't suppress the myriad thoughts that screamed in his head. *Arabella sitting alone on the horse—he couldn't take her with him. His home burned, destroyed. His mother and the others, where were they? His father, would he return in time to help? Gilchrist, staring at him while death came and stole him away. Aiden, and the guilt of leaving his younger brother to face the Vikings alone.* Yet, in all this, he knew he had to push on. He had to find his family.

The ground moved quickly beneath Kenneth. The green pines of Dalriada surrounded either side of the path north, yet they were lost from view. Kenneth remained absorbed in a world all his own. *Was this what it was like to be a man, to be a warrior?* He had seen his father heed the call and face battle, but he himself had never embarked upon the dreadful quest. His father had—Drostan had.

Kenneth's thoughts continued to churn. *Vikings. How many? How far ahead would they be? They couldn't be too far. Carrying captives would surely slow them—and Aiden, he wouldn't go easy, he would fight every step of the way.* The thought made Kenneth smirk. But his smirk quickly faded as he wondered if Aiden had gone at all.

The old hermit found the spot he'd been looking for. The large rock crag on the hillside would hide him from view and veil him from any riders heading north. And the thirty yards separating him from the trail was still well within the range of his old crossbow.

The trail running north and south along the western rim of Loch Lomond boasted dense patches of green pines. In most areas along the path, the pines grew nearly on top of one another, but here the pines thinned, some with long gaps stretching between them.

The old hermit found an opening in the pines that suited him—a place where he could hide with a gap large enough to spy passing riders.

The man had walked the trail a thousand times over the past forty years. And this was the spot he wanted. Through the opening in the row of pines, he could see the trail south for nearly fifty yards. To the north, he could see the trail for another ten yards before the pines thickened again and the trail curved out of sight. Once a rider passed and made the turn, the old man would become invisible in his rock crag. But it was the fifty yards to the south that gave him the line of sight he needed.

The old man rested his crossbow against his knee, loaded it, and leaned back against the rocks. Then he waited. He had nowhere to go and nothing to lose. He figured they would be back this way, though he wasn't sure when. He was willing to wait.

Time passed, and then the sound came. A low rumble echoed from the south. The thundering growl steadily grew to a roar that sounded something like a stampede of cattle.

The hermit sat, watching motionless from the rocks.

The first riders appeared from the south, donned with helmets and shields, axes and swords. He watched them come and let them pass. Dozens more followed. Occasionally, their numbers thinned with carts interspersed among the riders. The carts—and their human cargo—were surrounded and guarded by Viking horsemen.

The riders and their horned helmets were an ominous

sight. Their aura alone would terrify a rational man. But the old man was beyond rational. He had seen the horned savages in his younger days. The memory of their deadly raids years prior still crept among the dark places of his mind. They had taken from him—and now, he would take from them.

He wasn't frightened by his enemy, but seeing the carts and the people inside sickened his stomach. Over a dozen captives were locked within each cart. Wooden posts, mounted a foot apart, extended up the sides of the carts, forming cages, veritable wheeled prisons. The women inside held one another, and most were crying. The men sat lifeless, covered in dirt and soot. Their hair was mangy and disheveled. They stared off into nowhere with a glazed look on their faces, seemingly resigned to some unspoken doom.

Another cart passed the clearing in the pines, its captives weeping, wounded, and broken. The old man paused when he saw two younger Scots in the cart, young men holding on for their lives. One suffered severe burns on his shoulder and neck, and his head bobbed about as if fading in and out of consciousness. The other had a bloody wound along his ribs on his right side. A young woman was tending his injury, pressing a cloth against the wound to stop the bleeding.

Several minutes passed, and still the stream of Vikings continued. The old man watched in silence as they rode by. Biding his time, he waited. The army of riders eventually thinned and the old man prepared himself. The last of the marauders would be passing soon.

No more carts appeared. There had been three in total. The final riders rode in a detached line strung along the opening in the pines. There were five that trailed the pack, their horses spanning the fifty-yard gap.

The old hermit lifted his crossbow and let his fingers wander to find their grip. His index finger nestled against the trigger. Two of the five riders reached the end of the gap in the trees and vanished around the curved trail. Only three remained in sight.

The man lifted his bow and aimed the weapon at the last rider. He steadied his breathing. Calm, breathing—the hermit paused.

Shouts from more horsemen came from the south end of the path. The old man glanced to his right and counted two additional riders. He slowly moved the bow to the rider in the rear.

Seconds passed. The three front riders disappeared and the two trailing riders approached.

The hermit drew a deep breath. He steadied his hands and aimed his sights. The riders were separated by roughly twenty feet. He locked on the rear rider. His calloused finger slowly pressed through the trigger in a calculated, fluid motion. The bow neither strayed nor bucked when it snapped its cord forward and released its arrow. With the bow sights tracking a foot ahead of the rider, the timing of the two forward-moving objects were set on a collision course. The arrow soared on its trajectory straight and true.

Thunk.

The silent shaft came to a sudden stop in the neck of the Viking rider. The arrow sunk deep, piercing the man's throat.

The horned rider slid from his horse. His hands and arms twisted in the reigns, entangling him and knotting him to his horse. The horse jerked sideways to fight the tugging weight, and then slowed and wandered past the opening in the pines, dragging its rider out of sight.

The hermit grinned and cursed with exuberance. He rose to his feet and eyed the path, loitering in his rocky crag and wondering if the other riders would detect the slain man and return.

He strained to listen. He heard nothing.

He waited, guessing how far the horse may have carried on, dragging the man—

Hoofbeats.

The old man squatted in his crag. His heart pulsed. A thick blue vein running along his temple thumped with the beat of his heart. The salty sweat that beaded on his brow dripped into his eyes with a burn. He remained motionless, unflinching, cloaked in his hiding spot.

The hoofbeats drew closer.

The hermit loaded an arrow.

The sound grew from the south.

The old man lifted his bow.

The drumming hoofbeats approached.

A single trailing rider burst into the opening of the pines. Squaring his aim, the old man tracked the horseman and held him fixed in his sights. He would get two this day.

The hermit steadied himself. His finger found the trigger of the crossbow and began its rehearsed progression. As he pushed the bow's lever he flinched in shock—*a kilt, no helmet, a Scot!*

The arrow was gone.

The iron-tipped shaft drove hard into the shoulder of the galloping horse. The animal's front leg buckled and the creature crashed to the ground, hurling its rider sideways.

The rider struck the ground with a hard thump and tumbled several times on the dirt path, his limbs and torso flailing with each tumble.

The old man gasped and hurried from the rocks toward the path.

Lying on his side, Kenneth opened his eyes and gulped for breath. His impact with the ground had hit like a hammer against his skull. Confusion overwhelmed him. He sat up and shook his head to clear his vision. He staggered to his feet and fumbled for his sword. He tried to step but fell to his knees. Struggling, he lifted to his feet and craned his head to the left and right, searching for the enemy, but his eyes failed under the strands of disparate sunlight piercing through the towering pine branches.

For a moment his ears became his eyes. He heard the sound of hurried footsteps, and he turned toward a blurry figure. It was a man, thirty paces from him. The man was coming quickly and was holding something at his side. Kenneth caught the glow of the man's white hair beaming in the sun's bright rays.

Kenneth stood erect and lifted his sword. The man halted. Kenneth's vision began to clear, and he saw a crossbow in the man's hand.

"Your next arrow better kill me, old man!" Kenneth shouted.

The hermit surveyed Kenneth. It was clear the young Scot was desperate and angry. He dropped his bow and extended his hands. "Son, I mean no harm."

"Do you count me a fool? Why the hell did you try to

kill me?" Kenneth leveled his sword. It twitched in his grip as he pointed it at the man.

The hermit studied Kenneth, piecing clues together one by one. "You were going after the Vikings, yes?" the old man stated. "Forgive me, son. I thought you were one of them."

"They came this way. I know they did. I've tracked them and I aim to kill them, so either kill me or stay out of my way!"

"There's too many for one man, son. You might kill a few, but you'll die before you get'em all."

"They have my family. What do you expect me to do? Why did you stop me!" Kenneth made no attempt to control himself.

"I want'em dead too, son. I was trying to kill'em myself until you came through here. Fortunate for you, you don't wear a horned helmet. I tried to stop, but the arrow flew ... I'm sorry about your horse." The old man glanced at the sprawling beast. The animal wouldn't survive.

"What have you done—I need that horse!" Kenneth shouted. He panicked, realizing he was losing precious time—time he didn't have. "I've got to go after them!"

"Son, if you go after those Vikings in the condition you're in, they'll kill you in an instant. You won't help anyone. Let me give you some food and water. You need to rest a bit and get your wits about you," the man said, still keeping his distance from Kenneth.

Kenneth wiped his mouth with his wrist. He lowered his arm, and a long smudge of red lay smeared across the back of his hand. He didn't feel the blood resurface on his numb lip.

"When was the last time you ate or slept? Come with me. At least rest for a while. I'll see if I can find you some food and water ... and a horse."

﹫

The sun sat halfway between noon and dusk over Dalriada.

Coric and Donald led the group, riding side by side as they headed back to Renton. The deer they pulled on the wooden sled would be a welcome sight for those at home. The extra meat would be needed for the long trip north.

The two brothers trotted ahead and teased one another while the others rode behind. Donald insisted his deer was larger than any of the three that Coric had killed. Coric disputed the matter and wouldn't concede an inch to his little brother.

"One hill to go," Alpin called out to his sons and then again to the men behind him. Laise, the bowman from Milton, waved his hand from the rear of the line, signaling he'd heard.

"We should have the ladies bake some bread for our feast. Tonight we will eat like kings," Coric said, and cheers erupted from the men as his horse crested the hill behind Donald's.

"Father!" Donald shouted.

Coric's eyes shot up, and he stared beyond the hill at the ruins of his home. The sight struck him like a crashing wave. He ripped his dagger from his belt, turned in his saddle, and slashed the straps of his deer sled. Then he plunged his heels into his horse and the beast rushed forward.

Coric arrived first and jumped from his horse. The others of the hunting party galloped past. He paid them no attention. A heap of ash and blackened wood were all that remained of his boyhood home. The barn no longer stood, but sat as a pile of embers with a thin trail of white smoke emanating from its charred remains. The wooden fence of the sheep pen was nearly destroyed, and no sheep were in sight. The stone well, alone, had survived the raid.

Coric hurried to the front of what had been his family's home. There he found the bodies of three dead Vikings baking under the midafternoon sun. "Father, come see this!" Coric stared at the bodies, and a cascade of thoughts rushed through his mind. He spun, looking for his small home in the distance, afraid of what he might see. Across the field stood the humble dwelling he'd built for Ceana and himself. It peeked out from the distant tree line, unharmed.

"Go see if she's there, Coric."

Coric broke from his gaze and turned to his father, who now stood over the three dead bodies.

"Someone will pay for this," Alpin muttered, then he stooped to inspect the bodies. He peered up at Coric. "Go, check on Ceana. See if your mother and the others are there. I need to speak to Donald. We'll be right behind you."

Coric mounted his horse and raced across the field. A multitude of fears weaved through his mind. He prayed that Ceana was there—alive. "And God, by your grace, may Mother and the others be there, too," he uttered.

Laise caught Coric and rode beside him across the field to the small home.

The door to the house flung open, and Ceana ran out, her hands lifting her dress from the ground as she ran. Her eyes were red and swollen, and tears flowed down her cheeks. "Coric … Coric, they've taken everything," she yelled as she ran.

Coric stopped his horse and dismounted. He clutched

Ceana as she reached him and he held her tightly to his chest. She trembled in his arms.

Laise gasped in relief at the sight of his sister. He left the two alone and quickly trotted his horse in a wide arc around the outskirts of Coric's dwelling.

As Laise disappeared behind the building, Ena's slight frame emerged in the threshold of Coric's home. She stood motionless for a moment and then slowly stepped forward. Distress oozed from her countenance like sweat from her skin. It had been many years since Coric had seen his mother in such a state. She approached Coric and Ceana, and the three clung to one another.

Ceana tried to speak, but her sobs muffled her words.

"Ceana, shhh," Coric said. "It's alright. Tell me what happened. Where are the others?"

"Coric, these men … these men, they came and they took Aiden and Nessa," Ena said.

Coric stared at his mother in disbelief, the color draining from his cheeks. "Who took them? Where did they take them?"

"Men with helmets, with horns on their helmets," Ceana said. "They came this morning and circled the house and set fire to it—"

"I saw the men. They're dead. I saw their bodies," Coric said, trying to calm Ceana. Then he turned to his mother, "You said they took Aiden and Nessa. Are you sure?"

"Yes, we saw them—"

"What's happened here?" Alpin shouted. He dismounted his horse and helped Donald down from his.

Donald touched the ground and sprinted toward his mother.

Ena bent and Donald rushed into her arms.

"Mother, you're alright," Donald exclaimed and nestled in his mother's bosom. "Our home is gone, Mother. It's burned to the ground."

"Where are the children, Ena?" Alpin said.

"Mother, where are Kenneth and Aiden and Nessa?" Donald blurted out over his father, his voice laced with fear.

Ena glanced at Alpin before fixing her eyes on Donald. She placed her hands on her son's cheeks and spoke gently, "They're alright, Donald. They are not here now, but we will find them."

Alpin stepped to Ena and placed his arms around her with Donald pressed between them.

"It was awful, Alpin. They took Aiden and Nessa. Aiden fought them, but they captured him and took him. They burned everything and took the children, Alpin. They took them!" Ena cried between quivering lips.

"What about Kenneth?" Alpin asked. "What happened to Kenneth?"

"He went to see Arabella last night. He never returned," Ena replied. "I don't know if he's in Cashel, or if Cashel was attacked as well."

"Are you certain Aiden and Nessa are alive?"

"The three of us were outside when they came. Ceana was here. They came with torches and swords, there were several of them. One of the men grabbed me, and Aiden tried to stop him. The two started fighting, and I was pushed to the ground. There was more fighting, and they were moving through the fire and I heard them yell out. Oh, Alpin ... there were too many of them ... they took Aiden and Nessa."

Ena leaned her face into her husband's chest and she broke down and sobbed.

Alpin held her and gazed back at the blackened ruins of his home.

Coric stared at his parents, fighting back the boiling blood coursing through his veins. "Father, we must find Kenneth. And we must get the men and go after Aiden and Nessa!"

"Coric, we will find them," Alpin replied.

Laise rounded the corner of Coric's home. "It's clear. No sign of the enemy," he yelled.

"They can't be far, Coric," Alpin said with a sober anger in his eyes. "We'll find your brothers and sister ... and we will bring them home."

CHAPTER 19

"WAIT HERE," THE OLD HERMIT SAID, AND HE scampered down the curved path and vanished beyond the pines.

Kenneth watched the old man and then turned to his fallen horse struggling on the ground behind him. The animal fought to right itself, but with a broken front leg and an arrow protruding from its shoulder, the large beast had little hope.

Kenneth stepped forward and spoke calmly to the animal. He drew his sword. The horse's large round eye followed the movement of the emerging silver blade. In a single stroke, the animal's pain ended. Kenneth extracted the blade and wiped the blood on the rear quarters of the dead creature. Then he returned his sword to his belt.

Righting his frame, Kenneth gazed at his surroundings. The tall pines lining the muddy path stood like large green sentinels. Loch Lomond sat to the east not far behind him. He hadn't been this far north in years. He took a deep breath and wondered how he had gotten to this point. Everything was wrong, nothing was right. "What's happening?" he whispered to himself.

"Look here," the hermit shouted.

Kenneth turned toward the old man. He had reappeared, leading a horse behind him.

"I found this for you," the old man said. "The Viking who lost it won't be needing it any longer." He approached Kenneth. "Follow me," he said, and he led Kenneth and the horse away from the path in the direction of the loch.

The two stepped into a clearing. The opening before them was a broad expanse, covered with knee-high grass, thick and green. Its downward sloping terrain extended a few hundred yards before it stopped at the bank of the loch. Only a single oak and a lifeless pile of blackened wood and ash occupied the open field.

As the two approached the ash heap, the old man cursed and stepped past it. Kenneth stopped and stared at the pile of rubble. The smell of the burnt wood filled his nostrils.

The old hermit paused and turned to Kenneth. "They took all I had. For forty years, that pile of char was my home—survived a thousand storms, a few famines, and some awful winters. Those damnable savages felt they could take from me as they pleased. What could a tired old man do to stop them … they're animals!" He quieted and led the horse to the oak tree and tied it to its trunk.

"They burned your home?" Kenneth asked. "When did they do this?"

"Two nights ago," he said. "As the sun was setting, they came through. From the north, they rode south. They figured they'd stop and burn my home—why, I don't know … maybe because they're devils from hell?" He cursed again under his breath, then motioned to Kenneth, "Come with me." He left the horse and led Kenneth through the field.

The old man stopped beside a mound of broken grass. He bent down and cleared the grass, revealing a small wooden hatch in the ground. He lifted the hatch, moved it aside, and stepped down into the earth.

Kenneth followed.

The sloping ground eased into a dimly lit hole. Once inside, the old man picked up a burning candle and used it to light three others, illuminating the dank pit that served as a rudimentary cellar. The candlelight hardly filled the small room, but enough to reveal the old man's few meager possessions. A half-eaten loaf of bread sat on a small table next to a round of cheese and a tattered knife that looked to be a hundred years old. On the far end of the table sat a large basket of strawberries and two rockfish. The fish odor, mixed with the moist earthy musk, explained the cellar's unpleasant scent.

Kenneth stepped deeper into the cavity and found he had to hunch to avoid bumping into the clay ceiling above his head. He stared at the bread and cheese, and his stomach began to rumble. He hadn't realized how hungry he'd become.

"Sit. You should eat." The old hermit motioned for Kenneth to take the only stool in the makeshift cellar. Then he pushed the bread and cheese across the table toward Kenneth.

Exhausted, Kenneth sat down without uttering a word. He would not resist the old man's offer. He grabbed the bread and tore it in two. He consumed it as if he hadn't eaten in weeks.

"What's your name?"

"Kenneth," Kenneth replied tersely, not feeling much for talk.

A lengthy pause passed before another word was spoken.

"Kenneth ... what's your plan once you find the Vikings?" the hermit asked, and he found a wooden box that doubled as a stool and sat across from the younger Scot. He squinted at Kenneth, waiting quietly for a reply.

Kenneth's gaze lifted from his bread, and he stared at the old man. The light from the candle on the table made the old man look ancient. His deeply sunken eyes appeared as hollow pits in his head. Kenneth noticed that the man had an odd habit of biting the side of his lower lip when he wasn't speaking. Maybe it was something he did when he was anxious, or maybe he did it at other times too. Each time he bit his lip, his mouth curled, exposing his rotting teeth. Even the dim light of the cellar couldn't hide their crooked black edges.

Kenneth finally spoke, "I don't have a plan, except to free my family, who I believe are now the prisoners of those animals."

"From the way you rode after'em, you seemed hellbent on catching'em. Where are you from?"

"Renton. I'm the son of Alpin of Renton," Kenneth said before swallowing the piece of bread soaking in his mouth. Then he lifted the tattered knife from the table and cut into the round of cheese.

"You are the son of Alpin ... Alpin, son of Eochaid?" The old man's voice rose as he brushed off a once faded memory.

"Yes, son of Alpin, son of Eochaid ... how is it you know my grandfather's name, old man?" Kenneth asked and his brow lifted.

"You say I'm old, but there was a day when I was as young as you." The hermit lifted from his wooden box and stood. Because of his smaller stature, he didn't have to hunch as Kenneth did. "When I was a young man, probably not quite forty, I knew your grandfather, Eochaid. He was a few years younger than I was. He was a rare man, he possessed something few others possess—charisma. He had a way of winning the hearts and minds of others. With his tongue alone, he could change doubters to believers."

Kenneth set down his bread and cheese, waiting to hear more. He'd heard stories from his father, yet he'd never heard enough.

"In that time, the leaders of Dalriada in Kintyre came together at Dunadd to fight an enemy that came from the sea. It was at Dunadd that we battled the Vikings." He peered at Kenneth, "You know them monsters have been here before?"

Kenneth nodded, taking in every word.

"This encounter occurred about forty years ago. The Vikings struck hard, pillaging our abbeys for treasures and relics. In time, we drove them from Dalriada. Yet after they were pushed out, our own men began to fight over the leadership of our people. Two groups formed, and men took sides." The old man paused.

"So what happened between the two sides? Was my grandfather part of them?"

"No, Eochaid was not part of either group. There were two men who made claims of kingship, Gabran and a second Scot. The two claimed kingship over the Dalriadans, but their claims had no grounds—neither claim was just or right. Eventually, fighting began and we warred among ourselves. The fighting was wrong … it's awful for a man to die at the hand of his enemy, but far worse to die at the hand of his brother." The old man rubbed his face and stepped away from the table. "It was your grandfather who called out the Scots, daring them to turn from their recklessness and disavow those claiming to be king."

"And so ... go on," Kenneth insisted.

"Many men deserted the two vying for kingship, and they rallied behind your grandfather. Soon after, Gabran died in his bed with a knife in his throat—and his claim of kingship died with him. It was then that the other man claiming to be king vanished. He was never seen again in western Dalriada."

"And my grandfather?"

"Well, as I said, he held the hearts of the men. With Gabran dead and the other man missing, I believe your grandfather could've become king. But he didn't. No ... he didn't want to rule, he wanted to live. And he did. With the fighting over, your grandfather returned to his land, and there he tended crops and herded sheep."

"My father said he was killed in battle. Were you with him when he died?"

"He was killed in battle. He was killed by the Vikings, eight years after the civil war had passed. The Vikings reappeared in Dalriada, and many Scots lost their lives at Bunessan. It was there your grandfather lost his. He was a noble man, Kenneth. A man to be proud of ... he'd be proud of your courage in hunting them devils. Seems to be a family trait." The hermit mustered a toothy grin.

"How is it you know of my grandfather? Did you ever fight with him?"

"No. I never fought at his side. I was too foolish with my

own aspirations to have any real wisdom in those days," the old man said as he approached the table and slowly lowered to his stool-like box. His head sunk, his eyes dropped, and he ran his crooked fingers through his dingy white hair.

"I don't understand," Kenneth said. "How did you know him?"

The old man paused a moment before replying. "I spoke of Gabran and the other man, the two fools vying to be king. Kenneth—I was the other fool," he said sadly, staring into Kenneth's eyes.

Kenneth sat as still as a stone staring back at the old man.

The man spoke again, his tone low and subdued, "I was there when they buried your grandfather. I saw your father, he was still a boy, not yet a man. He was a good many years younger than you are now. Many came to the burial. It was near the small abbey in Iona. It was a dignified burial. A procession of men walked the Street of the Dead to the burial ground, the Relig Oran. I was no longer the man I'd once been. I had seen how pride tore apart lives … I spent eight years repenting of that pride. No one recognized me in the crowds at Iona. I made sure of that. It didn't matter though, I was a long-forgotten memory by then." The old man continued his confession, "I had come to Iona to pay my respects. In my heart, I wanted to give your grandfather something … something that was more his than mine."

The old man stood and stepped to the back of the dimly lit den. He stooped and grabbed the edge of a cloth that covered something on the floor in the corner. He removed the cloth and then grabbed a candle and held it above his head. "I want you to see this."

Kenneth stood and peered over the old man's shoulder. "What is it?"

"This, son, is a treasure that belongs to a people, not a man. It should be resting in Iona ... beside those men who were once great among us." He held up the light and let it shine over the old relic.

Kenneth gazed down at a large square stone sitting on the ground, worn and aged. "Is that the Stone—"

"The Stone of Destiny ... it is, son. Your father has spoken of it?"

Kenneth nodded, struck by disbelief and the irony that the once noble stone cut long ago now sat in the dreariness of an obscure and insignificant cellar.

The old hermit continued, "Legend says that the Lord Himself fashioned this stone for His people. It was this same stone that was given to us in ages past, the very stone that the patriarch Jacob rested his head upon after wrestling with God." The old man gave Kenneth the candle and ambled back to the table.

Kenneth held the small flame over the large square-cut stone. He reached to touch it and wiped his finger across a moist film of grime that covered its surface. The stone measured roughly two feet in length, over a foot in width, and stood a foot off the ground. Kenneth reckoned the stone weighed a couple hundred pounds. He had heard many tales of the Stone of Destiny, tales of kings and battles and treachery and war, but the stone had been missing for more than a generation. As kings of the past had faded from Dalriada, so too had the memories of the stone. Kenneth had always figured that no Scot would ever again lay eyes upon the stone, and yet here he stood beside it in the old man's cellar, beholding the stone with his own eyes and touching it with his own hands.

"The stone has not seen daylight in thirty years. Dalriada was once ruled by noble men, kings who saw beyond themselves. Those were seasons when the sun shone brightly upon Dalriada. But in time, darkness set in, and men with darkened hearts sought to be king." The old man grew more bitter as he continued to grumble. "I was willing to take men to their death for that stone ... willing to kill my own countrymen for it." The old man choked on his words. He stood and paced the ten-foot floor of the cellar, muttering under his breath as he moved.

Kenneth remained in the corner, watching the old man bathe himself in condemnation.

"That is not my stone!" the hermit burst out in anger. "It doesn't belong to a murderer, it belongs to better men ... noble men, men who gave themselves for their people!"

Kenneth's muscles knotted inside. He stood motionless, gazing at the old man, not knowing whether to despise him or pity him. He did both.

As the old man wrung his hands in torment, Kenneth eased from the stone and returned to the table. He sat for a moment, unsure of what to say, then he spoke, "There is good in Dalriada, much good ... there is life, and there are families and men who still fight for what is right ... why do you speak like this?"

"Good? What is left of good!" The old man threw his hands in the air. "All I have sits in a pile of ashes ... and you, you speak of family that you've lost to those Viking devils with no hope of stopping them from taking all of Dalriada—"

"Nonsense!" Kenneth shouted. "My father will come with a thousand Dalriadans! He waits in Renton now, where men from across Dalriada will join him to defeat our enemy!"

"Son, your youth blinds your vision. These men have no loyalty to your father. They will stand for a day ... but when their eyes see the blade of the Viking sword, or their bellies feel the emptiness of winter, they will drop their swords and run for shelter, only to be pursued by the Vikings and cut down from behind."

Kenneth glanced back at the dark corner and the ancient stone, and then he peered at the hermit. "Are you not the one who is blind ... blinded by your past, unable to see a future different from your own day?" The candle on the table flickered as Kenneth spoke, bending and stretching the shadows across the cellar walls. Kenneth stood and stared long into the hermit's small round eyes. "Apathy is no less evil then tyranny. One destroys the power to act and the other acts with the power to destroy. They are both grave evils, and I will not be guilty of either!" Kenneth exclaimed. His eyes narrowed and he shook his head in disgust. "Time will tell who is blind, old man. Time will tell."

Kenneth finished and stood motionless, his gaze remained on the hopeless hermit. Then he pushed past the old man and ascended the sloping entry of the musty cellar.

Escaping the dank hole in the ground, Kenneth rose from the earth, and the remaining light of dusk fell upon him as he stepped into the world above.

The thick mud of the worn path hid the large rock lying in the middle of the trail. The driver never saw it. In an instant, the cart's rear wheel hit the hidden fixture with a loud *thump.* The rock didn't move, yet the rear of the cart lifted into the air and crashed to the ground.

Snap! The hind axle of the cart split like a twig, and the rear left wheel broke free and wobbled off the path. The cart's back corner struck the ground and sunk like an anchor in the mud, tossing the captives backwards in the cage. The driver bobbed violently back and forth, and his skull struck the wooden posts of the prison cage behind him. Dazed, the man shook his head to collect his bearings, then he sat erect and quickly gathered his grip on the reins and yanked.

The horses bristled under the hard pull, bucking and fighting their harnesses. Their muscular necks flexed and heaved, and the ropes binding their chests drew tighter. A nearby rider dismounted and hurried to grab the leads of the beasts. The man tugged and leaned his weight into the ropes to settle the animals. After several moments, the horses eased and calmed, prancing in place and snorting at one another in frustration.

Inside the wooden cage, the captives lay pressed in a twisted heap at the rear of the cart. Some grabbed the wood bars to extract themselves from the pile of bodies, while others groaned and waited to right themselves.

Several Vikings slid from their horses and surrounded the cage. With swords drawn, they began shouting at the captives and striking their blades against the wooden posts. Two more Vikings dismounted and approached the rear of the cart. Dropping to their knees, they scooted through the mud to scan the underbelly and inspect the damaged axle. A man beside the cart shouted ahead for the procession to halt.

The forward pack slowed, and a dozen riders circled back on their horses, watching the chaos and even finding amusement in the captives' struggle. The less interested riders broke from the crowd and trotted to the creek beside the path to resupply their water.

Jorund, the largest of the Vikings, rode to the cart. Fuming with irritation, he dismounted his horse, dropped to the ground, and surveyed the wreckage. Sufficiently displeased, he lifted his head and shouted, "Get the prisoners out of there. Put them in the other carts. We can't fix this with them inside."

"But Jorund, the other carts are too full," one man replied. "They won't handle the weight."

"Shut your mouth and put them in the other carts. We can't leave until this gets fixed … now move!"

"What's the problem?" Halfdan yelled as he approached, his tone caustic and sour.

The Vikings surrounding the cart stirred and began to busy themselves.

Halfdan trotted his horse through the crowd of men with Kodran behind him.

"A wheel broke," Jorund replied. "We're moving the slaves to the other carts until we fix this one."

"The sun is nearly down. If your men can't fix it quickly, then we leave it here," Halfdan barked.

"It will take a good bit of time to fix—"

"Enough! If you can't fix it, then tie the slaves together," Halfdan said, pointing at the caged captives from his perch. "Tie them in a line behind a horse … they'll walk from here."

Halfdan turned his steed, and he rode between the men and disappeared.

"But Halfdan … if the cart doesn't get fixed, their walking will only slow us down."

"Then drag'em," Halfdan shouted without looking back.

Jorund yelled the new orders to the men. Two Vikings pried open the door of the wooden cage and motioned to the Scots.

The captives slowly rose, struggling to exit their prison and fighting to balance themselves on the tilted cart.

The first man out of the cage was a Scot named Gavin. He was a small-framed, thin young man just shy of thirty. He'd come to Renton for supplies early that morning when he found himself caught in the Viking raid.

Gavin stepped from the cart and planted his spindly form in front of the Vikings. He glared ahead as if the ground he occupied was his own, even daring them to take it from him. His diminutive build was of little threat to the husky Vikings encircling him. They waited for him to move, but he didn't. He stood stock-still, blocking the others from exiting the cage.

"Move, Scot!" Jorund hollered and shoved Gavin to the side.

The push sent Gavin sprawling several feet from the portion of earth he'd claimed. Gavin regained his balance and peered at Jorund, yet the hulking Viking paid him no regard. He was a mammoth of a man—one who suffered neither heroes nor fools.

Jorund turned to the next Scot, "Let's go!" The Scots quickly jumped from the teetering cart in a manner that suited him. Then Jorund walked away, glaring at Gavin as he departed.

Gavin stared back at the giant yet elected not to speak.

As the captives emptied the cage, the Scot with the wounded side eased to the opening. His diminished state had left him listless and frail. He slowly lifted one foot and took a long step down. When his second foot followed he stumbled and fell.

"Get up. Get up, I said!" a voice growled, and then a boot thumped the Scot's midsection, spinning him to his backside.

The Scot rolled and groveled in pain.

"Stop it!" Nessa screamed. She jumped from the cart and knelt beside the young man to check the cloth bandage she'd wrapped around his side. It was loose. She began to tighten it—

Suddenly, two hands gripped her shoulders. Her weight disappeared as she was lifted off her feet. A haughty laughter filled her ears, and then she was spun like a ragdoll. Her eyes landed on her assailant. The man was hideously ugly.

"This is a pretty one ... and isn't she sweet." The man ogled her figure up and down as he taunted.

Nessa closed her eyes and the man's hot breath raked across her nostrils. She summoned the courage to look again. The Viking's eyes were like coal. A scar ran across his left cheek and up across his eyebrow. His dark teeth were large and gray, but they were insufficient to shield his wretched breath, reeking of rotten fish. Nessa gagged and fought to free herself. Lifting her arms, she wedged her limbs between her body and his. Then she pushed with all her strength, but the man's grip only tightened.

The Viking laughed, and his jagged scar danced on his cheek. Others prodded with jeers and whistles. Suddenly, the man lurched forward to kiss her.

His mouth got no closer than a finger's width before his skull snapped back. His helmet tumbled from his head, and he staggered backward and fell to the ground.

Aiden released his grip on the man's ratty hair, having nearly ripped it from his scalp. In an instant, three Vikings were on top of Aiden, punching him and wrestling him to his knees. Two held his arms, and the third grabbed him around the neck, rubbing hard against his blistered flesh.

A guttural scream erupted from Aiden's throat, scattering even the birds of the treetops into flight.

Aiden had sustained multiple abrasions from his sword fight with the Vikings in Renton, but that was not what pained him. Rather, it was the severe burns he'd suffered during the attack. In the skirmish at his home, Aiden had fallen into the flames, suffering burns along the left side of his body. The burns on his shoulder, neck, and cheek had swollen into large blisters, leaving his skin raw and weeping.

The rip across Aiden's neck was more than he could bear. The pain sent him reeling. He lost focus and fell to his hands and knees, writhing from the burning sting. Drool ran from his mouth. He fought to gather his breath, and his mind faded in and out of blackness.

The Viking with the scarred eye erected himself. He watched as Aiden wandered aimlessly on the ground, panting and heaving to remain conscious. The Viking surveyed his spectators and then stepped toward Aiden. "Looks like the young Scot has lost his way," he mocked, attempting to veil the shame of having been tugged to the ground. He grabbed Aiden by the back of his shirt and jerked him to his feet.

Nessa ran to her brother but was stopped by the strong arm of a Viking. She kicked to free herself, yet she could only watch while clutched in her captor's grip.

Aiden stood upright. His knees wobbled as he labored to gain his balance.

The Viking with the scar squared face to face with Aiden. He peered at the shredded blisters lining the side of Aiden's cheek and the pool of ooze sliding down his skin. "Boy, if you hope to live another day, you had better not put a hand on me again." *Smack!*

The sudden slap twisted Aiden's head sideways. His body followed. The blow was crippling. Pain surged through his muscles and joints, and he blacked out before he hit the ground.

"Aiden!" Nessa shook herself free and ran to Aiden as he lay in a slump on the ground. She knelt beside him and lifted his head, then shook him gently.

He was unresponsive, his breathing faint.

"Get these Scots tied up," Jorund shouted. "We get this cart fixed now, or we'll have a slow day ahead of us. Night is coming soon."

Nessa's eyes gazed over her brother. His face was moist with ooze and blood while the remainder of his tired frame lay covered in dirt and soot. She didn't want to lose him. She sat with Aiden in her arms, and she pulled him close, pressing him against her small frame.

She closed her eyes, and in her heart she prayed for him.

Coric finished gathering supplies for the coming ride, wondering when his father would return from Renton, wondering how much damage had been done. He tied his last satchel to his horse and then grabbed a log. He tossed the wood onto the pit of fire and peered at the skinned carcass of the eight-point buck skewing over the pit's hot flames. His thoughts lingered and he turned his gaze toward the path to Renton.

The awful recollections of returning from the hunt and spotting the ashen remains of his family's home replayed in his mind. The image cycled over and over in his head before he broke from his trance, seeing his father approach in the distance.

Coric double-checked the food satchel and water sack tied to his horse. He was ready. Then he turned and waited for his father as he broke into the open field and rode across the blackened patches of burnt earth. Coric brooded in anger, wondering of the news his father had of Renton. He wanted to skew the murderers who had taken from his family. He wanted to kill them. He wanted to kill them all. He stood silently, waiting—waiting and brooding.

Alpin stopped his horse beside the fire pit and dismounted. His eyes met Coric's. The fact that he was troubled was evident, it was etched upon his face. And though the smell of searing venison struck him and his hunger stirred, he ignored it and kept his gaze fixed upon his son.

"It's not good, Coric."

"How bad is it?" Coric replied.

Alpin hesitated before speaking. "Renton is all but

destroyed ... burned ... many have been killed and others taken captive. And Coric ... I'm not sure ... I—"

"What Father? What is it?"

"Constantine sent a messenger from Cashel. He found me in Renton. Coric, Kenneth is not in Cashel."

"He's not in Cashel? What do you mean? Mother said he left for Cashel. Isn't Arabella there? He's got to be there!"

"Arabella is there. She's with Constantine," Alpin replied. "She and Kenneth were together last night. They came back here this morning and found the place burned and everyone missing. They went to Renton and were attacked by Vikings. Some of the villagers told me that Kenneth killed three of them and—"

"So where is he!" Coric demanded, his imagination spinning.

"The messenger reported that Kenneth sent Arabella back to Cashel and then he went after Aiden and Nessa, alone. Kenneth thought your mother had been taken, too. They didn't know Ceana and your mother were safe."

"So Arabella is safe ... and Kenneth is ... is alive, and he's gone after the Vikings alone? This is madness!"

"Coric, we have to keep our wits. We'll find them. Constantine sent word that he and the men of Cashel will arrive tomorrow."

Alpin eyed the setting sun. Soon its light would be scarce. He shook his head and gazed at Coric. "You're not going to like what I have to say, but we can't go after Aiden and Nessa tonight."

"Father, we must. We must leave now. We're ready. Laise and Ronan are ready. We've packed the supplies—we should go now while we can still find them!"

"Coric, like you, I am anxious to leave. I agree we should go, and soon, but tomorrow we will—"

"Father, we can't wait for tomorrow. We can't wait for every man in Dalriada to come. It'll take several more days for them to arrive. It'll be too late. We'll lose them … we must go now!"

"We're not simply waiting for the others. We're waiting for sunlight as well. We won't make any progress tonight, it's too late. We'll eat, we'll rest, and we'll be strong for the morning."

"Father, I don't like this. Every moment wasted is a moment we've lost."

"In the morning, we will have daylight and likely more men, and we'll need both. Constantine's scout said that the men from Cashel are assembling and could be here as early as tomorrow. And the men from Milton and Dumbarton will soon follow. They'll bring others from their surrounding towns and villages. Coric, we'll be stronger tomorrow."

"My brothers and sister may be dead tomorrow … ten thousand men won't help them then!"

Alpin's jaw clenched. He felt an urge to strike his son. He bit down harder and then took a breath. "Son, we will find your brothers and sister in time, but for now we must commit them to the mercy of God. I have nothing more to say."

Coric said no more, yet his anger still burned.

The two stood shoulder to shoulder, staring at the pit's red flames.

Alpin stepped to the fire and pulled a knife from his waist. He cut a piece of meat from the rear haunches of the deer. He chewed it and swallowed. "If the others don't arrive by quarter day tomorrow, then we'll go without them to find Nessa and your brothers and the others."

Coric nodded. "I'll be ready. Ronan and Laise will be ready."

"If we do leave before the others, I'll have Luag stay behind to assemble the men as they arrive. My hope is that they arrive in time … and we can go as one."

Alpin reached over the flames and cut another piece of meat. It would be ready soon. They would need to eat. They would need their strength. Much had been lost, and much remained to be found.

CHAPTER 20

KENNETH OPENED HIS EYES. LYING ON HIS BACK, he stared up at the dull blue sky and fought off the grogginess of a poor night's sleep. The morning sun approached the horizon, but had yet to crest the eastern hills of Loch Lomond. A dense fog hovered above the loch, covering its waters like a lofted blanket.

In some ways, this was but another day like all other days. The sun came up and the sky bore a tint of blue, yet for Kenneth the world had changed. Yesterday, he had awoken on a mountaintop holding Arabella, the girl whom he had wanted to hold all his life. But this morning was a different morning. This morning he awoke alone on the west side of Loch Lomond, wondering if it would be the last morning he'd ever wake. Indeed, everything had changed.

Kenneth sat up, his hair and clothes moistened from the early morning dew. The whickering of the mare startled him. He turned toward the horse. It was standing beside the tree where he had tied it. He sat silent for a moment and listened, his eyes glancing to the adjacent tree line and then to his rear. He neither heard nor saw a soul. All was quiet except the rustling of the trees and the wind gently blowing through their branches. His eyes returned to the horse.

He thought of the old man. The old man had given him the mare. Kenneth figured it was not much of a gift, since the old man had shot the horse he'd ridden from Renton. Giving Kenneth the horse of a dead Viking was the least the old man could do, yet a small part of Kenneth was grateful that the old man had provided him food and fresh water, as well as the mare.

Kenneth had parted from the old man the prior evening. He was in no frame of mind to stay the night. He'd decided it was best to move on. Today he would continue north following the path along the western shores of Loch Lomond. The Vikings thus far were heading north, though he figured they'd likely turn west—if he understood the scouts' reports noted by his father in Renton's meeting hall.

The night of rest brought salvation to Aiden. Sleep had given him just enough strength to march. His burns were severe, potentially fatal should infection set in. The hot, raw sting of his open flesh carried him in and out of coherency, as though his soul wished to cease with each surge of pain. The rest had helped, but he'd need much more rest if he was to heal—and the present march was sapping strength from Aiden like a leech from a corpse.

Nessa moved forward behind Aiden, watching her brother lumber with every step. She prayed he would stop resisting the Vikings, yet she knew he would fight if not for his ropes. He would eagerly fight five, even ten, of them—if only he had a moment of freedom and the strength to do so.

With the cart broken and abandoned, Nessa and Aiden and the others were now being led by a horse. Tied in a single line behind the animal, they were subject to the horse's pace. A second line of captives walked beside them, parallel behind a second horse. In some ways, Nessa was grateful that she was tied to Aiden and last in line.

Nessa trudged forward. The muddy path grew thicker with each step. The heavy rains and constant mashing of the horses' hooves turned the ground into a depressing sludge.

The mud crept over her feet as each step sunk into the brown mire. She had little concern of the filth, rather it was the dismal grind of the endless march and the uncertainty of things to come that plagued her most.

Nessa heard Aiden grunt, as he had done several times since they had begun that morning. She glanced up to see Aiden stumble. He fought to catch his balance. Mud hung to his hair in matted clods, mocking him and belittling his plight. He continued forward, his head sometimes facing up to the sky and other times bowing low to his chest as though he didn't care if his next step was his last.

She pitied him as she watched. She recalled his courage during the attack on their home. How he had fought with the strength of an army to protect his family. Without his father or brothers, Aiden had faced the Vikings single-handedly and fought like a warrior, even stopping the savages from killing their mother. Nessa winced as she remembered the horrid shrills of Aiden and his Viking foe when they fell into the fire. The blaze had sought to steal the lives of both men—and Aiden had paid a high price to keep his.

Tears welled in Nessa's eyes. She envisioned her mother lying on the ground, groaning helplessly. Then she thought of her father, which only made her heart ache more. *If only Father and the men had been there, it would have been different. They could've helped Aiden. They could've stopped them,* Nessa thought to herself. And now she was here, walking the road to hell, watching her younger brother die with every step.

Where are they taking us? Nessa asked herself. *Oh, dear God, let it not be to a foreign land where we'll never be found again.* Her father could spend every day for the rest of his life searching and still never come within a thousand miles of finding her. "Father, please come," she whispered. "Please, please find us."

"Pick up your feet and move!"

Nessa shuttered under the growl. She lifted her head as the Viking with the scarred eye barked from his horse, yelling at Aiden and the young man with the gashed side. The young man had tripped and stumbled in the mud in front of Aiden. His loss of blood was slowly killing him. Aiden steadied the young Scot and nudged him forward. Aiden gazed up at the Viking as if daring him to shout again. The Viking glared back and spat at him and then summarily coaxed his horse forward and harassed another captive.

Nessa shook her head, relieved the trouble had passed. She peered toward the line marching parallel and found Gavin. He was watching the man with the scarred eye. Then he looked over at Aiden and suddenly glanced back at Nessa, catching her gaze. He grimaced and looked away. She was unsure if he was angry or signaling some sign of reassurance.

She had never understood him. He'd always been somewhat of a recluse in Renton.

Searc sat on his horse with the sun high overhead. His body quivered with angst. The massive castle of Pictland towered in the distance. To Searc, the monolith of rock and stone was no less ominous in the light of day. He'd not expected his return to Perth would have come so soon. He'd hoped his prior visit to Oengus would have brought better things for the Scots, yet now his own village lay decimated in rubble far to the west in Dalriada.

Searc's demons attended him, haunting him on his journey to Perth. *Why did the Vikings suddenly attack Renton? Did they know the Scots weren't prepared?* He'd been certain Oengus had wanted to make peace with the Dalriadans and unite against the Vikings—he was much less certain now.

Searc trembled as his fears took hold, but he needed Oengus. He had to take the chance. He had no place to turn among his own people, no place but Taran. Yet with Renton now destroyed, Taran would never admit his complicity with Searc. Searc would have to speak to Oengus again, it was the only way—the Dalriadans needed the Picts now more than ever.

Searc took a deep breath and rode his horse forward.

"Pict! Pict!" Searc shouted to the guard high on the castle wall, slowing his horse and peering upward. "I must see your lord!"

"Who's asking?" the guard returned a cold retort.

"I am Searc, of Dalriada. I bring word of Renton. My people have been attacked by Vikings. I fear that Lord Oengus and the Picts may be next."

"Stay as you are," the guard shouted and disappeared.

Searc's horse stirred outside the castle doors. Doubt crept in as the moments passed. Searc hoped the guard would return soon. He wondered if the news of the attack would catch Oengus by surprise—or if he'd find the news surprising at all.

An uneasy feeling surged inside Searc. *What kind of fool have I been? How well do I even know this man? Should I even trust him?* In truth, he couldn't be sure—it was all happening so quickly. He knew he needed to speak to Oengus. He desperately needed to speak to him.

The clanking of the large latch sounded, followed by the creaking of the heavy castle doors. His chance to speak had come—and now there was no turning back.

Two men emerged from the opening between the large castle doors. Their arms bore the familiar painting of Pict warriors. They approached on either side of Searc and ordered him to dismount. From there, they led him into the entry corridor of the castle and through a dimly lit maze of hallways. The circuitous path ended at the castle's grand hall, a room boasting walls twenty feet high formed with large rectangular stones stacked one upon another.

Searc surveyed the vacuous hall. It was not the same room he had visited before. The hall's immensity reduced him, making him feel as a mouse in a lion's den. He swallowed and stared at the walls, second-guessing his decision to come. He slowly peered over his shoulder and considered retreat. Then he felt a forceful nudge from the rear escort and, reluctantly, he stepped into the grand hall.

A figure sat on a throne at the far end of the hall. It was Oengus. Two statue-like guards stood as armed bookends on either side of the Pict lord, each bearing a polearm glaive with a curved, twelve-inch blade. The hall was lined with large chairs arrayed along the walls, each slightly turned and facing the Pict lord's throne. The throne itself was ornate and impressive, dressed with fine red fabric and adorned with gold rivets and polished trimmings. Oengus filled the elevated throne, sitting several steps above the floor of the hall. He perched motionless between the two guards and gazed at Searc as the young Scot was escorted forward. The clicking of the guards' steps on the cold stone floor echoed through the hall as the three approached.

"Ahh, Searc of Renton, the young Dalriadan who wishes for peace in Britannia ... and who continues to search for that noble man who may bring such a gift to his people," Oengus spoke loudly, his voice bearing a sinister ring. He laughed a dry laugh when he finished.

Searc's heart weakened.

"My lord, you have heard of the Viking attack on Renton?" Searc framed his words as an uncertain question, purposely avoiding presumption. Assuming Oengus hadn't heard of the news may be as regretful as assuming he had.

"Yes Scot, I'm aware of the attack that occurred on Renton. You see, I have eyes and ears as well."

"My lord, I beg of you ... you sought to unite with the Dalriadans to join us in our fight against the Vikings?"

"So you say," Oengus replied.

"Do not the Vikings attack my lord when they attack the Dalriadans?"

"No," Oengus said. He peered down at the Scot. "An attack on Renton is not an attack on Perth."

"But my lord, our leaders will listen to you. Guaire and Taran are respected among the Dalriadans. They will unite with you, if only you would speak to them and offer your pledge as you did to Alpin—"

"Enough!" Oengus exclaimed. "My pledge of unity came on a day that is now long gone. Alpin and the Dalriadans had their chance to pledge fealty to the Pict crown and they spurned their opportunity. They knew this day would come, and in their arrogance they were certain they could stand. Their fate is their own."

Searc shuttered at the Pict lord's apathy. Fear gripped him. "My lord, you cannot leave our people like this. They are now the slaves of these Viking savages. Would not our people help the Picts should they—"

"Boy!" Oengus rose from his throne, "Do not dare accuse me of some malicious treachery—that I am one to sit idle and do nothing. Indeed, your beloved Alpin has to be prodded and shamed into helping his own people, and you have the audacity to claim that he would rush to help the Picts? You are either blind or a fool ... or both." Oengus paused. Without turning his eyes from Searc, he lifted his hand and circled his finger in the air.

The escorts and guards departed, leaving the two alone in the large hall.

Oengus slowly descended the steps and approached the young, petrified Scot.

Searc's body trembled. There was no place to flee, no

place to hide. Had he the courage to speak, he couldn't, even if he wished to. For though Oengus often spoke with a deceitful tongue, his charge had not been untruthful.

Oengus stepped to Searc, looming over him. His lips pursed tightly together and air hissed from his nose as he breathed. "Young Scot, was it not you who came to me under the cloak of darkness, searching for a means to dethrone your mighty Alpin? In your sedition, did you not hope to dispel Alpin, the man you despise ... was it not the whisper of your own voice persuading you to bring him down, even if it meant treason against your own people!"

The indictment scorched Searc's soul. He stepped back from the Pict lord and turned away.

Searc tried to reason with himself, that he was only wanting to help his people—help them when Alpin wouldn't. *How did it come to this? Had Oengus conspired with the Vikings, aiding their attack on Renton? Or worse, had he orchestrated it, even planned it?*

Searc wanted to be strong. Summoning what little courage remained, he gazed at Oengus and spoke, "My lord, did you ... did you tell the Vikings of—?"

"You sniveling child!" Spittle erupted from Oengus' mouth and sprayed across Searc's face. "Your pathetic mind tells you lies that you wish to hear, and you are foolish enough to believe them. You came to me in the dark of night because you wanted Alpin dead! Do not pretend that you had some grand noble cause to save the world. Your heart yearned for one thing—Alpin's death! You nearly got what you wanted, and now your soul cannot bear to live with your heart!" Oengus leaned toward the young Scot, his hot breath pouring over Searc's skin. With a cutting whisper, he spoke, "You ... you are the enemy, not me."

The Pict's words could have pierced armor. Searc had played the fool. Every word exchanged with Oengus in their plan to unite was a lie, even his own. His stomach tightened in dread and his legs fell limp.

Searc dropped to his knees, slumping on the steps at the foot of the Pict throne. He cupped his face in his hands. He had offered his soul to the devil and the exchange had been consummated. With his veil of lies now uncovered, he realized the pain of truth known only to traitors.

Oengus stood over the broken boy, stirring in contemplation as he looked down at him. "You may feel as if Renton is lost ... that you are lost, but there is always a path to redemption."

Searc lifted his bloodshot eyes and gazed at the Pict lord. "What is left? What is done cannot be undone," Searc muttered.

"I'm not suggesting that all is done, I'm suggesting that you finish what you started," Oengus said. "You see, I have no love for these Viking animals. I'd be quite pleased to never see them again in this land. Your Taran sounds willing to ... how would you say it ... *to work with me.*"

Staring up at Oengus, Searc sat like a corpse in the shadow of the Pict lord, fear-struck of what would be said next.

Oengus folded his arms across his chest and rubbed the hairs of his chin. "I understand that Alpin was not present when the attack came on Renton ... that was most unfortunate ... it is true, not all plans are perfect. But let's say that I am working to rectify that mishap." Oengus began to pace. He continued, "I suggest that you visit with this Taran and remind him of whom he should rely on for aid, for protection ... for security. Help him to see the merit of pledging fealty to my crown and sharing this wisdom with the others of Dalriada."

A tiny door cracked open in Searc's heart. He allowed himself to listen again to the small voice born the day he saw his father lying dead in the cart that had carried him back from Ae. Here was a possibility to fix his folly, to finally be done with the one man who had plagued him since that awful evening long ago. Searc lifted his sullen frame and gave a venal ear to the Pict lord.

Oengus halted his pacing and peered at Searc. "If Taran is the man you say he is, then he would be wise to take heed of my words. And Scot, you should know ... should your lips breathe word of this to those in Dalriada, you'll be forever known as a traitor. And should you open your mouth to those in Pictland, you'll hang before the sun is able to fall. Either way, your tongue is mine. Share it with others, and you'll lose it ... along with your life."

"Guards!" Oengus called out.

Four armed men instantly appeared.

"Please escort our friend to the castle door."

Gazing at Searc, Oengus smiled and said, "Good-bye, Scot." Then he turned and walked away, his shadow following him as he disappeared from the hall.

Searc mounted his horse and rode from the castle. He had saved himself, yet his conscience refused to quiet, ever whispering its recriminations. He couldn't escape the one person that he would hurt the most—Aiden. Thoughts of his lone companion crept into his mind. His stomach began to turn. He fought to suppress his anxiety. Nausea overtook him, and he dismounted his horse and vomited.

Shame and fear taunted his spirit. His old demons had vanished for but a moment, and now they had returned, more vile than before.

Searc began to question himself. Aiden had always been his friend, his only friend. How could he now take Aiden's father, as his father had been taken?

Searc mounted his defense, rationalizing—even justifying—his deeds. For all he knew Aiden was dead. Searc had remained hidden when the Vikings attacked Renton. He had watched as Aiden was carried away in the cart, badly burned and hardly able to move. And having Taran and Oengus together may be the only means of saving Aiden, if indeed he was even alive.

Searc returned to his horse and pulled himself up. He jabbed his heels into the animal's belly and spurred the beast forward. He wanted to move on, to press on, to escape himself were it possible. He fought to quench his guilt and rid his mind of the thoughts that sickened him.

He rode, though to where, he didn't know.

CHAPTER 21

SUMMER CLOUDS SWELLED IN THE SKY OVER Renton. Beaming rays of sunlight pierced here and there through the porous covering. It was noon. A quarter of the day had passed.

The time had come. Dalriada's sons had yet to appear in Renton. And Coric had waited long enough.

Coric would join his father and, together with Laise and Ronan, the four would settle their plans with Luag and head north to hunt for Kenneth and the others.

Coric stood beside his horse and glanced back at the empty doorway of his home. He untied the animal from its post and grabbed the lead. Looking back one last time, he stopped. The doorway now framed the petite figure of his young bride. She stood small in its hollow entry, silently staring back at him.

Coric left his horse. His gaze fixed upon Ceana as he approached. A heavy frown hung from the corners of her mouth, clothing her countenance in sadness. Coric shook his head, silently pleading with her to let go of her fear. She turned and faded from the doorway, receding back into the protection of the four walls.

"Ceana … Ceana." Coric ran to the empty doorway.

Inside, Ceana sat in a small wooden chair, wiping her eyes and refusing to cry.

Coric entered and knelt beside her.

She turned, not willing to glimpse his gaze.

"Ceana, look at me," he said, groping for words to console her. "We must find my sister and brothers and the others. When we find them, we will return. By then, the men of Dalriada will be here. It'll be alright."

Ceana's face fell to her palms and her body crumpled— Coric's words had fallen like a pebble on a mountain.

"I know you're upset, Ceana … please try to understand?"

"I do understand! That's why I'm upset. I know you must go, but should I be happy that you must? That you may be killed and never return!"

"You can't get rid of me that easy." Coric tried to ease her mood. "I have my father's sword and your brother's bow protecting me … it's the Vikings who should be afraid," he said, and he grinned at her.

"You are not taking me seriously, Coric. I was here when they attacked! I saw them. I know what they can do." A lump filled her throat. She fought to speak, "I know you have to do this. I accept that … but it may mean I have to accept much more."

Coric stood and took a deep breath. His eyes moved across the room. A small tin vase sat on the table filled with white wild flowers she'd picked. A rug that she'd saved for and bought in Renton lay nestled by the fireplace. She had made their house a home. He loved her for that. He eased his hand to her shoulder and spoke, "Ceana … I know you are troubled. I understand … I know the Vikings are dangerous and this will not be easy. We'll have to be careful in getting them back, but we have to try." Coric wished she would listen, he wished she would trust him. "I'll be back ... don't worry, I'll be back for you."

Ceana pulled away. A tear ran down her cheek.

Coric reached to her and caressed her hair, "What is it?"

Ceana gazed into Coric's eyes as if looking into his soul. "Coric, I am not worried only about myself. Coric ...," she glanced down at her stomach. The tiny bulge that she now carried in her midsection was hardly discernable. Her eyes moved upward and found Coric's. She closed her lips without finishing her words.

"What? Ceana ... what is it?"

Ceana pushed back her tears, stood abruptly, and then stepped across the room. She swallowed and composed herself. "I'm worried about everyone—Nessa, Aiden, Kenneth ... you and Laise and ... Coric, this is all so scary. I just don't want to lose you. I can't lose you."

Coric moved close to Ceana, put his arms around her waist, and held her. Several moments passed before he let go. He lifted his hands to her face. "You won't lose me," he promised.

She nodded.

He quietly mouthed the words, "I love you." His smile was warm and his words were genuine. He kissed her lips and then released his hold of her, and he turned and walked out the door of their small quiet home.

She watched him from the doorway as he rode away. And she longed for his return.

Coric rode to the charred remains of his once

childhood home. There he joined his father and Laise. Coric acknowledged the two with a nod and then gazed down at the black pile of ruin, his thoughts consumed with what had been taken from him and his family. The night dew had evaporated in the warm day leaving the air bitter and burnt—the odor stoked Coric's hatred of his new enemy.

Together, the three Scots pushed their horses hard and raced toward Luag's home where Ronan waited to join them. Once at Luag's, Alpin conveyed his orders for the men who would soon arrive in Renton. Luag remained behind to carry them out.

Departing Luag's home, the four headed north along the west side of Loch Lomond and followed the trail of the Vikings. As they rode, thoughts of Ceana riddled Coric's mind. He was unsettled with how he'd left her. Though he'd tried to reassure her, she never seemed comforted. He assured himself that his mother would be a help while he was gone, that if anyone could console Ceana it was her. His mother was a strong woman, and she'd seen her husband leave for war. Maybe she could settle Ceana's heart.

Coric rode forward. He welcomed the warm wind that blew against his face. It was like a balm that soothed his conscience and focused his mind. He had to find Nessa and his brothers, and though he couldn't be sure they were still alive, he was determined to try. He vowed to repay those who'd brought trouble upon Renton—and upon his family.

Under the steady drumming of the horses' hooves, Coric's mind wandered back in time. He was sixteen. It was the last day he saw Drostan alive. His brother sat high on his horse, full of courage. Coric stood next to Kenneth and Aiden, staring up at Drostan. On that day, Coric had wished he could have been the one showing his strength and testing his mettle in the march against the Britons. He could still hear Drostan's voice, still see his taunting, teasing grin—the grin of an older brother. His gut wrenched as he recalled the anguish that day had brought.

Memories of the past continued to hound Coric—the rains drenching him and his brothers as they dug Drostan's grave. He was standing in the pit next to Kenneth, watching as Kenneth dug deeper and deeper into the cruel earth to prepare a resting place for their brother. That day had been a cold day. It was a day that cut deep, and its scars, though faded, would never be washed away.

Coric rested his mind. He wanted to look ahead, for the day he lost his older brother had long passed. He would now find Kenneth and the others, and they would take their revenge on the Vikings. Coric fed on his fury. It compelled him forward. He could taste the fight as he rode.

He snapped the reigns of his horse and pulled in front of the three to ride lead. They had much ground to cover.

Kenneth was closing on the Vikings. The steam wafting from the horse dung littering the trail evidenced they weren't far ahead. He wanted to see the army. He wanted to know their size, their strength. He wanted to find his mother, his sister, his brother, and his people. To do this he would need to be close, dangerously close.

The Vikings would likely keep to the path through the lowlands, staying near the rivers and streams as a water supply for the men and horses. Kenneth gambled. He broke from the trail that pushed through the valley and rode into the hills.

Riding through the forest of the mountainous terrain would be difficult, but being a single rider, he held an advantage. The Vikings, moving a small army on horseback and pulling carts and captives, would be forced to move slowly. Kenneth would follow the sun as a bearing. He would need to plot his course well if he was to intercept the Vikings passing through the valley below.

Kenneth rode along the woody ridgeline, eyeing the sun as it lowered. Reaching a clearing on the ridge, he trotted toward the ledge and stopped his horse. He gazed below but saw nothing. Then he closed his eyes and paused to listen. Only the aspens' quaking leaves offered a sound, fluttering and dancing in the wind.

A bird of prey suddenly lofted from a nearby tree, startling Kenneth. He sat for a moment before dismounting and watched the bird soar in a wide elongated circle. The bird looped a second time and then a third before disappearing south beyond the tree tops. Kenneth snapped from his daze and slid from his horse. He stepped to the edge of the ridge to gain a better view.

Below lay a path with a small river running beside it. Hundreds of hoofprints pocked the path. From high above, the tracks appeared faded and aged. They also headed east, and the Vikings were returning west—maybe the gamble had paid off.

Kenneth led his horse into the trees along the ridgeline. There he tied the animal to a branch and returned to the rocky ridge.

The sun was setting and evening was approaching. Dusk would come soon. Kenneth eased precariously along the ledge of the ridge, searching for a perch where he could spy his enemy from above.

Ambling a dozen yards along the edge, he found two sizeable rocks sitting next to one another with a small nook between them. The nook formed a roost embedded in the ridge, a vantage point from which he could peer down and remain invisible from passersby on the trail below. Kenneth lowered himself into the nook and sat.

He adjusted left then right, trying to settle against the jagged surface of the nook. Its protruding bumps became a nagging irritant. Kenneth sat still for another moment, then rearranged himself to sit more erect. Despite his efforts, he found himself unable to avoid a particularly annoying rock that poked his kidneys, and he resigned himself to ignoring it.

As time passed, the damnable rock felt more like a dagger than a stone. Kenneth likened the irritant to the old hermit, amusing himself and even snickering as he recollected the hermit's spunk in shooting the Vikings with an old worn-out crossbow. At that moment, Kenneth peered down at his simple knife and sword and grimaced, wishing now that he had requested the old man's bow.

As Kenneth waited in his nook of granite, a dozen scenarios played in his mind. He considered that maybe not having a bow was better. Maybe he didn't want to start something he couldn't finish, at least maybe not at the moment. He wondered if the Scots had gathered in Renton. He hoped they weren't far behind now that a day and a half had passed since his leaving.

Dusk was near, and the lack of light would soon become a hindrance.

Kenneth rose in his perch. He began to wonder if the Vikings had stopped, or maybe even turned off the path. He grew anxious and tried to reassure himself that he was watching the right path, that the Vikings would be coming his way. He tried to be patient, realizing that trouble would come soon enough, and he didn't need to spend time worrying of its arrival.

Kenneth lowered again. He turned sideways in an attempt to keep the small irritating rock from jabbing his back. He looked west at the sun fading on the horizon, wedged between the cotton clouds. The image took him back to the hilltop with Arabella two evenings prior. He could see her gazing at the sunset, and he remembered how she'd caught him gaping at her. A gush swept over him and he smiled at the thought. *What would it feel like to hold her again, to hear her laugh?* He pictured her at home in Cashel, waiting for his return. He wanted to be with her.

A faint clip-clopping sound shook him from his daydream. He ducked lower in the nook and waited a moment, then peeked out from the two rocks and scanned the path below, tracing it back as far as he could see.

The path crested in the distance. And though he couldn't see any riders, by the sound of the steady hoofbeats, there were more than a few.

Kenneth slunk back. His heart raced. He glanced down at his sword and ran his thumb across its sharp metal blade. Then he lifted to a squat and placed his hand on the large rock to his left to steady his balance. Staring up at the sky, he whispered a prayer, "Good Lord, keep me and grant me courage."

He drew a deep breath and peered past the rocks.

Vikings! Men with horns lifting from their heads. Their dull metal helmets and dark leather garments displayed an ominous, villainous appearance. They rode large beastly horses and marched down the path as if the ground beneath them had forever been theirs, as though the earth was their own.

Kenneth watched the mystical procession with peculiar fascination. More and more men poured over the distant hill, and in a matter of time they would be below him.

As the army of riders approached, none appeared to notice him or even glance in the direction of his nook. Indeed, his perch was an invisible hideaway.

He waited silently and tried to count the men as they drew near. Two dozen had passed when he spotted a particular rider. The man rode proud on his horse, shoulders straight and eyes focused. His leather covering was black and darker than the rest. It was long with tassels lining the shoulders. Unlike most of the others, the man wore no helmet, rather he wore a thick black band around his head that pulled his hair off his brow.

Kenneth's gaze left the man when his ears caught the sound of creaking carts. Peering back along the path, he saw a horse and cart crest the hill. The cart was suited with a large wooden cage mounted to its bed.

At first Kenneth strained to study the captives inside the moving prison, but his nerves pulsed with angst and drew his attention back to the procession of men passing below him. He glared down at the horned riders. They were exchanging words in a foreign tongue, often gesturing to one another as they moved forward on the path. Kenneth hovered above like a phantom hawk peering at its prey, watching as they carried on with one another.

One by one, the riders passed. From front to back, they formed a stream of men and beast countless in number. In the middle of the procession, a single Viking, boasting bright golden hair, broke from the line and rode past the other riders. He called out, "Halfdan … Halfdan."

The man in black stopped his horse only yards ahead of Kenneth's perch.

Kenneth twisted in his nook for a better view. As he did, a small rock rolled from under his foot and tumbled along the slope toward the edge. He gasped and froze, then lurched forward and grabbed the stray stone an inch before it would disappear off the ledge. His pulse quickened, and adrenaline pumped through his body, churning a gut-wrenching mixture of fear and fury in his belly. He took in a gulp of air and could feel the blood in his head thumping to the beat of his heart while his muscles were begging to release their pent up anger.

Below, the golden-hair rider glanced upward and slowed his horse.

"What do you want?" Halfdan growled.

The golden-hair rider quickly lowered his gaze and rode to Halfdan.

As the Vikings spoke, Kenneth stole a glance from his hidden perch and glimpsed the two. They were speaking in words that Kenneth couldn't understand. The rider pointed to the small river running along the path and then pointed forward in the distance.

When the two finished, the rider with the golden hair returned to the procession, and the one called Halfdan remained not far below Kenneth, watching the riders move past. The man loitered for a moment and then merged into the pack. The clopping of the army continued as the horses' hooves pounded the muddy path and marched forward.

Kenneth's focus returned to the cart. The first of now two carts was approaching. Kenneth counted eleven people inside and recognized each of them, but saw no sign of his family. The captives were filthy and disheveled, and some badly beaten. He wanted to call to them, to say something, anything. Yet he denied the urge and remained silent.

The second cart approached and passed, carrying a dozen more prisoners. Still no family.

Were more carts coming? Kenneth asked himself as he lowered and knelt on one knee, relieving the muscles now burning in his legs. His gaze returned to his enemy, and he watched them closely as they streamed over the eastern hill. *No more carts. Where are they?* Trouble and despair welled in his gut.

Then something strange appeared in the distance. Kenneth squinted to make out the image.

A pair of horses, escorted by Viking horsemen, had crested the hill with what appeared to be two rows of people trailing behind. As the lines drew closer, it was clear the people were captives, bound together with ropes tied around their waists. Once the last of the captives crested the hill, no other riders, captives, or carts passed over the hilltop.

The captives slogged forward, inching on without purpose, moving as if their feet were lead and their legs putty. Their steps were like those of a death march.

Excruciatingly, they approached.

Kenneth lifted and tucked himself within the rocks of the nook. Then he eased his head outward. He surveyed the lines and saw the listless faces of the marching prisoners.

Nessa! His heart jumped in his chest. *She's alive!*

His mind went wild.

He caught his breath.

He gripped his sword.

He stepped to the edge, then suddenly lost his balance. He leaned back to stop himself and quickly ducked. His eyes raced forward to the lead riders, slowly combing the procession from front to back, all the way to the rear. No one had noticed.

He eased to a stance. The two lines of captives were directly underneath him and Nessa would soon pass below. And then she would be gone.

He closely scanned the two lines, searching for his mother and Aiden. There were no other women in the line. *Where was Mother?*

He retraced the lines a second time. *Where was Aiden?*

His heart sank. *Had the savages killed them?*

Kenneth closed his eyes. He gripped his sword and tightened his hands, squeezing the leather-wrapped handle until his knuckles fell white.

He took a deep breath and then lifted his bicep to wipe the sweat from his brow.

He wanted to see Nessa again. He leaned forward in his perch. She was nearly below him, and he watched her as she slowly advanced. Then the prisoner in front of her tripped, and Nessa reached and grabbed the man's waist. Kenneth shuddered when he caught sight of the young man.

A bloody cloth wrapped the man's head, and his neck was charred with open sores. What remained of the man's shirt was burned across the left side, exposing a fleshy shoulder pocked with blisters and jellylike blood.

Nessa released her grip from the man's waist and Kenneth heard the young man groan.

The voice—Kenneth's mind spun. The man's head suddenly bobbed back, lifting his burnt face to the sky—*Oh God, Aiden!*

Kenneth convulsed in shock, and he ducked his head to hide. His eyes shut tight, wincing at the sight of his brother and fighting back his rage.

Kenneth paused and let a moment pass, then he glanced down at his feet and peered over the edge. He guessed he was twenty to thirty feet from the ground. He wondered if he would survive the jump.

Placing his feet at the lip of the ledge, he closed his eyes and exhaled. Then he clutched his sword with both hands and pressed it against his chest, pointing it downward.

He opened his eyes and looked below to prepare himself.

Aiden was passing under him.

Nessa gazed up. She stopped in her tracks when she saw her brother peering down. She gaped at Kenneth and their eyes locked.

The rope around Nessa's waist suddenly tightened and tugged her forward. She lurched and staggered. After regaining her balance, her eyes lifted again to Kenneth. Her face hung with sadness, desperately wanting him near her—and far away—at one and the same time.

Kenneth's eyes widened as he stared back at his sister. He nodded his head ... *yes*.

A tear rolled down Nessa's cheek, and she shook her head, *no … no, Kenneth.*

She tore his heart.

He watched her pass.

She turned her head to look back.

He was gone.

CHAPTER 22

TRACKING THE VIKINGS THROUGH THE northwest mountains of Dalriada was akin to tracking game for Kenneth. Yet for this hunt, the stakes were higher—much higher. Kenneth had left his hidden overlook and had now tracked his enemy for some distance, cloaking himself along the forested ridgeline and following the Vikings' movement through the valley.

At nightfall the Vikings stopped. When they broke for camp, Kenneth dismounted his horse and hid the animal deep in the high timbers. He left behind his water and sword and carried only his knife, tucked in his belt. Checking it twice, he made certain it was secure.

A steep but traversable slope separated Kenneth above from the Vikings below. Lumbering pines and small scrub trees dotted the sloped hillside. Without a sound, Kenneth scampered beneath the dim moonlight until finding a location where he could survey his enemy. His lookout was a large evergreen amid a patch of aspen trees midway down the hill. Satisfied it was safe, he crawled below the evergreen's low sprawling branches and shoved aside a host of fallen pinecones. Then he lowered to a position on his belly and watched the camp move busily below.

From what he could see, the Vikings had posted three guards at the camp's perimeter, one to the east, one to the south, and one to the west. To the north, the camp was bordered by a river. The rope-bound Scots and the two carts loaded with captives were clumped together in the center of the camp and encircled by Vikings. With the darkness and distance, Kenneth couldn't distinguish his brother and sister from the others.

Hours passed before the campfires slowly died and the muttering of men faded. Kenneth lay watching, waiting in silence with only the dull rush of the river sounding under the dark sky.

The night grew long before the Vikings had fully retreated to their slumber. Though Kenneth had no set time and no set plan, he felt the urge to move. He prayed for strength. Then he wedged his fingers in the dirt below the tree branches and pulled himself forward. Carefully, he crawled from the protection of the evergreen. Once removed from its cover, he remained prostrate in the grass with the moon's light shining down on him. He waited and surveyed the camp below to see if he'd been detected.

No one stirred.

He crawled again.

Over and over, Kenneth pulled himself forward in the knee-high grass, inching toward the guard at the south edge of the camp. He stopped thirty feet from the guard, and again he waited.

Kenneth quietly lifted his head to see above the grass. The south guard remained seated on a stone, illuminated by the moon while facing the hill behind Kenneth. From what Kenneth could see, the guard didn't appear to be looking at him, but Kenneth knew he'd be spotted if he moved too abruptly.

He needed a distraction. *Maybe the guard will relieve himself, or better, maybe he'll fall asleep,* he thought.

Lying in the grass, Kenneth surveyed his surroundings. The Viking horses were spread across the camp, three or four tied to one tree or another. He needed a plan. He would need to free Aiden and Nessa, and somehow he would need to get a horse. Then Kenneth wondered if Aiden would even be able to ride.

The night pressed on. Kenneth's legs and back began to stiffen. He kept an eye on the moon, measuring his time before the sun would return. He couldn't be caught lying in the grass when the night ended—he'd be dead for sure if he didn't get back to the woods before dawn.

Kenneth buried his face in the ground. He thought of Aiden and his awful burns. Then he recalled Nessa, envisioning her along the path, staring up at him and pleading to him—pleading for him. Kenneth hated the Vikings.

A rustle stirred in the grass ahead.

Kenneth eased his forehead off the ground and listened.

Footsteps.

Faint at first, then closer.

Kenneth lifted his eyes, yet dared not lift his head. The grass was too tall to see over and too thick to see through.

The steps drew nearer.

And then they stopped.

Kenneth's heart pounded in his chest. He breathed slowly in and out of his mouth, fearful of making a sound.

Silence.

A chill ran over his body.

Would they come closer?

Stillness.

Eternity passed before he heard the footsteps again. This time the steps grew more and more faint.

Kenneth mustered his courage and peeked above the grass.

The guard was returning to his stone—no, he was passing it.

Kenneth lifted his head higher.

This was it.

It was the moment Kenneth was waiting for. The guard passed the stone and disappeared into the darkness of the camp. Kenneth pulled his feet beneath him and crouched in the grass. Keeping low, he moved toward the camp. Once past the guard's stone seat, he hid behind a wide clump of yews. Quietly, he ducked and peeked between the shrub's branches.

A new guard was coming. The man ambled from the camp and walked past the yews.

Kenneth turned, watching the man as he passed.

The guard headed to the seat and plopped down on the stone. He sat as the other guard had sat, facing the hill.

Twenty feet away, Kenneth stared at the backside of the guard. Not long after the guard took his perch, his head slumped downward and then suddenly popped up. Kenneth watched the guard battle against slumber's seduction. The battle was short-lived. Not many moments passed before the man's head went down in surrender.

Kenneth's pulse accelerated. He wanted the man dead, he wanted the man to sleep forever. Kenneth's hand dropped to his waist in search of his knife. His fingers found its handle, and he removed the blade from his belt. He stepped from the yews and eased toward the guard. His heart raced. His blood pumped. His flesh pounded. He had killed men in Renton, but that was in defense, they were attacking him. This would be different. It would be calculated and purposed. It would set things in motion from which Kenneth could never turn back. The Vikings would know he was near—either in hours or in minutes—but they would know.

Kenneth moved closer.

The guard's head bobbed and then rested. He remained a prisoner of sleep on his lonely stone.

Kenneth slid behind the man. He drew a silent breath. With his left hand hovering beside the man's mouth and his right hand holding the knife to the man's throat, Kenneth executed his cut with precision. The guard gasped for breath, but his covered mouth and opened throat robbed him of any ability to breathe. The man twitched and fidgeted and then stilled. Kenneth held tight for a long moment and then lowered the guard's body to the ground.

Kenneth glanced left, then right. The two remaining guards sat uncaringly in the distance, neither seeming to notice the commotion. In silence, he stepped away from the dead man and moved into the camp. He crept toward the carts like a fox in the night, sliding from shadow to shadow between the streaks of moonlight that splintered down through the tree limbs above.

Kenneth skirted past a mass of sleeping men, wishing he could call down fire from heaven to kill them all where they slept. Moving past them one by one, he reached the carts. The two carts sat fifteen feet apart with a dozen bound captives lying between them.

Kenneth gazed over the prisoners, recognizing the villagers of Renton, fellow Scots that he had known his entire life. He wondered how he could possibly free them all. He shook his head, as if to clear a fog that clouded his mind. Freeing them all would only bring their demise, and likely his. They would never make it out of the camp alive. He needed to free Aiden, or his brother would likely die.

Without warning, a horse snorted. Kenneth froze and peered back at the Vikings. A few stirred in their sleep. It was then that Kenneth abandoned any thought of freeing the others.

Kenneth stepped lightly, passing by three captives before he found his sister. Lying beside her was Aiden. He was asleep, but his breathing was labored and husky. Kenneth knelt beside his brother and studied his face. His burns were severe on one cheek, but the other appeared uninjured. Guilt swept in. *If only I would've stayed home with you, this would've never happened … what misery did you suffer to stay alive?*

Kenneth turned to Nessa. He grabbed her shoulder and shook her softly. "Nessa," he whispered.

Nessa stirred.

"Nessa," he whispered again.

Nessa's eyes slowly opened. When she realized it was Kenneth she lunged toward him, hardly able to hug him with her rope-bound hands. She pulled back and gaped at his face. "How did you get here? How did you find us?" she whispered, excited and scared.

Kenneth held a finger to his mouth, wanting her to remain quiet. He drew his knife and cut her ropes, then he pointed to Aiden, "We need to get him out of here. Where's Mother?"

Nessa looked at Kenneth, surprised. "Kenneth, she's not with us. They left her behind ... in Renton."

"She's alright?"

"Yes," Nessa whispered.

"Thank God," Kenneth said. "She wasn't there when I returned. She must be with Ceana." Kenneth glanced at Aiden, "He looks bad ... Father and the others should be close behind, but we need to take Aiden now. Wake him up."

Nessa nodded, and she reached to wake her brother.

Kenneth sliced the ropes binding Aiden's hands and feet. He returned to Aiden's side, leaned over him, and whispered, "Aiden—"

Kenneth never saw the Viking looming behind him.

He never saw the large axe.

The blade shimmered in the moonlight as the man lifted it high.

"Uhh." Kenneth heard a sudden groan. He startled and swiveled.

The Viking stumbled. A kick to his calf had caused him to teeter. A second kick struck the Viking's knee, twisting his leg awkwardly and throwing him off balance.

The Viking tumbled toward Kenneth. Kenneth caught the man and spun him to his back, then pinned him to the ground. He pressed his knee into the man's throat and drove his knife twice into his chest.

Kenneth's eyes lifted, and he locked stares with the Scot who had delivered the blows to the Viking. It was Gavin. He was sitting up, legs extended, and nodding in approval.

Kenneth scanned the darkness for more Vikings. Everything was silent except the ambient chortling of the passing river. He gazed back at Gavin under the dim moonlight and then crawled to him. "My father is coming with men," Kenneth whispered. "I have to take my brother away from here. I can't take you … but we'll come back soon for you and the others."

Gavin's countenance displayed more than a small measure of grief. He glanced at his fellow captives and then at Aiden before peering back at Kenneth. "Take him, but please, come back for us."

"I will," Kenneth vowed, then he reached out his arm and clasped Gavin's. "Thank you. I owe you, Gavin."

Kenneth crawled back to Nessa as she tended their brother. "Can he travel?" he asked.

Hearing the voice, Aiden's hand lifted and he reached for Kenneth. He clasped his fist to Kenneth's shirt and pulled him close. "I can move. We should go," he muttered in a broken whisper.

Kenneth pulled back and gazed down at his brother. Aiden was smiling at him with the same silly grin he wore as a boy. "Alright … we will go," Kenneth said, returning his brother's grin.

It was rest, and likely hope, that seemed to have revived Aiden. He moved more ably now—now that he was unbound and had no scar-faced Viking barking at him. Kenneth was pleased to see the improvement. *We may get out of here alive after all*, he thought. Kenneth led the way, guiding Aiden through the shadows of the camp.

Nessa followed the two. As she crept away, she glanced back at the captives and saw Gavin sitting up in the darkness. He'd been watching the three, but then he turned and began digging at the dead Viking beside him. He pulled something from the dead man's belt.

Nessa glanced ahead to her brothers. She'd fallen behind, and she hurried to catch them.

Kenneth led Aiden to the cluster of yews and stooped behind them to wait for Nessa. The camp and the hillside slowly blackened as the moon disappeared behind a large cloud that floated overhead like a ship in the night sky.

Nessa approached and Kenneth signaled the two to follow. He retraced his steps, moving south in the direction he had come. The three moved in a single file line, with Kenneth leading and Nessa trailing and Aiden pinned between his brother and sister. As they neared the edge of the camp Aiden staggered and stepped on a fallen tree branch. The dead limb cracked in two beneath his heavy foot. In the crisp night air, the noise sounded like a thunderclap in Kenneth's ears, even startling the nearby horses.

Kenneth dropped to the ground and pulled Aiden beside him. Then he turned and motioned to Nessa to duck.

Kenneth cupped his ear to listen and thought he heard voices. The three lay flat in the tall grass, waiting for several moments. Then Kenneth slowly lifted his head in the direction of the guard to the east.

The man was staring at him.

A wave of terror splintered through Kenneth's body, yet he denied even the slightest twitch.

The man was looking at him, watching him—or was he? Was the darkness playing tricks on him?

Moments passed and the man stood. He stretched his arms into the air and then sat again. He now seemed to be facing away from the three.

Did he see us? Were my eyes fooling me? Kenneth asked himself. He waited a moment longer before finding the courage to move again. Then Kenneth's head turned like an owl's as he gazed west to spy the other guard. The man was sitting farther away than the eastern guard. From appearances, he seemed to be sitting with his back to the camp.

Kenneth glanced again toward the eastern guard. The man was still facing the opposite direction.

Kenneth crept beside Nessa. "Watch Aiden. I'm going to get those horses," he whispered and pointed to two horses tied to a nearby tree. "Then I'll come get you ... we'll have to hurry!"

Nessa nodded.

Kenneth scampered through the darkness to the two horses. He quickly cut their ropes and freed them. When he turned to guide them away, he noticed a crossbow and quiver tied to the larger horse. He checked the quiver—arrows!

Kenneth led the horses toward Nessa and Aiden and motioned for them to join him.

Nessa helped Aiden from the grass and the two hurried to Kenneth.

"My horse is in the trees at the top of this hill," Kenneth whispered. "We'll move up on foot and I'll lead the horses. Nessa, take Aiden's good arm and help him up the hill. We'll be exposed in the moonlight at times, but we'll move among the trees for cover. Freeze if you hear anything, but if they see us, get up the hill as fast as you can. At the top, we'll mount the horses and ride."

"Kenneth, is Father coming?" Nessa asked.

"I am certain he is, but we must go."

"When will he get here—"

"Nessa," Kenneth interrupted. "Not now. We must go."

Kenneth started up the hill, holding the horses' leads and towing the animals behind him. Nessa and Aiden followed.

Halfway up the hill, Kenneth veered toward the large evergreen that not long prior had been his hiding spot. He steered the horses behind the tree and caught his breath, waiting in the dark for Nessa and Aiden.

Nessa rounded the evergreen, her arm on Aiden's waist, guiding him as he ambled wearily beside her.

"We can rest here, but only for a moment," Kenneth said. "How's he doing?"

Aiden stood hunched with his hands on his knees. He was breathing heavily and wheezing as he inhaled.

"He's getting tired," Nessa said. "I don't think he can make it to the top alone."

Aiden straightened himself and peered at Kenneth. "I can make it," he said, gulping for air. "I can make it."

Kenneth nodded to Nessa, "Let him try."

Kenneth left the horses and walked to the side of the evergreen. He peeked through the branches to the Viking camp below. Scanning for movement, he saw none. Then he turned and glanced up at the sky. "It's getting lighter. The sun will rise soon. We need to get to the top of the hill, before they realize what has happened," he said. "You ready?"

"Ready," Nessa replied.

Kenneth led the horses and headed uphill.

Nearing the hillcrest, Kenneth paused and glanced behind him. Nessa and Aiden were struggling to keep pace. Nessa had wrapped Aiden's arm around her neck and was coaxing him forward. The two ascended several more steps latched to one another, but then, without warning, Aiden fell to his knees. Kenneth released the leads and hurried to his brother.

"Nessa, you get the horses. I'll take Aiden!"

"Oh Kenneth, we—"

"Go, Nessa!"

Nessa rushed up the hill toward the horses.

Kenneth squatted in front of his brother. "We can do this, Aiden," he said.

Aiden wheezed and nodded his head.

"Get on my back," Kenneth said, and he turned and motioned for Aiden to climb on.

Aiden shuddered when his body touched Kenneth's, his burns pressing against Kenneth's back. He winced and exhaled, then wrapped his arms around Kenneth's neck.

Kenneth lifted. The tightened muscles in his thighs felt as though they were aflame with fire. He glanced up the slope at Nessa. Then he put his head down and plowed forward as quickly as he could, ascending the steep and unforgiving hillside.

Kenneth was twenty yards from Nessa when he heard her shout. "Kenneth, they're coming!" Kenneth glanced over his shoulder. The two guards were moving up the hill and passing the large evergreen.

Kenneth hurried forward with Aiden clutched to his

back. Each step pressed their two bodies hard against one another, and Kenneth found himself grimacing as Aiden's pained grunts echoed in his ear.

Kenneth kept moving. As he neared Nessa and the horses, he was startled by a quick, chilling hum—the buzz of an arrow passing his ear. The horse closest to him bucked and reared up on its hind legs and released a shrilling cry. When the animal's front feet returned to the ground, Kenneth saw the arrow lodged in its side.

The horse fought and kicked and tore its lead from Nessa's hands. The panicked beast turned in a circle and then disappeared beyond the hilltop.

"Nessa, the horse took an arrow. Hold on to the other one," Kenneth yelled, still ten yards from his sister but approaching fast.

A second arrow flew past Kenneth and struck the ground a stride ahead of his front foot. Kenneth struggled forward with Aiden in tow, working every muscle as he hastened his pace.

Nessa hurried to the top of the hill with the remaining horse behind her.

"Get on, get on!" Kenneth shouted.

Nessa mounted the animal.

Kenneth reached his sister and he stooped to release Aiden. His thighs were burning as he squatted, but relief came when Aiden let go. His brother's feet hit the ground and he tottered. Kenneth spun and balanced him, then he moved behind Aiden. "Pull him on," Kenneth said, and he placed his shoulder under Aiden's rear and pushed him upward. The two wrestled to lift their brother, careful not to harm the injured portions of his seared flesh.

With Aiden mounted, Kenneth glanced down the hill. The guards were coming fast and closing quickly.

Kenneth sprinted toward the woods, ignoring the angry muscles aflame in his thighs. He shouted back to Nessa, "Follow me, we'll get my horse. I'll take Aiden when we get there—we don't have much time."

Nessa steered her horse behind him.

When they reached Kenneth's horse, he untied the lead. "Nessa, we can't get Aiden down and back on my horse. There isn't time," Kenneth said. "You take my horse and I'll ride with Aiden."

"Kenneth, won't they follow us?" Nessa asked, dismounting.

"Yes, but it's our only chance. Get on."

Nessa mounted Kenneth's horse.

Kenneth pushed Aiden forward and mounted behind him. He put his arms around his brother and grabbed the reigns.

"Let's go!" Kenneth yelled, and in an instant they were moving.

They rode through the trees, pushing their horses along the woody ridgeline as fast as the beasts would carry them.

Then a horn blew in the distance. A loud horn— blowing with all the fury of hell.

A shudder raced down Kenneth's spine.

CHAPTER 23

DAWN CAME TO CASHEL.

Arabella tossed in her bed. She was awake. She tried to clear her mind and return to sleep, but sleep refused her.

Her house was silent.

Arabella rose from her bed and donned her shawl from the back of the wooden chair sitting in the corner of her room. She could no longer stand the emptiness of the house and wanted to escape its silence, its numbing silence. She prayed the outdoor air would rid her of her endless thoughts—those terrible thoughts that pierced her mind like a thousand tiny needles.

Arabella stepped outside and followed the pebble path leading to the well.

The morning sun sat below the eastern horizon, promising its early light to the surrounding hills of Loch Lomond. The loch was still, and the air was wet with a hovering fog. Birds flittered in the treetops, chirping and clicking to one another. Arabella was deaf to it all. The cool air cleared her thoughts but could not dispel her sullen mood. She felt as if she was lost in a fog, a fog thicker than that of the loch and one harder to escape.

I must stop thinking of him! she scolded herself.

She didn't want to dwell on Kenneth—her thoughts and her fears only took her to places she didn't want to go.

She would walk to the well and draw a pail of water. The chore would ease her mind, maybe even hold her focus and help the time to pass. And she would need the water anyway.

The pebbles on the path made a grinding sound under her feet as she stepped. *I wonder how Father is doing?* She forced herself to think of Constantine. He and the men of Cashel had left the prior day for Renton. Arabella was still somewhat angry with her father for his insistence that she stay in Cashel. She had pleaded with him to let her join him in Renton. His dogmatic insistence that Renton was unsafe had sharply ended their discussion. She would have to stay in Cashel with the women, children, and older men who had stayed behind. In her heart, she wanted to be in Renton to wait for Kenneth. Cashel promised her nothing, nothing but a silent home and distant thoughts.

Arabella halted when she saw the well. Her hand rose to her lips as she gasped. The sight of the well seized her, taking her back to a happier day—Coric's wedding day.

She remembered the well. She remembered Kenneth. She remembered their first kiss. She treasured the kiss. He had surprised her. She loved him for surprising her. She could see his eyes, his hair. She could feel his embrace and hear his laughter as they tumbled to the ground. She remembered how the warmth of his body made her feel alive. *If only once more*, she thought, and then the image faded.

Her lips tightened and her brow fell.

She stood alone on the pebble path.

Slowly she took a step, then another step. Step by step, she eased toward the well.

Once at the well, she stopped and stared at its round stone wall, and then her eyes lifted to the drawing bucket. Extending her arms, she grabbed the bucket from its hook on the post. She held the bucket in her hands, turning it, inspecting it, tracing the seams of its wood slats and letting her fingers linger over the knots in the weathered pine. She'd used the bucket a hundred times before. It was the same bucket she'd always used.

She set the bucket on the well ledge and then placed her hands to either side.

Her mind's eye slowly lost focus, fading from the wooden bucket back to Kenneth.

Arabella.

Arabella.

His voice.

She snapped from her trance and spun to look behind her.

An empty path of pebbles.

She looked right.

Trees sleeping in silence with their slumbering branches wandering aimlessly in the breeze.

She looked left.

The lonely loch and a white fog nestling above it.

Her gaze eased back to the empty bucket.

She dropped to her knees and leaned against the cylindrical stone wall of the well, alone.

Her head lowered into her hands and she cried.

◎

The two horses galloped through the forested hills high along the ridgeline. The illumination of dawn crept through the canopy of pines and lifted the darkness.

Kenneth pushed his horse forward, keeping an arm securely wrapped around Aiden's torso. Climbing the hill had depleted much of his brother's strength, leaving him in a hapless slump as the three raced to distance themselves from the Vikings.

"You alright, Aiden?" Kenneth asked, trying to rouse his brother. "Aiden … Aiden, are you alright?"

"I'll live … I think."

"Well think hard … I didn't free you from those animals to die out here." Kenneth glanced back at Nessa and slowed his horse to let her come alongside.

"He's holding on, but barely," Kenneth said.

"Do you have any water? Maybe he needs a drink."

"I have a water sack, but we can't stop now. We have to keep going. They'll be coming for us … they likely aren't far behind." Kenneth checked the rear for riders. It was clear. "We need to stay on the ridgeline while we can. The trees will hide us."

"Alright," Nessa replied. "Are Father and the others near?"

Kenneth sensed her fear. "I don't know." He tried to be honest. "I hope they are." He glanced ahead and then back at his sister.

She glimpsed toward Kenneth but said nothing. Then she faced forward and stared at the path as it passed below her.

Kenneth was sure he saw tears in her eyes.

"Nessa, if they get close, I want you to split up from us. I want you to ride—"

"Kenneth, I am not leaving you and Aiden."

"We will only slow you down. With Aiden like this, we won't ..." He elected not to finish. He started again and tried to speak calmly, "Nessa, I need you to split up from us and find Father. Aiden and I will make it ... but you have to find Father."

"Kenneth, I don't want to leave you."

Kenneth didn't reply. He glanced over his shoulder once again to see if the Vikings were coming.

After a few miles of mountainous, woody terrain, Kenneth's horse began to fatigue. The animal slowed under the double load, and the gap between him and his sister was widening.

"Nessa," Kenneth called ahead.

Nessa looked back at her brothers, now a dozen paces behind. "Kenneth."

"Go, Nessa ... you must go, this horse can't keep up. Head east to Loch Lomond. Father will be coming that way with the men. Find him. Aiden and I will break from the trail and keep hidden. We will find our way home, but you must go." Kenneth didn't want to separate from his sister, but he had to. "Tell Mother we love her ... and Coric and Donald, as well. Tell Father we will fight until we see his sword."

"Kenneth, Aiden—"

"Nessa, go ... you must go now. You must hurry!"

"Alright, Kenneth." Her voice cracked as she spoke. Her eyes fell to Aiden. "I love you, Aiden ... you were brave. We'll be waiting for you."

"Ness," Aiden uttered a single garbled word.

Nessa's eyes found Kenneth's. "Stay alive ... I love you both." A tear streamed down her face.

Kenneth smiled for her. "Love you too, Ness. We won't be far behind."

Nessa prodded her horse forward, knowing that leaving her brothers and finding her father was the only way to save them.

"Nessa," Kenneth called out. Her head swung back toward her brother. "Tell Arabella that I love her ...," Kenneth said, wanting to say more. "Go Nessa, keep hidden and go!"

Nessa nodded and tried to smile. Then she shook her reigns and headed deeper into the woods.

Kenneth coaxed his horse and steered the animal southward. He rode for a moment and then stopped to watch his sister as she moved east.

Kenneth sat in silence, holding Aiden upright. His eyes inspected the oozing wound on the side of Aiden's neck. "We're going to get you home, Aiden. Hang in there."

Aiden moaned something unintelligible.

The birds in the trees startled and stirred, then lifted into flight.

Kenneth gazed at the frantic flock as they flew overhead, scattering in every direction.

He sat still, listening.

Hoofbeats. Vikings!

Kenneth glimpsed east and caught sight of Nessa moving through the distant trees. He forced his horse south, wanting to stretch the ground between him and his pursuers. Time was precious. They needed to disappear quickly.

Kenneth veered through the trees, which thinned and grew less dense as they neared the edge of the forest. Soon, the two reached the timberline and rode across the open ground beyond the veiling trees.

Kenneth slowed and again surveyed the woods for Nessa. She appeared now and again among the far trees, moving as a speck in the forest.

He glanced west in the direction of the oncoming hoofbeats. The enemy was drawing closer.

His stomach furled when he saw the first rider emerge among the trees. The man's helmet of horns magnified the sinister appearance of his dark leather garb. Steam-like breath billowed from the horse's snout in rhythmic bursts. A pack of five more riders appeared behind the first. Like wolves, they moved through the trees undaunted, predators in pursuit of prey.

Kenneth sat stone-still just beyond the tree line. "Keep quiet, Aiden," he whispered. His eyes followed the Vikings as they tore through the forest, their horses pummeling the ground in fury. When the riders reached the place where Kenneth had left the path, they continued forward, oblivious to the two on horseback at the edge of the woods.

The reality of the enemy's forward trajectory suddenly hit Kenneth like a stone to the forehead—they were following the path Nessa had taken. If they saw her, even in the distance, she would never escape.

Kenneth kicked against his horse, "Yaah, yaah!" His horse shot forward as if launched from a bow. The two rode east along the edge of the forest. It was suicide and Kenneth knew it.

Without breaking stride, the pack turned like a swarm of bees and cut a diagonal path toward Kenneth and Aiden.

The south slope along the ridgeline rose upward into

a treeless vista. Kenneth pushed his horse up the slope. He spotted a cluster of boulders speckled high along the ridge and snapped his reigns, steering the animal toward the patchwork of large rocks.

As the brothers approached the boulders, the slope grew too severe for the exhausted horse to carry them farther. The animal slowed and then stopped. Kenneth thrust his heels into its side, but the horse refused to move. The beast wheezed and huffed, then sidled to balance itself.

Kenneth dismounted and pulled Aiden off. He reached to the rear of the horse and untied the crossbow and quiver. The Vikings had broken into the clearing and were fast approaching. Kenneth ducked his head under Aiden's arm and the two moved up the slope toward the ridge crest.

At the crest, the ground ceased.

Kenneth helped Aiden to sit, and then he peered over the edge. There was no downward slope to the other side, only a drop-off—a fifty-foot cliff. Below ran a wide rushing river with waters churning angrily against a smattering of rocks.

Kenneth stepped from the edge and returned to his brother. He lifted Aiden and led him to a large granite rock of brown and red. "Aiden, stay here and don't get up … just sit!"

Aiden nodded and dropped to his rear beside the rock.

Kenneth ducked low and scampered to an adjacent boulder. He rose and glanced over it, peering at the advancing Vikings below. The six had crossed the clearing and were fanning into a half circle, riding their horses methodically up the slope as though surrounding a wounded animal and cutting off any path of escape.

Kenneth dropped behind the rock. He grabbed the

crossbow. He wished for his sword and cursed as he realized it was tied to Nessa's horse. "Find Father, Nessa," Kenneth whispered under his breath. He pulled the arrows from the quiver. *Only three!* Six Vikings and three arrows was not promising. He loaded the first arrow into the crossbow.

Again, Kenneth peeked over his rock. His enemy was closer, but the hill had proven too steep for the horses and the men were dismounting. Once on foot, the six slunk through the lower rocks, hunting for the Scots.

Kenneth elevated his crossbow and aimed at the Viking to his far left. He waited. It needed to count. He pulled the trigger. *Click.* The arrow launched and struck the man square in the chest. The man fell backwards and hit the ground.

The other men instantly turned, gaping at their fallen comrade.

Another arrow struck, catching a second Viking below the temple. The man tumbled down the slope. His body came to an abrupt stop, thumping against a rock while his helmet snapped off and continued down the hill.

The remaining four Vikings leapt for cover behind the closest boulders.

Kenneth kept his head down for a long moment and then lifted to steal a glimpse. Below, he saw a single pair of horns bobbing behind a rock. Kenneth reloaded the bow. His last arrow. He vowed that if this was the end, he would not die without a fight—he would take down as many men as he could before he fell.

Kenneth stood. He pointed his weapon at the pair of moving horns, then he waited for the man to lift.

In a blink, three Vikings stood and dashed from the rocks, rushing the hill toward Kenneth and screaming a cry of war. Two held swords, one carried an axe, and all stormed forward with blades raised high.

Images raced through Kenneth's head—images of Arabella, of Father, of family.

Kenneth squeezed the trigger.

The arrow released and sunk into the shoulder of the nearest man, twisting the Viking's body and knocking him into the man behind him.

The third Viking, brandishing the axe, charged Kenneth and swung his weapon with a fury.

Kenneth jumped backwards, and the axe struck a boulder with a loud steely *clang*. Kenneth drew his knife and jabbed at the large man. The Viking dodged the blade, then twisted his wrists, circled his axe, and swung. The axe thumped Kenneth's knife and sent the weapon sailing over the cliff.

The big man gazed at Kenneth and grinned. He lifted his axe above his head—

"Jorund!" a voice shouted. "Keep him alive!" It was Kodran. He had circled the boulders when the others had charged and was now standing behind Kenneth.

Jorund lowered his blade and glared at Kodran, "He killed two of my men at camp and now two more. He should die!"

"It's not your decision, Jorund," Kodran said, approaching. "Halfdan ordered it." He peered down the slope toward the other two Vikings, and then he turned and his gaze found Aiden. His lips arched to a smirk when he saw the young Scot sitting by the rock. "This one however, is a different story." He pointed to Aiden.

Kenneth inched toward his brother. He had taken only a step before Jorund's axe pressed against his ribs.

"That's far enough, Scot," Jorund growled.

The two Vikings below rose to their feet. The injured one leaned against a rock and moaned in pain. The other moved up the hill toward Jorund and Kodran, cussing with each step.

When the man reached the others, he saw Aiden sitting on the ground, leaning against the brownish-red boulder. A devilish grin formed on his face, and he strode toward Aiden and hovered over him. He snickered. "He must be important to you," he said to Kenneth. "What fool would risk his life to save a dead man?"

Kenneth couldn't help but notice the long scar cutting across the man's eye, leaving a wide hairless gash in his eyebrow. "Go to hell!"

"I'll show you hell!" The man spun and stomped his foot into Aiden's ribs.

Aiden gasped as the man's boot jarred his frame.

Kenneth lunged toward the man, but Jorund's arm caught his gut and stopped him instantly.

"This roach has been a bother to me since we captured him. It would be a pleasure to kill him here and let his body rot. The birds can feed on him and clean the meat from his bones … if they don't first vomit from his hideous burns." The man grinned and released a ghoulish laugh.

Kenneth shoved Jorund's arm and drove his shoulder into his large body, knocking him backwards. Then he dashed toward the Viking with the scarred eye.

Kodran's foot struck Kenneth's stomach in a blur. He never saw it coming. Kenneth doubled over and Kodran finished with an elbow to his back, dropping Kenneth flat on the ground. Kodran's fighting skills were second to none among the Vikings, and he showed little effort in restraining them.

Kenneth lifted his head and spat dirt from his mouth. Before he could lift to his knees, Jorund jerked his arm and dragged him away from Kodran. Then Jorund lifted him and shoved his arm up and under Kenneth's. He pulled Kenneth's hand downward and locked Kenneth to his chest.

"Indeed, this boy must be special," Kodran said.

"He's my brother," Kenneth muttered, wiping the dirt from his lips with his free hand. "I'll die before I let you kill him."

"Oh, you'll die Scot … when I say you'll die," Kodran replied. Kodran peered at Aiden and then at the man with the scarred eye. "He won't last in his condition. He's of no use to us. Do what you please."

The man's ugly lips curled into a smile. He grabbed Aiden and lifted him to his feet.

"No! You can't do this. My father, he … you can't!" Kenneth yelled. He wrestled to free himself from Jorund but couldn't match the strength of the massive Viking.

The man with the scarred eye pushed Aiden's shoulders back and forced him to stand erect.

Aiden shook his head, trying to dispel his stupor. He gazed at the man and recognized the scarred eye. He stared at the scar for a moment and smirked, as if amused that fate had brought the two together again. Aiden slowly turned his head, and his eyes fell upon Kenneth, his expression spoke a thousand words—and none were good.

The Viking drew his sword. He poked the tip into

Aiden's belly and prodded him backwards. Again the man prodded, and again Aiden inched back.

Aiden glanced down. His heels hung on the edge of the cliff. Small rocks and broken clods of earth loosened below his feet and fell lifelessly into the river below.

No more steps.

Aiden lifted his eyes, and a swift backhand struck his face. Ooze slung from his cheek and sprayed out over the cliff.

Kenneth tugged furiously against Jorund's hold until his arm nearly snapped. But it was futile. Kenneth settled and studied Aiden. He appeared coherent, but with a visage resigned to the finality of things. Childhood memories flooded over Kenneth—how many days and seasons had they endured together? How many struggles had he shared with this younger reflection of himself? Much like Kenneth, Aiden bore a strong resemblance to their father, with a touch of their mother shaping his eyes. The look on Aiden's face terrified Kenneth, yet he refused to let his brother go. He would not let it end, not here, not now, not to these animals.

Kenneth called to Aiden, trying to draw him back to the present world, "Aiden … Aiden … I …"

Aiden stopped him, "Kenneth, this is as Father told us … there is a day for every man in which his life will be asked of him … Kenneth … on such a day, we shall be willing."

"Aiden, no!"

The scar-eyed man spat at Aiden and then extended his arm and thrust his sword at Aiden's chest.

Aiden twisted as the sword jabbed forward. He grabbed the Viking's shirt and pulled him to his chest.

The skirmish was sudden.

The precipice was unforgiving.

The two disappeared over the cliff.

"Aiden!" Kenneth watched as his brother vanished before his eyes. He heaved and wrenched his arm free and ran to the edge.

Nothing.

The rocks dotting the tortuous currents below claimed no victims. The river alone claimed ownership. Its cold waters had opened up and swallowed them both.

Kenneth's gaze blurred. His eyes closed to the misery that was the world. *Aiden. Lost. His father's heart would be forever broken. A second son, stripped from him. Was God a hater of men? A hater of him? A hater of his father?*

Two lifeless bodies surfaced on the river below, dragged along by an uncaring current. Nessa hid behind a giant oak tree, seeing it all, sobbing, numb. *How could this be?* All that was precious in life was being robbed from her, piece by bloody piece.

She had watched her brothers on the cliff from the shadow of the distant oak. She stood sullen for a long moment then closed her eyes in disbelief.

Kenneth stared down at the cruel merciless river. He could do nothing but watch his brother's body float lifelessly away from him.

Kenneth turned to the three remaining Vikings. Only the wrath of God and hell bore more fury.

Kenneth's legs erupted below him and he lunged like a hurled dagger at Jorund. He wrapped his arms around the large Viking's tree-trunk waist, knocking him off balance and sending the two tumbling backwards. Their fall didn't stop when the two hit the sloped hillside. They descended in a twisted knot, rolling over one another and throwing punches and kicks as they tumbled and wrestled like rabid dogs desperate for a kill.

Kenneth grabbed a patch of grass to stop himself. Jorund rolled past and groped to find something to halt his descent.

Kenneth stared up at the blue Dalriadan sky. He took a deep breath, trying to suck in the cool, damp air. Images flew through his mind—he hated these men with every fiber of his being. It was then that he heard his enemy grunt.

Kenneth's head swiveled. Jorund was coming. Kenneth rose from the ground. "This is for my brother!" The words sprung from Kenneth's lips as he leapt into the air and delivered a hammer blow to the lower jaw of the overgrown giant. Jorund teetered and Kenneth plunged his shoulder into the Viking's belly.

Their bodies fell as a single mass and the struggle continued headlong down the hill. In an instant, the tumbling melee stopped when the two collided hard against a massive boulder. The fight ended when Kenneth lost consciousness.

His last thoughts were of Aiden—and Arabella.

END. BOOK I

EPILOGUE

THE FATE OF DALRIADA TEETERS AT THE EDGE OF a portentous precipice, clouded under the ever-darkening shadows of Viking conquest and Pict treachery. Will Alpin and his clansmen rise up to secure their precious freedom, or will their savage enemies overtake them and imperil their land forever? Read the continuation of the saga in Book II, *Dalriada: Edge of the Blade*, as the epic twist of love, honor, and fury unravels in search of a hero and king.

GLOSSARY

Dalriadan Men:

Alpin – Leading Dalriadan in Renton; father of Drostan, Nessa, Coric, Kenneth, Aiden, and Donald

Drostan – Alpin's oldest son

Coric – Alpin's second oldest son

Kenneth – Alpin's third oldest son

Aiden – Alpin's fourth oldest son

Donald – Alpin's youngest son

Eochaid – Alpin's father

Malcolm – Alpin's grandfather

Constantine – Alpin's cousin who lives in Cashel; Senga's husband; adopted Arabella

Ronan – Coric's good friend; Luag's son

Luag – Alpin's right hand man; Ronan's father

Laise – Dalriadan from Milton; strong with a long bow; son of Latharn and brother of Ceana

Latharn – Leader of Milton clan; father of Laise and Ceana

Gormal – Dalriadan from Renton; father of Searc

Searc – Dalriadan from Renton; Gormal's son

Taran – Dalriadan from Dumbarton; Guaire's son

Guaire – Dalriadan from Dumbarton; Taran's father

Feragus – Blacksmith in Renton

Gilchrist – Cleric in Renton

Gavin – Young man from Renton, prisoner of Vikings

Dorrell – Dalriadan whose village is destroyed; uncle and cousin are killed by Vikings

Gabran – Dalriadan who vied for kingship in the days of Alpin's father

Dalriadan Women:

Arabella – Pict by birth, adopted daughter of Constantine and Senga

Ena – Alpin's wife; mother of Drostan, Nessa, Coric, Kenneth, Aiden, and Donald

Nessa – Alpin's daughter; sister of Drostan, Coric, Kenneth, Aiden, and Donald

Sorcha – Dalriadan woman from Milton, wife of Latharn, mother of Laise and Ceana

Senga – Constantine's deceased wife; adopted Arabella

Ceana – Young Dalriadan woman from Milton; daughter of Latharn; wife of Coric; sister of Laise

Rhiannon – Young Dalriadan woman whose father and brother are killed by the Vikings

Picts and Vikings:

Oengus – Pict Lord

Deort – Oengus' right hand; captain of the Pict guard

Halfdan the Black – the Viking leader

Kodran – Nimble Viking, second in command

Jorund – Large Viking, third in command

Alrik, Magnus, and Fox – Vikings who serve Halfdan

Gudrod the Hunter – a Viking king; father of Halfdan

Printed in the United States
by Baker & Taylor Publisher Services